THE APOSTLE PAUL, CHRISTIAN JEW

Faithfulness and Law

EDWIN D. FREED

Professor Emeritus, Gettysburg College

UNIVERSITY
PRESS OF
AMERICA

Lanham • New York • London

Copyright © 1994 by
Edwin D. Freed

University Press of America,® Inc.
4720 Boston Way
Lanham, Maryland 20706

3 Henrietta Street
London WC2E 8LU England

Library of Congress Cataloging-in-Publication Data

Freed, Edwin D.
The apostle Paul, Christian Jew : faithfulness and law /
Edwin D. Freed.
p.   cm.
Includes bibliographical references and index.
1. Paul, the Apostle, Saint.   2. Bible. N.T. Epistles of Paul—
Theology.   3. Justification—Biblical teaching.   4. Paul, the
Apostle, Saint—Views on Jewish law.   I. Title.
BS2506.F74   1993   225.9'2—dc20   93–43078 CIP

ISBN 0–8191–9425–5 (cloth : alk. paper)
ISBN 0–8191–9426–3 (pbk. : alk. paper)

 The paper used in this publication meets the minimum requirements of
American National Standard for Information Sciences—Permanence
of Paper for Printed Library Materials, ANSI Z39.48–1984.

Ann and Julie,
Wife and Daughter

CONTENTS

There are a myriad books on Paul, and many of them, of course, are very good. So, you may ask, "Why another book on Paul?" But this is not just another one. It is different in conception and content.

In the interpretation of Paul's ideas there has been far too much emphasis on the Reformation doctrine of justification by faith in Jesus Christ, not by works. Accordingly, then, that doctrine is regarded as central in the thought and letters of Paul. However, evidence presented in this book will show that such views on Paul have been wrong. Paul does not even mention believing in or faith in Jesus in the seven letters universally regarded as genuine, and he is really only secondarily concerned with beliefs about Jesus.

Paul's primary concern is faithfulness toward God, with a simultaneous concern that Christian converts live moral/ethical lives under the power of the Holy Spirit. That dual concern is the central message of all Paul's letters. And, according to Paul, moral/ethical probity is necessary for justified converts in order to gain ultimate salvation in the future.

This work was actually written long ago and was of a rather different nature. It was first written as a polemic against several scholars who were greatly exaggerating and misrepresenting Paul's idea of justification by faith and related ideas. At the suggestion of the late Professor Samuel Sandmel, who read an early draft of the manuscript, I have dropped the polemic and tried to write in a way that would be appropriate not only for scholars but also for open-minded lay persons, whose intelligence many scholars underestimate, who want to learn about Paul and his ideas.

Only recently have I been able to return to this work. During the last twenty years discussions on the subjects covered have intensified considerably. Meanwhile, I have scanned important older and recent works on the subjects treated, and I have found nothing to change my conviction about the understanding of Paul presented here.

Although the book is intended primarily for scholars, it is written without the technical language used in most scholarly studies on Paul and his work as an apostle. At the same time, I sometimes define or explain some things that scholars will know, but the lay reader will not. And there are even no footnotes. Instead of looking for notes to check for substantiation or refutation of what I say, I hope scholars will look for fresh insights and suggestions and then check them against the texts and contexts of what Paul himself says.

I think it was a president of Oberlin College who once said, "A professor is a person who thinks otherwise." In this work I have tried to do that. Doubtless, some persons, hopefully not too many, who read this work will also think otherwise on a number of points. For those readers who want to compare the results of my study with a wide variety of views of other scholars there is an extensive bibliography, both older and recent works at various levels of difficulty, on Paul, his letters, and his thought at the end of the volume. The bibliography is not intended, of course, to be complete but to present diverse points of view.

My purpose for writing, then, is not to debate the opinions of other scholars. Rather, my aim is to consider the letters of Paul that by all scholars are regarded as authentic and to present his ideas as objectively as I can. I hope that many scholars will find some new insights into the views of Paul and that lay readers will better understand what Paul really says.

I have tried to understand Paul as a Jew who became a follower of the Jesus movement, who lived in the middle of the first century A. D., and who believed that God had called him to preach his message of faithfulness toward the God of the Jews, especially to Gentiles.

My procedure has been to begin with Paul's earliest letter, 1 Thessalonians, and to present his ideas on justification, faith, the law, grace, and salvation as they evolve from that letter through Philippians. From the beginning I resolved to stick to the texts of Paul himself, to pay special attention to key words in their contexts, and to try to be influenced as little as possible by secondary sources. But, naturally, throughout the years I have learned much from scores of authors, both American and foreign. Therefore, in a general way I hereby express my gratitude and appreciation to all whose ideas may sometimes be reflected in this work. Any works by which I may have been influenced are sure to appear in the bibliography. Sometimes the language I use here may be reflected in my <u>The New Testament: A Critical Introduction</u> (Belmont: Wadsworth, 1986, 1991), published long after this work was first written.

I want to express special appreciation and thanks to Kim S. Breighner, Computing Services, Gettysburg College, who has prepared the final manuscript of this book for publication.

Except where indicated otherwise, the translations from Biblical texts are my own. However, I have frequently consulted older and newer translations, including the <u>New Revised Standard Version</u>, which appeared as I was finally preparing the manuscript for publication. Sometimes my translation agrees with one or the other, frequently with none. Translations from Greek and Roman authors are also my own.

This book is a radical one, radical in the original sense of the term. The word "radical" comes from the Latin word <u>radix</u>, meaning "root." I have tried to get to the root of Paul's ideas. Sometimes the task has been difficult, not only because Paul's language is frequently hard to understand but also because his thought is not always consistent. Yet, I believe that this book presents many new insights into Paul's language and thought.

The Apostle Paul, Christian Jew:

Faithfulness And Law

Introduction

It is not necessary to be a literalist to accept as true the words of 2 Pet 3:15-16 that "our beloved brother Paul" wrote some things in his letters that are "hard to understand." Anyone who reads Paul's letters will discover that the writer of 2 Peter knew what he was talking about.

Paul is the best known of early Christian leaders, and the record of his life and work is more complete than that of Jesus to whom he was so devoted. Yet, in spite of that, the objective interpreter of his letters has real difficulty when trying to understand Paul's religion. And because many interpreters approach Paul with their own presuppositions, especially those of Reformation theology, it becomes even more difficult for persons who want to learn about Paul's ideas to know what he really says. Perhaps part of the problem is Paul's diversity of approach. Just when we expect him to be consistent, he is not. Instead of a theology that is worked out systematically, we find one grand muddle. From that grand muddle, I want to try to convey Paul's ideas about the relationship of justification on the basis of faithfulness to the Jewish law and the imperatives of that relationship, according to Paul, for Christian life and ultimate salvation. In order to get to the root of Paul's ideas and the reasons for them, it seems best to begin with a few comments about his letters as a group and about his personal religious experience.

Paul's Letters as a Whole

Of the thirteen letters that purport to be from Paul there is universal agreement about the authenticity of seven: 1 Thessalonians, 1 and 2 Corinthians, Galatians, Romans, Philippians, and Philemon. The views in this book are based on those seven letters. There is no unanimity of opinion about the chronological sequence of the letters. However, I subscribe to the view generally held among New Testament scholars that 1 Thessalonians is Paul's earliest letter and that he wrote

1

Galatians before Romans. These are the only points in the sequence of Paul's correspondence that bear on my arguments.

Things to Remember When Studying Paul's Letters

With the exception of Romans, and possibly Philemon, Paul wrote letters to communities he had previously visited and which he had helped to establish during his mission travels. So Paul's letters are situational or occasional, that is, they address specific situations or occasions or deal with particular problems in the communities addressed. His letters, therefore, provide information about specific Christian communities during the middle of the first century A.D., their members, and their problems.

We have, then, definite contexts for Paul's letters. This is in strong contrast to the contexts of Jesus' teachings which were often no longer known to the gospel writers. Those writers frequently invented contexts for teachings of Jesus, so the original contexts of those teachings are mostly unknown to us. It is much different with Paul. In fact, only by Paul's responses to problems in his churches can we determine his views. Moreover, if people in those churches had always agreed with Paul, we would know little about his religious insights, since he wrote in response to what people in his churches were thinking and doing.

Paul's letters were all written within the broadest context of the Roman Empire, the chief cultural feature of which was Hellenism, Greek culture as spread outside the Greek mainland. Within the cultural context of Hellenism, which included political, social, economic, and religious aspects, there were Jews in every large city who kept Diaspora Judaism alive in environments that were often very threatening. Although Paul certainly was familiar with Diaspora Judaism and with many aspects of Hellenism, only occasionally do some things in his letters allude to society outside the church groups to which his letters are addressed. However, the letters are not intended for the larger society. Rather, Paul is concerned almost entirely with specific communities of Christian converts themselves.

The letters of Paul do not represent a systematic statement of doctrine but are a diverse collection of writings directed toward diverse situations. With the possible exception of Romans, no letter was carefully thought out in great detail and planned before he wrote it. Although the content of his letters was largely his, Paul did not write them in his own hand. Rather, he dictated them to a secretary, as we know, for example, from Rom 16:22: "I, Tertius, who have written this letter, greet you in the Lord." Sometimes Paul wrote a notation at the end, as in 1 Cor 16:21: "The greeting in my hand from Paul" (see also Gal 6:11-18; Phlm 19). Paul's letters, then, reflect spontaneous and hastily dictated thoughts through which we learn his feelings and his advice to converts in the Christian communities he helped to establish. Therefore, we must try to understand each letter in relation to the situation that occasioned it. We must also try to understand Paul's ideas in the contexts in which they appear, not in light of our own religious training or theological convictions.

A point to be remembered and stressed is that Paul was not writing to persons who had long been Christians and whose families had been Christians. In fact, the word Christian was not even in use among Christians themselves in Paul's time. So, the word is actually an anachronism, one, however, that can hardly be avoided in a work of this sort (see chapter 6 of this work for comments on the word).

How long before Paul wrote his first letter he had become a follower of the Jesus sect of Jews we do not know. But we do know that he was writing to persons who had only recently become Christians or were even still in the process of becoming Christians. It is more appropriate, therefore, to refer to the recipients of Paul's letters as converts than as Christians. Paul and the converts in his churches all were of the first generation of persons belonging to the Jewish Jesus sect. None of Paul's adult converts was born into a Christian family where Christian faithfulness and life were assumed, much less practiced. Indeed, many converts formerly worshiped Graeco-Roman deities or belonged to a mystery cult and practiced lifestyles quite different from those advocated by Paul, in accordance with his strict Jewish monotheism and moral upbringing. And Paul was often fearful that some of his converts, especially Gentiles, would revert to their former status of unfaithfulness and immorality. This was always one of Paul's main concerns and a fact constantly to be remembered.

Not only should we be aware that Paul was writing to recent converts, but it is also extremely important to realize that Paul was, therefore, writing to persons of his own time. When Paul wrote, he surely did not have in mind Christians of later times, much less of our own time. This is true because he expected the end of the world to come soon, perhaps even before he died (see, for example, 1 Thess 2:19; 3:13; 4:12-5:4; 1 Cor 4:5; 10:11; 11:26; Phil 1:19-24). When considering Paul's ideas, we must not overlook the fact that he was not writing for people today. Yet frequently not only from the pulpit, but also in scholarly meetings as well, we often hear words such as these: "Paul says that we are saved by the grace of God, not by our works" or "We are saved by our faith, not by our works." But Paul did not have us in mind at all when he wrote. Of course, this does not mean that we cannot learn about Christian life from what Paul writes, but he was not telling us what to believe or what to do.

When studying any of Paul's ideas, we should always remember, then, that the contexts of those ideas are always those of new converts and the problems they faced after becoming converts. Consequently, we should stress, as Paul does, the emphatic requirement of moral/ethical probity for former pagans who had just become converts in a Christian community to which he was writing. Paul's ideas about justification by virtue of faithfulness and not by works of the law actually occur only in Galatians and Romans, nowhere else. Therefore, we must not read those ideas into his letters where they do not appear. And Paul's ideas about faithfulness, justification, and grace are frequently overemphasized and misrepresented in discussions of the Reformation doctrines of "justification through faith alone" (sola fide) or "salvation by grace alone" (sola gratia). Those doctrines became deeply imbedded in Reformation theology in spite of the fact that the words used to express them are nowhere to be found in the undisputed letters of Paul. And in none of the undisputed or disputed letters of Paul is the word "alone" used with "faith" in his discussion of either justification or grace.

We should also remember that, in contrast to the people in Paul's churches, we are familiar with all of his letters at the same time. It is easy for us, then, to read an idea that occurs in one letter into another where Paul did not have that idea in mind at all. The probability that people in one of his churches knew what Paul had written to other churches would, indeed, be very slight. This is true, of course, because he was addressing specific problems in each church. In fact, the only problem existing in every church that Paul had to be concerned about was the behavior of the converts, individually and socially.

Occasionally Paul mentions other churches with regard to this point when writing to a particular church. He writes to the Corinthians that he sent Timothy to remind them of his "ways in Christ," as he teaches "them everywhere in every church" (1 Cor 4:17). Here the word translated as "way" (hodos) refers to the moral/ethical standards Paul required of himself and his converts. It is the equivalent of the Hebrew halakah ("rule of conduct") and of the Greek peripateo in its moral/ethical sense of "conduct one's life" or "live."

Paul also tells the Corinthian converts that his rule in all the churches is that all persons should live in the way God called them, with the same standards and without deference to social status (1 Cor 7:17; see also 1 Cor 11:16; 14:33; 16:1; 2 Cor 8:1-7).

Another thing to remember--one too often forgotten--is that when persons speak about faith versus works, understood by the average Christian in the sense of "good works" or deeds of kindness, they completely miss the point Paul is making about justification on the basis of faithfulness, not works. Paul sometimes uses the Greek word ergon, meaning "work," with reference to something good to be done (for example, 1 Cor 15:58; 2 Cor 9:8-10; 11:15; Gal 6:10; Rom 2:4-10) or to some evil to be avoided (for example, Gal 5:19-21; Rom 13:12). But when he speaks about justification, faithfulness, and works, Paul does not mean works as most Christians usually understand them. Rather, he means works of Jewish law. And when he contrasts faithfulness and works of the law (Gal 2:15-16; 3:2-5, 10-12; Rom 3:20-28), it is crucial to understand that he does not mean all aspects of the law. He usually means works of the law in a specific and limited sense, mostly with reference to circumcision and dietary regulations, not the law as a whole, and certainly not works in the sense of good deeds.

That Paul did not negate all Jewish law for converts is clear from several statements in both Galatians and Romans. To the Galatians he writes, for example: "The whole law is fulfilled in one word: 'You shall love your neighbor as yourself'" (Gal 5:14), a statement clearly addressed to Gentile converts. He writes the same way also in Rom 13:8-10.

At least once Paul uses the expression "work of the law" in an ethical sense. In Rom 2:14-16 he says that Gentiles who do "the work of the law" willfully, without having the Mosaic law, do not need that law when they appear before God in judgment. Then their consciences and their ethical deliberations are enough to account for their deeds.

With respect to faithfulness versus works, Paul stands in contrast to the writer of James, who does place faith and works as deeds of mercy in antithesis (James 1:25; 2:14-26). If, indeed, the writer of James knew Paul's letters, he misunderstood Paul because Paul never places faithfulness and deeds of kindness in antithesis. Some early Christian writers after the New Testament period also misunderstood Paul in the same way. For example, the author of 1 Clement (c. A. D. 90-100), who writes as though Paul was speaking for his time, reveals the same kind of antithesis: "We, who through his [God's] will have been called in Christ Jesus, are not justified (made righteous) by ourselves or by our wisdom or understanding or piety or works that we have done in holiness of heart, but through faith by which Almighty God has justified all persons" (32:4). Although the author of 1 Clement places faith and good works in antithesis in a way that is contrary to Paul, he does reflect Paul's view of justification precisely when he associates justification with conversion, not with salvation. The writer of 1 Clement continues:

> What, then, shall we do . . .? Shall we desist from doing good and forsake love? May the Lord forbid that this should happen, at least to us, but let us hasten to accomplish every good work with perseverance and willingness. . . . Let us observe that all the righteous [dikaioi] have been adorned with good works; and the Lord himself adorned himself with good works and rejoiced. Having, therefore, this model, let us follow his will without delay; let us work the work of righteousness [ergon dikaiosynes] with all our strength (33:1, 7-8).

If Paul could have read this passage from 1 Clement, I think he would have agreed with the author completely.

The dichotomy of faith and good works as deeds of love and kindness, not works of the law, is false. It is contrary to what Paul himself says at every phase of his development and writing as a Christian Jew. Therefore, we must stress Paul's prevailing emphasis on moral/ethical probity as necessary for life in the communities of brotherhoods with which he was concerned and for ultimate salvation (see chapter 7 of this work).

The Jesus Movement and Paul's Special Religious Experience

Before Paul began his mission work Christianity was a sect within Judaism that shared the beliefs and practices of Judaism. From that Jewish sect, Paul received the teaching that Jesus of Nazareth was in some way God's long-expected Messiah, that God had raised him from the dead, and that he would come again. This threefold teaching was essentially all that Paul received from the Jesus sect of Jews when he became a member.

Before Paul joined the Jesus movement he belonged to that vast majority of Jews who did not accept Jesus as their long-expected Messiah. He not only did not accept the messiahship of Jesus; he also persecuted those who did (Acts 7:58; 8:1-3; 22:4-5; 26:9-15). Paul writes to the Galatian converts about his persecution of Jesus' followers: "You have heard of my former life in Judaism, how I persecuted the church of God violently and tried to destroy it" (Gal 1:13; see also 1:23). And to the Corinthians he says: "I am the least of the apostles, unfit to be called an apostle, because I persecuted the church of God" (1 Cor 15:9; see also Phil 3:6).

When Paul joined the Jesus movement, it was beginning to spread out from Palestine, the land of its origin, into the Graeco-Roman world northward and westward into lands north of the Mediterranean. This happened as the result of dissensions between Jewish and Gentile converts in the mother church in Jerusalem. Paul, the Greek-speaking Jew, appeared at just the right time to accelerate the spreading of Christianity. Perhaps only someone like Paul, who did not know the earthly Jesus who lived by the law, could reject certain requirements of the law regarded by some other Jewish converts as crucial for those Gentiles wanting to join the Jesus movement. As Paul looked back on his career as a Christian Jew, he came to believe that, as with the Hebrew prophet Jeremiah, God had called him even before he was born for religious work (compare Jer 1:5 and Gal 1:16). Paul believed God had called him specifically to preach God's Son among the Gentiles (Gal 1:16). Only Paul, who believed he had a special spiritual religious experience, could imagine Christ as a spiritual being and life in Christ as spiritual. Only such a person also, without personal knowledge of the earthly Jesus, could enthusiastically help to spread the Jesus movement from its Jewish origins in Jerusalem to lands of the Gentiles.

Besides Paul's letters, the book of Acts is the only other source in the New Testament for information about Paul and his association with the Jesus movement. Although the information in Acts is not always in agreement with that in Paul's letters, both sources agree on essential aspects of Paul's life and mission activity. He was a strict Pharisaic Jew (Acts 23:6; 26:5; Phil 3:4-5; see also Gal 2:15). As a Pharisee Paul would have believed that the law (Hebrew, <u>Torah</u>, which more accurately means teaching or instruction concerning God's will for Jews) was sacred and to be observed scrupulously and that circumcision was its most significant requirement (see Acts 15:5). As a Pharisee Paul would also have believed in the one God with his justice and mercy and his righteousness and wrath; a final judgment, with a resurrection of at least the righteous dead; and in the existence of angels and demons (1 Cor 4:9; 8:4, 6; 11:10; 13:1; Gal 1:8; 3:20; 4:14; Rom 3:30).

According to the writer of Acts, while Paul was going to Damascus to look for Christian Jews to bring them to Jerusalem for trial (Acts 9:1-2; 22:4-5; 26:9-11; see also 8:3), something happened that helped to change his own life as a Jew. Although Paul mentions that he was in Damascus on two occasions (2 Cor 11:32; Gal 1:17), he never says anything about any special event or experience while he was on the way to that city. One might wonder, though, how much those who helped Paul escape from Damascus (2 Cor 11:32-33) influenced his decision to become a convert to the Jesus movement. At least, he went back to Damascus again of his own accord (Gal 1:17).

Although Paul's special religious experience is usually referred to as a conversion, that term is not wholly appropriate. It is very difficult to determine the nature of the phenomenon usually known as Paul's conversion and even more difficult to explain it and to determine how much it influenced his thought and work. But we must try to understand it from his perspective, not ours. Paul would not have thought he was completely converted in any sense of the term. He neither completely changed from no religion to religion nor from one religion to another. He did not even change from Judaism to Christianity because he never gave up his Jewish beliefs. His beliefs about Jesus were simply added to his Judaism. That is why it is most appropriate to call Paul a Christian Jew in order to distinguish him from Jews who did not become converts to Christianity and even from some who did.

Although Paul's letters indicate that he never completely forsook his Judaism, they sometimes reveal an inner struggle concerning his old ways of Jewish life under the law and his life under the Spirit as a Christian Jew. It is probably better, therefore, to think about the phenomenon that is reported in Acts--if, indeed, it was a phenomenon that occurred as reported--as a special religious experience rather than a conversion.

Effects of Paul's Special Religious Experience

Paul seems to have been a kind of mystic who believed he had a renewed experience of God through Jesus as the risen or spiritual Christ whose Spirit became a reality in his life. Although Paul's special religious experience had a very positive effect on him, we should not assume that it transformed him to the extent that it was the sole motivation for all his ideas after he became a Christian Jew. This is the view of Eusebius (c. A.D. 264-340), who writes about Paul:

> Paul, most powerful of all in preparation of words and most competent in thought, transmitted in writing no more than short letters, although he had a myriad things to say, since he touched visions of the third heaven, was snatched up to the paradise of divine majesty itself and thought worthy to hear there unspeakable words (Ecclesiastical History 3:24:4; see 2 Cor 12:2-4).

Although Paul's special religious experience had some influence on shaping his ideas, we must not think that they were given him from heaven. Rather, in light of both that experience and the situations in the communities of Christian converts he helped to establish, Paul worked out his ideas as he tried to meet the challenges in one community after another.

How was Paul influenced by his special religious experience, and how did it affect his relationship to the Jesus movement? In the first place, in contrast to the accounts in Acts, which nowhere mention God in connection with Paul's experience on the road to Damascus, Paul himself says that God was responsible for what happened. God "was

pleased to reveal his Son" to him (Gal 1:16). In all of the accounts in
Acts it is always the risen Jesus who speaks to Paul (Acts 9:4-6; 22:8;
26:14-18).

In the second place, after his special religious experience, Paul
changed from rejection to acceptance of Jesus as the long-awaited
Messiah. He believed Jesus became the Messiah through his suffering,
death, and resurrection (see 1 Cor 1:23; Rom 5:6-11; 6:4, 9; Phil 2:8-
11). This Messiah, a descendant of David, was sent by God as the one
on whom the Gentiles should hope (see, for example, Rom 1:3; 15:8-
13, an idea quoted from Isa 11:10). A similar view is reported in Acts,
whose writer says that in the synagogue at Thessalonica Paul argued
with the Jews "from the scriptures, explaining and proving that it was
necessary for the Christ to suffer and to rise from the dead, and saying,
'This Jesus, whom I proclaim to you, is the Christ'" (Acts 17:2-3; see
also 18:5, 28; 26:23).

Although Paul apparently shared the view that Jesus was a
descendant of David, as Messiah he did not bear a title or fill an office.
Paul did not regard him as a present or future king. That is why so
many times for Paul Christ was only a proper name. For Paul the
greatest thing about Jesus as the Messiah was to be found not in his
person but in his faithfulness toward God. That faithfulness functioned
to motivate God to keep his promises to Abraham and his descendants
in order that the blessing of Abraham might also come upon the
Gentiles (Gal 3:14; Rom 4:13-17). Paul lived in that same kind of
faithfulness and expected his converts to do the same.

Paul's most creative and characteristic expressions "in Christ" and
"Christ in" indicate that he also came to believe that he shared in Jesus'
crucifixion and resurrection by a kind of mystical union or spiritual
experience of the risen Christ that inspired his life. Perhaps Paul's
feelings are best summarized in Gal 2:20: "I have been crucified with
Christ; it is no longer I who live, but Christ who lives in me; and the
life I now live in the flesh I live in the faithfulness of the Son of God"
(see also 2 Cor 12:9; 13:5; Rom 8:10-11; Phil 3:8-11; 4:13; and the
discussion of Gal 2:20 in chapter 4 of this work).

As a result of his special religious experience Paul developed
keener insights into God's faithfulness, his righteousness, and his will
for humankind. For Paul, as a Jew, having also become a Christian,

faithfulness toward God, certain beliefs about Jesus, and an utmost concern for moral/ethical probity for himself and fellow converts all became the focus of his renewed life.

As with other ideas of Paul, the idea that God was responsible for his mission activity as a Christian Jew developed more fully as he progressed with his work and writing. In 1 Thessalonians he says nothing about himself personally being called, but the conviction that God is responsible for the activity of him and his fellow workers is quite clear. He writes to the Thessalonian converts: "Our gospel came to you not only in word but also in power and in the Holy Spirit and with much conviction" (1 Thess 1:5). He says "our gospel." Later in 1 Thess 4:7 he writes that "God has not called us for uncleanness but in holiness." Thus, from the beginning of his mission activity Paul believed that the call of him and his fellow workers included a moral purpose, as is clear from the contexts of both passages cited. Along with faithfulness toward God, the moral/ethical imperative became the dominant emphasis in all of his letters.

The first and simplest statement of Paul's own call is in 1 Cor 1:1: "Paul, called through the will of God to be an apostle of Christ Jesus" (see also 2 Cor 1:1). In the letter to the Galatians, where Paul opposes his adversaries most strongly on the basis of his developing convictions, the statements about his call become more personal and extensive: "Paul, an apostle not from humans nor through humans but through Jesus Christ and God the Father" (Gal 1:1). Whereas in 1 Thess 1:5 Paul refers to the message of the missionaries as "our gospel" (see also 2 Cor 4:3), in Gal 1:11 he says emphatically: "For I want you to know, fellow converts [Greek, "brothers"], that the gospel which was preached by me is not according to human (authority), for I did not receive it from a human being, nor was I taught it, but through a revelation of Jesus Christ." Then Paul goes on to say about being called specifically to preach to Gentiles.

When writing to the converts in the church at Rome, Paul's statements about his call and its purpose are more detailed and also include a summary of his theology. Perhaps the reason for this is that he is writing to a church he did not help to establish, or even ever visit. In Rom 1:1-5 he writes: "Paul, a slave of Christ Jesus, called to be an apostle, set apart for the gospel of God . . . concerning his Son . . . for the purpose of the obedience of faithfulness among all the Gentiles for the sake of his name."

That Paul believed his call included mission work among Gentiles is quite clear. The same conviction is put in words of Paul by the writer of Acts: "We turn to the Gentiles. For so the Lord has commanded us: 'I have set you to be a light for the Gentiles'" (Acts 13:46-47, from Isa 49:6; see also Acts 9:15; 22:21; Rom 11:13; 15:15-21). As "an apostle to the Gentiles" (Rom 11:13) Paul is addressing mostly Gentiles when writing as he does.

When Paul boasts of "visions and revelations of the Lord" (2 Cor 12:1), he does not appeal to them as the basis for his work, even though he can boast of such experiences. Rather, Paul wants his converts at Corinth to take as evidence for his mission work only what they see in him or hear from him (2 Cor 12:6). In this instance his authority has its origins in the power that comes from his sufferings (2 Cor 12:7-10). In Gal 1:11-17 Paul also appeals to his religious experience, and there his appeal is presented not as the basis for his views but as the reason for his preaching among Gentiles.

Paul's conviction that God had set him apart as an apostle to the Gentiles and the situations in his churches helped him develop a peculiar mission character, so to speak. That character manifested itself at least partly in the way he wrote, especially in his use of the first person, whether singular or plural. This is probably the best way to explain Paul's use of "we" in certain contexts (for example, 1 Thess 2:13, 17-3:5; 1 Cor 1:23; 4:8-21; 9:1-12; 2 Cor 12:11-21; Gal 2:18-21; Rom 8:22). As a mission character Paul, naturally, differed from other mission characters, whether friendly or adversarial.

As a mission character Paul was always deeply involved with the communities of converts he addressed. When ministering to a community confronted with specific problems, Paul's mission character developed more fully only as he helped each community discover its own communal character. So each community as a character of its own tended to focus on the character of the apostle ministering to it. Other missionaries had their distinctive mission characters, and when they ministered to one of Paul's communities, some persons began to focus on them instead of on Paul. But Paul differed from his adversaries in that he expected his converts to focus not only on his message (1 Cor

1:10-17; Gal 2:4-10) but on his personal behavior as well (1 Cor 4:16-17; 11:1; Phil 3:17).

Although Paul felt that he had been a superior Jew (Gal 1:14; Phil 3:4-6), he would have had to live and practice his trade (see 1 Thess 2:9; 1 Cor 4:12; Acts 18:1-4) among Gentiles as well as Jews. While practicing his trade and doing mission work at the same time among Gentiles, it would not be too difficult for Paul to moderate his attitude toward the Jewish law in order to make his work more effective. He found it convenient to become all things to all persons that he might win some. To the Jew he became a Jew to win Jews. Although not himself under the law, he became as one under the law to win those observing the law. To those without the law, he became like one of them to win some of them, though not himself without law toward God yet under the law of Christ (1 Cor 9:19-23).

When eating among Gentiles he probably could not obey all Jewish dietary laws. Even Peter, the more conservative Jew, learned that such observance was not practical (Gal 2:11-14). Both in and outside of Palestine there were Jews as individuals and as groups who ignored some external observances but observed other laws. Where it was impractical or impossible to obey certain legal requirements, it was easy to conclude that they were no longer valid. Apparently Paul's personal religious experience helped to lead him to precisely that conclusion. Converts living by the Spirit did not need to observe the ceremonial aspects of the law, such as circumcision and dietary regulations. This is evident from his words to the Roman converts: "Now we are discharged from the law, dead to that which held us captive, so that we serve not under the old written code but in the new life of the Spirit" (Rom 7:6). Led by the Spirit, converts were not under ceremonial aspects of the law such as circumcision and dietary regulations (Gal 5:18). There were, however, "just requirements of the law" that Paul still believed were valid for all converts (see chapter 8 of this work).

Before his special religious experience Paul thought that the law separated Jews and Gentiles, but after that experience, he came to believe the law should no longer be a barrier to either Gentiles or Jews who wanted to join the Jesus movement. During Paul's former life as a strict Pharisaic Jew, faithfulness toward God and the law were the determining factors in his life. But after his special religious experience, in addition to his profound faithfulness toward God, he learned certain beliefs about Jesus, along with a renewed concern for moral/ethical life, life by the Spirit. All of these became central in his life as a Christian Jew. The law should not prevent Jews or Gentiles who were faithful toward God and held certain beliefs about Jesus from becoming members of the new "Israel of God," for whom neither circumcision nor uncircumcision was important, "but a new creation" (Gal 6:15-16). According to Paul, converts who joined the Jesus movement and pledged faithfulness only to God (see chapter 1 of this work) took the first step toward their ultimate salvation.

Theologically, Paul's changed attitude toward Jesus found expression in the conviction that Jesus Christ was Lord. This is the only theological conviction evident in every letter. But as Lord Jesus did not take the place of God, or even equal God, in the faithfulness of Paul. Paul's view of Jesus as Lord is best stated, perhaps, in 1 Cor 8:5-6: "For if indeed there are so-called gods whether in heaven or on earth, even as there are many gods and many lords--yet for us there is one God, the Father . . . and one Lord, Jesus Christ" (see also 1 Cor 12:3). Paul preached "Jesus Christ as Lord" (2 Cor 4:5), and he wanted "every tongue (to) confess that Jesus Christ is Lord, to the glory of God the Father" (Phil 2:11; see also 3:8; Rom 10:9; Phlm 5). It was this Lord who would soon return to bring an end to all things (1 Thess 3:13; 4:13-5:23; 1 Cor 15:51-57; Phil 4:5; see the discussion of Jesus as Lord in chapter 5 of this work).

There is no conclusive evidence that Paul ever saw the earthly Jesus. Apparently Paul thought of his special religious experience as a kind of vision of the risen Jesus. When Paul alludes to that experience, the vocabulary in his allusions is that used with reference to a vision. In defending his own authority as an apostle he writes to the Corinthian converts: "Am I not an apostle? Have I not <u>seen</u> Jesus our Lord?" (1 Cor 9:1). When narrating the resurrection appearances of Jesus, Paul writes to the same Corinthians: "Last of all, as to one untimely born, he <u>appeared</u> also to me" (1 Cor 15:8; emphases mine). The underlined words are part of the vocabulary normally used to describe visionary experiences.

Paul's changed views of Jesus became his main argument against his adversaries. When Peter and others who had known the earthly Jesus argued that Gentile converts should be circumcised and obey Jewish law, they could appeal to their association with the earthly Jesus. In contrast to them, Paul centered his arguments on the death and resurrection of Jesus. Jesus became more than the human Messiah. He became "Son of God . . . by his resurrection from the dead" (Rom 1:4). Paul's experience of the risen Jesus convinced him that he had greater authority as an apostle than his adversaries did.

As a Jew who could speak and write Greek, Paul was a Hellenistic Jew. Since he could also use Hebrew (see 2 Cor 11:22; Phil 3:5; Acts 21:40), he belonged to that large group of people who used two languages, Hebrew (Aramaic) and Greek. If, as Acts reports, Paul's home was in Tarsus (Acts 9:11; 21:39; 22:3), the Graeco-Roman environment of that city would have provided opportunities to listen to philosophers and to observe some of the many pagan religious cults. We know from Philo of Alexandria (c. 20 B.C. - A.D. 50) that Jews living outside of Palestine had begun to question the relevance of at least some of their Mosaic law in the Hellenistic communities of which they were a part.

As a Hellenistic Jew who associated with Gentiles, Paul not only found himself in situations when it was impractical, if not impossible, to observe the whole law (see Gal 5:3; Rom 2:17-29; 4:15; 5:13-20; 7:7-11). As a Christian Jew he also became convinced that it was God's will that he preach to Gentiles and that the rites of circumcision and dietary observances were too burdensome for them. Indeed, Paul may have shared the attitude toward his Pharisaic fellow Jews put in words of Jesus in Matt 23:3-4: "They talk, but do not act. They bind heavy burdens, hard to bear, and place them on persons' shoulders; but they themselves are not willing to move them with their finger" (see also Luke 11:46). For Paul as a Christian Jew the whole law was summed up in one commandment: "You shall love your neighbor as yourself" (Lev 19:18; Gal 5:14; Rom 13:8-10).

Paul accused Peter and other Jews at Antioch of insincerity because they ate with Gentiles until those who wanted Gentiles to be circumcised came there. Paul reprimanded Peter for such insincerity: "If you, a Jew, live as a Gentile and not as a Jew, how can you compel the Gentiles to live as Jews?" (Gal 2:14).

As a Hellenistic Jew who remained a diehard monotheist but who had difficulty with some aspects of the law, Paul found it easier to become better assimilated into the Jesus movement than into Hellenism. His unshakable faithfulness toward the one Jewish God, made even stronger as the result of his special religious experience, as he confronted the polytheism of the world in which he lived, may well have been the biggest single factor that triggered the theological direction Paul took. Consequently, he found himself comfortable within the Jesus movement. And Paul's background as a Hellenistic Jew made it easy for him as a Christian Jew to gain and maintain contact with Jerusalem and with Antioch in Syria, the two main centers of the early Jesus movement.

Although Paul entered the Jesus movement rather early, he was regarded as a recent arrival on the scene by the first followers of Jesus. But Paul never thought that because he was a later participant in the movement he had any less authority as an apostle than any of the first apostles. Indeed, from the Corinthian letters and Galatians we learn that he turned what his adversaries considered a disadvantage into an advantage. His vision of the risen Christ more than compensated for his late arrival in joining the new movement and gave him, he believed, a decided advantage over his rivals.

In another instance Paul also turned a disadvantage into an advantage. The writer of Acts reports that he "was ravaging the church" (Acts 8:3), and Paul himself admits that fact several times (1 Cor 15:9; Gal 1:13, 23). Apparently he admitted that he persecuted the church before joining it in order to demonstrate his integrity. The fact that he persecuted members of the Jesus movement became one of his qualifications as an apostle having himself become zealous for the movement whose members he had persecuted. Those who were skeptical about him were won over, as we know from Paul's words in Gal 1:23: "The one who once persecuted us is now preaching the good news of the faith he once was devastating. And they glorified God on my account." Apparently Paul's character was persuasive, even if his speech was not (see 2 Cor 10:10).

Paul as a Christian Jew

Three passages are important for understanding Paul as a Christian Jew. The first is 2 Cor 11:21-23 where, in referring to his adversaries, he writes: "But in whatever any one dares to boast . . . I also dare to boast. Are they Hebrews? So am I. Are they Israelites? So am I. Are they descendants of Abraham? So am I. Are they servants of Christ? I am a better one." Notice that in speaking about his Jewishness, as well as about his devotion to Christ, he says "am I," not was I."

The second passage is Rom 11:1, where Paul uses his own Jewishness to show that God has not rejected his people, the Jews. "Has God rejected his people? By no means!. For I (myself) am an Israelite, descended from Abraham, of the tribe of Benjamin." Here Paul's Greek for I am is even more emphatic than in 2 Cor 11:21-22 (kai gar ego eimi). The ego ("I") with the verb makes it more emphatic than if it were not used with the verb.

The third passage is Phil 3:4-16 and is most important for understanding Paul's heritage as a Pharisaic Jew and his life as a Christian Jew: "If any other person seems to be confident in the flesh, I am more, circumcised on the eighth day, from the people of Israel, of the tribe of Benjamin, a Hebrew born of Hebrews; with respect to the law, a Pharisee, with respect to zeal, a persecutor of the church, with respect to righteousness under the law, blameless." As in 2 Cor 11:21-23, Paul does not try to deny his Jewishness: "I am more," that is, more "confident in the flesh" than his adversaries. Again, Paul says, "I am," not "I was." But as a Christian Jew he has to confess that fellow converts are "the circumcision, who worship God in Spirit and proudly glory in Christ Jesus and do not put confidence in the flesh" (Phil 3:3). As a Christian Jew Paul stresses the Spirit, not circumcision (see also Gal 6:12-15; Rom 2:25-3:2). As in the Corinthian passage, in Phil 3:7-11 Paul goes on to stress his relationship to Christ:

> But whatever gain I had, I counted these things as loss for the sake of Christ. Indeed, I count all things as loss because of the surpassing worth of knowing Christ Jesus my Lord, for whose sake I have suffered the loss of all things . . . in order that I may gain Christ and be found in him, not having a righteousness of my own, on the basis of law, but that which is by virtue of the faithfulness of Christ, the righteousness from God on the basis of

the faithfulness of [Christ] that I may know him [Jesus] and the
power of his resurrection, and the sharing of his sufferings,
becoming like him in his death, that if somehow I may attain the
resurrection from the dead.

Although Paul says that whatever gain he had he counted as loss
for the sake of Christ and that he thinks of everything as loss for the
sake of being superior in knowing Christ Jesus his Lord, he does not
deny his Jewish heritage. Rather, he summarizes his ideas as a
Christian Jew as they had developed from his experiences with the
churches in Corinth and Galatia and after he had written the letter to
Rome. Obviously, he stresses his Christian life, including, of course,
his unswerving faithfulness toward God. However, as a Christian Jew
he believes the advantages that he thought he had before his special
religious experience became disadvantages. Knowing and experiencing
the spiritual Christ are also extremely important. By virtue of the
faithfulness of Christ (see discussion of this phrase in chapter 4 of this
work), not on the basis of the law, he now feels God's forgiveness.
This is true because Paul believes that he shares in Christ's faithfulness
toward God.

Paul also thinks his own sufferings are like those of Christ, and
through them he knows the meaning of Christ's resurrection. Because
of Christ's resurrection converts have the hope for attaining a similar
resurrection in the future. Having submitted to God's righteousness on
the basis of faithfulness toward him, not on the basis of works of the
law, as a Christian Jew Paul wants to attain the ultimate goal of his
life--resurrection from the dead. But that goal is still future; he has not
yet reached it. "Not that I have already attained this or am already
perfect; but I press on to make it my own, because Christ Jesus has
made me his own" (Phil 3:12).

The Greek verb translated as "am perfect" is teleioo, which
literally means "bring to completion" or "complete." With reference to
persons it means "bring to ethical or spiritual maturity" or "to be
completely good or mature in character." But what does Paul really
mean by the use of the word? Does it refer to the resurrection from the
dead (Phil 3:11) or to leaving this life to be with Christ (Phil 1:23)? At
any rate, in the verses that follow the moral implications become
emphatically clear.

In the language of an athlete Paul tells his Philippian readers that his experience as a Christian Jew is not complete: "Forgetting what lies behind and straining forward to what lies ahead, I press on toward the goal for the prize of the upward call of God in Christ Jesus." Yet, at the same time, in typical fashion, Paul speaks of being perfect: "Then let as many of us who are perfect think this, and if you think anything otherwise, even this God will reveal to you. However, to what we have come, let us hold to it" (Phil 3:15-16). Do not fail to observe that even in this passage, the most christological in Paul's undisputed letters, the thought of Paul returns to God, who is still behind all his thinking about Jesus. In my literal translation the word for "perfect" is the adjective teleios from the verb teleioo used earlier. As with the verb, the adjective, of course, refers to moral character.

In the passage from Philippians Paul is influenced by the Jewish scriptures. In Deut 18:13, where the writer is having Moses report to the children of Israel what he believed God had told Moses at Sinai, we read: "You shall be perfect before the Lord your God" (LXX). The Greek word translated as "perfect" is teleios and renders the Hebrew word tamim, which has the meaning unblemished or with no imperfection. When used with reference to humans, it denotes persons without moral blemish, or morally blameless. For example, God says to Abraham: "Be blameless" (Gen 17:1; see also 2 Sam 22:26; LXX = 2 Kgs 22:26). It seems, indeed, that the law itself was the motivation for Paul's goal of moral perfection as a Christian Jew. Paul expected no less of his converts (see 1 Cor 2:6; 14:20; Rom 12:2; see Matt 5:48).

Paul appeals to his fellow converts at Philippi, as elsewhere (see 1 Thess 1:6; 2:14; 1 Cor 4:16; 11:1), to "be imitators" of him and to observe those "who so conduct their lives as they who have a model in us" (Phil 3:17). The Greek verb that I have translated as "conduct their lives" is peripateo and literally means to "walk." In the Septuagint it usually translates the Hebrew word halak, which means to "walk," "go," "travel," and also to walk in the sense of "lead a life" or "live." In the New Testament it is usually translated as "live" and is thus used Hebraistically in an ethical sense and means "conduct one's life." The words in Phil 3:18-19 describe persons who do the opposite of what Paul is striving for. They are those "whose end is destruction, whose god is the belly, and (for whom) the glory is in their shame, who set their minds on earthly things." Such persons conduct their lives "as enemies of the cross of Christ." (For further comments and suggestions concerning Phil 3:7-16 see chapter 7 of this work.)

Paul, Man of Feeling, Not Intellectual Acumen

Throughout his letters Paul reveals a variety of emotions, perhaps made more sensitive as the result of his special religious experience. Distressed because of the behavior of some Corinthian converts, he writes to them "out of much affliction and anguish of heart and with many tears" (2 Cor 2:4; see also 1 Cor 3:1-4; Phil 3:18). He shares in the pain, joy, sorrow, and fears of others (1 Cor 2:3; 2 Cor 1:23-2:11; Gal 4:19-20). Sometimes Paul is patient and tolerant (1 Corinthians 8; Romans 14-15), sometimes intolerant, impatient, even angry (Gal 1:1-24; 2:4-5; 4:16-17; 2 Cor 7:8-9). Paul confronts the Corinthians "in weakness and in much fear and trembling" (1 Cor 2:3) and with speech "not in plausible words of wisdom, but in demonstration of the Spirit and of power" (1 Cor 2:4). And the Corinthians say that Paul is humble when present but bold when absent (2 Cor 10:1). When dealing with his adversaries, Paul's language is often polemical and coarse (2 Cor 10:2; 11:12-15, 20-21; Gal 1:6-10; Rom 16:17-18; Phil 3:18-19). Sometimes his emotions got the better of him. To be specific, he wishes the troublemakers at Galatia would "be castrated" (Gal 5:12), and he calls his adversaries at Philippi "dogs" (Phil 3:2). Paul was emotionally strong because he survived numerous dangers and hardships (2 Cor 11:23-27; see also 1 Cor 4:9-13; 2 Cor 1:7-10; 4:7-12; 6:4-10; 7:5; Phil 4:10-13), besides feeling "the daily pressure" and "anxiety for all the churches" (2 Cor 11:28).

Paul was not a systematic theologian. Nothing in his letters indicates that he was intellectually discerning or even that he had a superior education. Rather, Paul was profound in feeling, not in intellectual acumen. And evidence indicates that he was driven more by personal faithfulness toward God and powerful moral/ethical convictions than by systematic thought. Perhaps those convictions came partly as the result of his special religious experience. But the crisis at Galatia caused by the troublemakers of the circumcision party did more than anything else to shape Paul's peculiar ideas.

In the following chapters I try to present Paul's ideas, as clearly and objectively as I can, on justification by faithfulness, grace, the law, and the relationship of those ideas to his views of Christian life and ultimate salvation.

Chapter 1

Basic Ideas Of Paul

In this chapter I summarize basic ideas of Paul and then in subsequent chapters I consider them in more detail as they appear at varioius places in his letters.

The so-called doctrine of justification by faith <u>in</u> Christ is not the basic idea of Paul. In fact, there is no such doctrine in the undisputed letters. There are three reasons why I say this. First, although doctrine means something that is taught, the word implies that what is taught is formally worked out and carefully and consistently presented. This is not true for Paul because he develops his ideas to meet particular situations he is addressing in one church after another. I say "ideas" because he usually has more than one idea on most theological subjects, and his ideas are not always consistently presented.

Second, the ideas of justification are not at all central in his letters because they appear in only two of them--Galatians and Romans. And third, evidence presented in this work will show that the phrase "faith <u>in</u> Christ" is not a genuine Pauline phrase.

Faithfulness Toward God

At the root of all Paul's ideas is his profound faithfulness toward the God of the Jews. I say faithfulness toward God because for Paul, as with most Jews of his time, such faithfulness was expressed with reference to the polytheism of the pagan world. This faithfulness toward God, not to the gods of the pagans, is a tradition in Judaism that the Jews believed went back to Moses and the Decalogue: "I am the Lord your God who brought you out of the land of Egypt, out of the house of slavery. You shall have no other gods besides me" (Exod 20:2-3).

Paul's faithfulness toward God, along with his renewed conviction of God's own faithfulness in dealing with his people Israel, is the key to understanding all of his ideas on theology and ethics. Indeed, in every letter God, not Christ, is Paul's main concern. This will become evident as we proceed with our investigation, but here I mention only several passages that provide the basis for my view and that are crucial for beginning any study of Paul. However, before I discuss specific passages let me mention something of a more general nature that is important for understanding Paul's emphasis on faithfulness toward God and what he thought it meant for converts to the Jesus movement.

By Paul's time philosophers were beginning to question the actions and even the existence of the Graeco-Roman gods that often were thought to behave worse than humans. For Paul, however, as for most Jews of his time, the existence of God was taken for granted, not debated. Also, for such Jews religion was not a matter of reason or of the mind expressed in theological propositions. Rather, religion was a matter of heart and life, one's very existence, which was regulated by strict moral/ethical discipline under the law. Jewish converts to Christianity never lost that sense of discipline.

Jews believed that holiness of character was the highest expectation of the law and that the greatest achievement and the deepest religious experience was the realization of righteousness. A basic text for such belief was Lev 19:2: "You shall be holy, for I the Lord your God am holy" (see also Lev 11:44-45; Num 16:7; Deut 26:19; 28:9). Indeed, holiness (kedushah) was the primary virtue in a higher mystical concept of a person's relationship with God that was expressed by the Hebrew word chasiduth, meaning "saintliness" (see the discussion of Christian converts as saints or holy ones in chapter 6 of this work).

Jewish converts to Christianity would, then, already understand what Paul meant when they read words such as these: "For God has not called us for uncleanness but in holiness" (1 Thess 4:7) and "I appeal to you, fellow converts, through the mercies of God to present your bodies as a living sacrifice, holy and acceptable to God" (Rom 12:1). And it would not be difficult, either, for Jewish converts to understand the meaning of being a new creation (Gal 6:15) as the result of their baptism and the forgiveness of their past sins. In other words, it would not be too difficult for Jews to adapt to the stringent moral/ethical requirements demanded by life lived under the power of the Holy Spirit.

On the other hand, for pagans, whose understanding of religion was more a matter of mind and reason than of heart and life, it was extremely difficult not to tie in their old attitudes toward their gods with their lives as new creations under the influence of the Spirit. Or, to put it in another way, it was hard for Gentile converts not to associate old attitudes toward their pagan gods with their lives as new creations as part of their faithfulness toward the one God who expected them to be holy or righteous as he was holy or righteous. Generally, then, most prospective Gentile converts would not have the vaguest notion of what Paul was talking about. All of these things made the tasks of Paul and other missionaries extremely difficult and help us to understand why Paul has constantly to exhort Gentile converts to conduct their lives as they were expected to do.

With these things as background, I turn now to specific passages that show Paul's main concern in his mission to the Gentiles was faithfulness toward God and the imperatives of that faithfulness for Christian life.

Examples from Paul's Letters

Paul's first letter, 1 Thessalonians, provides the basic clue to understanding his ideas about faithfulness toward God and the practical implications of that faithfulness for converts. Paul compliments the converts at Thessalonica because their "faithfulness toward God" has gone out to every place and because they "turned to God from idols to serve a living and true God" (1 Thess 1:8-9). Conversely, he chides the

Corinthian converts by saying that when they were pagans, that is, before they turned to faithfulness toward God, they "were misled and led to dumb idols" (1 Cor 12:2). Paul and his fellow laborers worked hard not to burden any of the Thessalonian converts while they preached the good news (gospel) of God to them (1 Thess 2:9). These passages make it clear that from the beginning of his mission activity Paul was primarily concerned that pagans turn from idolatry to the God of the Jews. Therefore I use the phrase "faithfulness toward God," rather than "faith in God." Faithfulness of converts is to be directed toward God, not toward idols. Paul writes similarly to the converts in the churches of Galatia: "But then when you did not know God, you were slaves to beings that by nature are not gods; but now that you know God or, rather, are known by God, how can you turn back again to the weak and beggarly elements to which you want to be slaves once again?" (Gal 4:8-9).

Paul was primarily concerned that converts turn to faithfulness toward God and only secondarily with their beliefs about Jesus. So he can quite naturally write about "the church of the Thessalonians in God the Father and the Lord Jesus Christ" (1 Thess 1:1) and about fellow converts as "beloved by God" who chose them (1 Thess 1:4). Paul speaks several times about "the gospel of God" preached to the Thessalonians and about "the word of God" that they had heard from him and his fellow workers (1 Thess 2:2, 8, 9, 13). He exhorts the Thessalonian converts to conduct their lives worthy of God who calls them into his own kingdom and glory (1 Thess 2:12; see also 4:7, 9). He calls Timothy "a fellow worker of God in the gospel of Christ" (1 Thess 3:2).

As with 1 Thessalonians, in every other letter God is uppermost in Paul's thinking. Paul writes to "the church of God that is in Corinth" (1 Cor 1:2; 2 Cor 1:2) and thanks God for "the grace of God" given to the Corinthian converts "in Christ Jesus" (1 Cor 1:4; see also 1:9). He says that he and his companions are "fellow workers of God" and that the Corinthian converts are "the field of God, God's building" (1 Cor 3:9). The converts at Corinth are "the temple of God"; God's Spirit dwells in them (1 Cor 3:16). Paul and his fellow workers are "servants of Christ and stewards of the mysteries of God" (1 Cor 4:1). What pagans sacrifice they "sacrifice to demons and not to God" (1 Cor 10:20).

Paul uses the expression "church of God" not only for a particular Christian community, as with the one at Corinth, but also for several churches as a group. He expresses his joy that the Thessalonians "became imitators of the churches of God that are in Judea" (1 Thess 2:14; see also 1 Cor 11:16). He also uses the expression for the church as a whole. To the converts at Corinth and Galatia Paul laments the fact that he persecuted "the church of God" (1 Cor 15:9; Gal 1:13; see also 1 Cor 10:32). It is important to observe that, in contrast to the phrase "church of God," the expression "churches of Christ" occurs only once in an undisputed letter of Paul, in Rom 16:16, a passage that may not have been written by him.

In 1 Cor 1:9 Paul assures the converts at Corinth that God who called them into the fellowship of his Son will, by his faithfulness, sustain them to the end. In 2 Cor 1:18-20 Paul invokes God's faithfulness in defending himself against the Corinthians' accusation that he had vacillated in his plans to visit them: "It is because God is faithful that our word to you is not 'yes' and 'no.' For the Son of God, Jesus Christ, who was preached among you through us . . . was not 'yes' and 'no,' but in him was 'yes.' For however many are the promises of God, in him they are 'yes.'" The promises of God are, of course, those made to the Hebrews as the result of Abraham's faithfulness toward God (Gal 3:16; Rom 9:4; 15:8) and those concerning the coming of the Messiah (Gal 3:14; Rom 1:2).

Because the promises of God are fulfilled by virtue of Christ's faithfulness, converts say the "Amen" through him for the glory of God. The centrality of God in the thought of Paul and in his life is emphasized in his summary statement in defense of himself and of his fellow workers: "But it is God who confirms us [both missionaries and converts] with you in Christ and has anointed us [that is, with the Spirit]; he has set his seal upon us and given us the down payment of the Spirit in our hearts" (2 Cor 1:21-22). Later Paul writes that the confidence of him and his fellow workers comes by virtue of Christ but that their competence comes from God, who made them competent to

be ministers of a new covenant, not of the letter but of the Spirit (2
Cor 3:4-6).

Paul reminds the Galatian converts that it was in accordance with
"the will of our God and Father" that Christ gave himself for converts'
sins. And Paul marvels that the converts are so quickly deserting God
who called them into the grace of Christ (Gal 1:6).

To the Galatian converts Paul also writes that the churches of Judea
"glorified God" because of him (Gal 1:24). He calls God to witness in
his own behalf (Gal 1:20; Phil 1:8). While Paul's imprisonment is for
Christ, most of his fellow converts are more bold to speak the word of
God fearlessly (Phil 1:13-14). In contrast to his adversaries at Philippi,
Paul and his Christian friends are "the true circumcision who worship
by the Spirit of God and glory in Christ Jesus" (Phil 3:3). Paul's God
will fill every need of the Philippian converts according to his riches in
glory in Christ Jesus (Phil 4:19).

Paul addresses his letter to the Romans "to all those in Rome
beloved of God" (Rom 1:7) and thanks his God through Jesus Christ for
all of them (Rom 1:8). According to Paul, Gentiles who did not
become converts "did not glorify God as God" but "changed the glory of
the immortal God into images like mortal humans" (Rom 1:23). His
whole discussion in Romans about Gentiles indicates that the God of
Paul and of other Jews and of God's faithfulness to them was the
utmost concern in his mission to a church he had not founded. Toward
the end of Romans he expresses his satisfaction with the converts at
Rome and says that he wrote to them boldly about certain things
because of the grace given to him by God for him to be a minister of
Christ Jesus to the Gentiles (Rom 15:14-16). Then Paul writes: "I have
pride in Christ Jesus with respect to the things I do for God. For I will
not dare to speak anything except what Christ effected through me for
the obedience of Gentiles" (Rom 15:17-18). Because of vocabulary and
style, the doxology in Rom 16:25-27 was probably not written by
Paul. But although the author of the doxology writes in his own
peculiar idiom, he has certainly understood the goal of Paul's mission
activity correctly: to bring about the obedience of faithfulness of all the
Gentiles toward the only wise God. This is precisely what Paul himself
had said in Rom 1:5: his apostleship was for the purpose of "the

obedience of faithfulness [toward God] among all the Gentiles for the sake of his [Jesus'] name."

These examples are typical of Paul's writing about God and Christ and show that God is uppermost in his thinking. There are several contexts in which Christ does seem to predominate as, for example, in 1 Cor 11:23-32; 15:3-9, 12-19; and Phil 2:5-11, all in traditions that Paul probably had received from earlier Christianity. But in the contexts of those passages Paul himself is always concerned about God. Before the passage in 1 Cor 11:23-32 Paul asks the Corinthian converts if they "despise the church of God" by misbehaving at the Lord's Supper. Then he introduces the traditional account of the institution of the Supper that he had received after he had become a Christian Jew. In the context of 1 Cor 15:3-9 Paul says that he is what he is by the grace of God that is with him in his working harder than anyone else (1 Cor 15:10). In the context of his discussion of the resurrection in 1 Cor 15:12-19, Paul says that when the last enemy--death--is overcome, "the Son himself will be subjected" to God who subjected all things to himself "in order that God may be all things to all persons" (1 Cor 15:28). And even in Phil 2:5-11, one of the highest christological passages in Paul's letters, God is supreme. Christ "did not think being equal to God a thing to be snatched at" and confession of Jesus as Lord is to be done "for the glory of God the Father" (Phil 2:6, 11).

God is also at the center of Paul's eschatological thinking. Ultimately God, not Christ, is responsible for converts' ultimate salvation or condemnation. "God is not mocked. For whatever a person sows, that will that person also reap. For the person who sows to his own flesh from the flesh will reap corruption, but the person who sows to the Spirit from the Spirit will reap eternal life" (Gal 6:7-8). "We shall all stand before the judgment seat of God" (Rom 14:10; see also Rom 2:5-11).

<u>Observations and Summary</u>

Paul's experience of the spiritual Christ in his life by the grace of God was a strong motivation for his mission activity, especially for converting Gentiles to faithfulness toward God and Jews as well as Gentiles to certain beliefs about Jesus. But God was always uppermost in Paul's mind. This is confirmed not only by the evidence presented

"acquit," "make pure," "set free from," and "justify." It is used of God's action toward humans, both with reference to the righteous and to the unrighteous. King Solomon prays to God "to justify the righteous, to give him according to his righteousness" (3 Kgs 8:32, LXX; [3 Kgs in the LXX = 1 Kgs in the Hebrew and English Bibles]; see also Ps 81(82):3; Isa 53:11). According to Isaiah, "God blots out all transgressions" and expects his people to confess their sins "in order to be justified" (Isa 43:25-26; see also 50:8). "By the Lord should they [the children of Israel] be justified" (Isa 45:26).

Dikaioo is also used of a human's action toward other humans. According to Exod 23:7, the laws of justice require that persons "not justify the wicked because of gifts" (see also Isa 5:23) but "justify the righteous and condemn the wicked" (Deut 25:1). And the prophet Micah asks: "Shall the lawless person be justified in the balance?" (Mic 6:11).

In the apocryphal writing of Sirach (c. 180 B. C.) the Jewish author uses dikaioo with reference to various persons and phenomena. For example, "Unrighteous anger cannot be justified," nor can one who has sworn needlessly (Sir 1:22; 23:11). "The person who loves gold will not be justified" (Sir 34:5). "A huckster will not be justified from sin" (Sir 26:29). The writer of Sirach says that one should not be ashamed in making a judgment to justify the ungodly (42:2). On the other hand, he writes that the ungodly will not be justified until Hades (9:12). Perhaps this coincides with the psalmist's view that no one living shall be justified before God (Ps 142(143):2). The obverse of the psalmist's idea may be reflected in Paul's statement "The person who has died [that is, symbolically in baptism] has been justified from sin" (Rom 6:7). Here Paul's Greek expression "justified from sin" is almost identical to that of Sirach in 26:29, and the meaning is exactly the same. This means, then, that justification and the forgiveness of sins are thought to be the same thing for both some writers of the Septuagint and Paul.

In the Septuagint the words "justification" and "salvation" are sometimes used synonymously as, for example, in the following two passages. "My justification quickly draws near, and my salvation shall go forth as light, and on my arm Gentiles shall hope" (Isa 51:5). "I have brought near my justification, and I will not delay the salvation that is from me" (Isa 46:13). In the first passage God is speaking to the remnant of Israel who have survived the downfall of their nation and the Exile. In the second passage it is the Gentiles who are addressed, and they are offered the same possibility of God's salvation as the Israelites. Although Paul never uses the nouns "justification" and "salvation" in parallel, he does use the verbs "justify" and "save" in that way (see Rom 5:9 and 10:10 and the discussion of those passages later in this chapter).

Observations and Summary

These examples from the Septuagint are important for understanding Paul's concept of justification, and they show the distinctive differences between the use of <u>dikaioo</u> in the Septuagint and in Paul's letters. Nowhere in the Septuagint is the idea of faithfulness associated with the verb "justify," as it is in Galatians and Romans. On the other hand, Paul uses the verb "justify" only with respect to God's action toward humans, never of humans' actions toward other humans. Nor does Paul share the idea of God justifying the righteous, as in some writings of the Septuagint, but only that of justifying the ungodly or impious. According to Paul, God "justifies the impious" (Rom 4:5), an idea he shares with the writer of Sir 42:2. The idea that God justifies the ungodly or unrighteous on the basis of faithfulness toward him is part of Paul's creative contribution to theology. And this study shows that there are aspects of Paul's ideas of faithfulness that are different from those usually presented in studies on Paul. The same is true for his ideas of justification.

In sum, according to Paul, "God is the one who justifies" (Rom 8:33). Converts are justified or declared righteous or "righteoused" (that is, forgiven of their past sins) through the grace of God by virtue of the faithfulness of Christ (see chapter 4 of this work), not by works of the law. Justification or forgiveness takes place symbolically through baptism, during which, Paul believed, converts received the Holy Spirit. Baptism was the initiation rite by which converts became members of the renewed covenant community of God (see chapter 7 of this work). Forgiveness is for past sins, not sins committed after baptism. Members who had received the Holy Spirit were expected to live moral/ethical lives by the Spirit and not to sin (see Romans 6 and the discussion of that passage in chapter 6 of this work). The ultimate salvation of all converts depends on their continuing in their faithfulness that includes remaining in a state of righteousness, free from sin, by living by the Spirit. Because converts live by the Spirit, circumcision, dietary laws, and other ceremonial aspects of Jewish law are no longer necessary for righteous life. Paul's idea of justification occurs only in the letters of Galatians and Romans, and it emerged from and was developed fully only after he had to deal with the crisis in the churches of Galatia (see chapter 4 of this work).

Faithfulness and Justification as Related to Salvation

Salvation belongs within the framework of Paul's eschatological thought in the broadest sense. Paul shared the usual Jewish eschatology, including the idea of two ages, the present age and the age to come. As with other Jews of his time, he believed that the present age was evil; but unlike non-Christian Jews, he believed that Jesus had come as the Messiah, in accordance with the will of God, to deliver persons from that evil age (Gal 1:3-4). Paul often implies that the present age is only temporary (1 Cor 1:20; 2:6-8; 3:18-19; Rom 12:2). As with other Jews of his time, he believed that the end of this age would soon come, sometimes that the end was already dawning (1 Cor 10:11). He eagerly anticipated that end because for him as a Christian Jew, but not for non-Christian Jews, it meant the coming again of Jesus (1 Thess 4:13-5:11; 1 Cor 1:7-8; 15:23-28). For Paul, as for all other writers of the New Testament, except for the writer of John's gospel, judgment, salvation, and eternal life were phenomena thought to belong to the future age. Although there are passages in John that reflect the same understanding of those phenomena (for example, John 5:25-29; 11:23-24), others stress salvation or eternal life as beginning here and now with the present existence of believers. Persons are already judged on the basis of their belief or disbelief in Jesus, and for believers eternal life has already begun because of their faith in Christ. "The person who believes in him is not condemned; but the person who does not believe is condemned already, because that person has not believed in the name of the unique Son of God" (John 3:18). According to John, Jesus says to the Jews: "Truly, truly, I say to you, the person who hears my word and believes him who sent me, has eternal life and does not come into judgment, but has passed from death to life" (John 5:24).

After raising Lazarus from the dead, Jesus is reported as saying to Martha: "I am the resurrection and the life; the person who believes in me, though that person die, shall live, and every one who lives and believes in me shall never die" (John 11:25-26).

Paul nowhere reflects such a concept of the judgment and eternal life, probably the Johannine equivalent of salvation. And he never talks about believing in Jesus as the writer of John does. For Paul, judgment and salvation belong to the future. The transition of believers from the joys and tribulations of human life to eternal bliss can come only after the divine judgment. This view, precisely that of contemporary Judaism, was in early Christian circles supplemented with the idea that the last judgment would be preceded or accompanied by the second coming of Christ.

In Romans the terms "justify" (dikaioo) and "justification" (dikaiosyne) are used with past, present, and future meaning, but always with reference either to the present experience of believers or to the anticipated state of prospective converts. Never can it be definitely shown that by justification Paul ever means ultimate salvation. With the possible exception of Rom 5:8-11, never does the justification of converted sinners even imply the ultimate salvation of those persons. Only the hope of that salvation seems to be assured (see Rom 8:24-25), provided, however, the converts continue to live their lives in accordance with the required moral/ethical instruction (see Rom 13:11-14).

In Rom 5:9-10 the verb "save" is in the future tense, where as future it stands in contrast to being justified and reconciled: "Much more, then, having now been justified by his blood, shall we be saved through him from his wrath. For if while we were enemies we were reconciled to God through the death of his Son, much more, now that we have been reconciled, shall we be saved in his life." This passage may appear to be the Achilles' heel in my statements that Paul thinks of ultimate salvation by God as happening in the future. Rom 5:9-10 is the only passage in all of Paul's letters (but see comments on 1 Cor 1:8 in chapter 3 of this work) that seems to imply the certainty of ultimate salvation for converts who are justified and reconciled to God. But it must not be taken by itself and must be considered in light of what

Paul says about salvation elsewhere in the complex and confusing contexts of Romans. And although the conditions of being justified and reconciled are present experiences of new converts, any notion that converts as justified persons are on an automatic course to final salvation is positively and emphatically dispelled in Romans 6 and elsewhere (see the discussion of Romans 6 in chapter 6 of this work).

It is significant to observe here that whereas believing or faithfulness is usually mentioned in connection with, or as a requirement for, justification, believing is mentioned with salvation (eis soterian, "toward salvation") only in Rom 1:16 and believing with being saved only in Rom 10:9-10. In both of those passages (discussed later in more detail) Paul is clearly referring to the potential experience of converts, both Jews and Gentiles, who become justified or forgiven of their past sins. Nowhere in Romans is faithfulness mentioned in connection with the convert's ultimate salvation. Equally significant is the fact that the word "grace" is not once used in any passage where the word "save" or "salvation" occurs.

With reference to Paul's ideas on justification and salvation in Romans let me comment briefly about his idea of predestination. It may appear to border on the idea of universal salvation (Romans 8-11) and, therefore, make the idea of a future judgment, with reward for the righteous and punishment for the wicked, irrelevant. However, his idea of predestination can be understood only in light of the idea of a future judgment. According to Paul, God was working through him for the ultimate salvation of Jews as well as Gentiles. From the beginning God had predestined certain persons, but the point is that they were predestined for justification, not for ultimate salvation (Rom 8:28-30). This is a very important point in the theology of Paul.

Unlike the terms "predestine" and "justify," which are used together in Rom 8:28-30, the terms "predestine" and "save" never occur together in the undisputed letters of Paul. In spite of this fact, I am a bit perplexed by Paul's concluding phrase in Rom 8:30: "whom he justified, those he also glorified." This is the only place that he uses the verb doxazo ("glorify") in that way, whatever way it is, especially since it is in the past tense (edoxasen) and, so, can hardly refer to salvation in the future. In Rom 8:17 Paul uses the verb syndoxazo (a hapaxlegomenon in the New Testament) in the aorist subjunctive with future meaning: "in order that we may also be glorified with him [Jesus] if we suffer with him." In 2 Cor 3:18 Paul speaks of converts being transformed from one glory to another and in 2 Cor 4:17 of being prepared for an eternal weight of glory exceedingly. These passages speak of future ultimate glorification. If by "glorified" in Rom 8:30 Paul means that the final glorification of justified converts is assured, it is the exception that proves the rule. The rule is stated in Rom 5:2: "We boast in the hope of (sharing) the glory of God." Justified converts have only "attained access to the grace in which" they stand (Rom 5:2).

Salvation in the Disputed Letters of Ephesians and Colossians

Several passages in Ephesians and Colossians reveal how the ideas of the authors of those works, who surely were familiar with Paul's letters, differ from those of Paul himself.

In Ephesians, as sometimes in Paul's letters, the verb "save" occurs as the equivalent of being converted or justified by the grace of God and becoming a member of the Christian religion. The context of the only passage where "save" occurs makes that clear: "When we were dead with our transgressions, he [God] made us alive with Christ--by grace you have been saved--and raised us with him and made us sit with him in the heavenly places in Christ Jesus, in order that in the coming ages he [God] might show the extraordinary wealth of his grace in kindness toward us in Christ Jesus. For by grace you have been saved by virtue of faithfulness; and this is not of your own doing, but the gift of God, not on the basis of works, lest anyone should boast" (Eph 2:5-9).

The author of Ephesians does not understand that when Paul speaks about works he means works of the law, not good deeds. This is quite clear from the next verse: "created in Christ Jesus for good works . . . that we should conduct our lives in (doing) them" (Eph 2:10). And the author exhorts his readers not to "share with others in the fruitless works of darkness" (Eph 5:11, 15-18). At the same time, though, this shows that the author of Ephesians is aware of the real Paul's emphasis on moral conduct and deeds of love.

Moreover, the context of Eph 2:5-9 conveys Paul's idea of justification, not of salvation, although expressed in the language of the epitomizer of Paul. That the author of Ephesians is referring to the time of the converts' forgiveness of past sins is clear from the words "when we were dead with our transgressions." And that he is referring to their baptism at the time of their becoming converts is clear from the words "he made us alive with Christ," presumably, symbolically of rising from the water of baptism. Presumably also, this is a foretaste of what is to happen in the coming ages. However, the words "made us sit with him in the heavenly places"--whatever they mean--are quite unlike anything Paul himself says. And, yet, the twice-repeated phrase "in Christ Jesus" and the expression "made us alive with Christ" may indicate that by "the heavenly places" the writer means some spiritual experience. This is quite likely, it seems to me, and would come close, then, to Paul's ideas of life by the Spirit or of experiencing the spiritual Christ.

The combination of being justified and believing or faithfulness is common in Galatians and Romans but not the idea of being saved and believing, as in the passage from Ephesians. Nor does the combination of being saved and grace ever occur in the undisputed letters of Paul. So, we could substitute "justified" for "saved" and have Paul's meaning precisely. In fact, the epitomizer replaced Paul's characteristic term "justify," which does not once occur in Ephesians, with "save." And the use of the perfect tense with reference to salvation is quite unlike Paul who prefers the future or present passive to represent salvation as a process still continuing and culminating in the future. Only in Rom 8:24 does Paul use a past tense (aorist) when referring to salvation, but there it refers to the time when the readers became converts and is qualified by waiting and hoping for redemption that is still to come. According to Paul, converts have only "the firstfruits of the Spirit" (Rom 8:23).

Ephesians contains only two passages in which a noun that means "salvation" is used. One of them includes the phrase "the helmet of salvation" (Eph 6:17), a part of converts' armor of God to be used in defending them against the evils of the eschatological age. Here the Greek word for salvation is soterion, a word that Paul himself never uses (compare Paul's words, "a helmet the hope of salvation" (soteria) in 1 Thess 5:8. The other passage in Ephesians where a noun meaning salvation occurs is 1:13-14: "In him [Christ] you also, who have heard the word of the truth, the gospel of your salvation, and have believed in him, were sealed with the promised Holy Spirit, which is the down payment of our inheritance, toward the ransoming (redemption) of the obtaining of it, to the praise of his glory." The phrase "believed in him," with Christ as the object, as expressed here (en ho kai pisteusantes) occurs nowhere in the undisputed letters of Paul.

Again, the writer of Ephesians conveys in his own words the essential meaning of Paul's message. The reference is clearly to the justification of those who had heard the gospel, became converted, and received the Holy Spirit, presumably during baptism. As in Paul's own letters, that experience, which was only begun but not completed in the past, continues under the influence of the Spirit in the present but is still to be consummated in the future.

Several words and phrases in Eph 1:13-14 make reference to the future, as well as the past, clear. The word translated as "down payment" is arrabon, a Semitic word that probably came into Greek from the vocabulary of traders. It was a down payment to seal a bargain and obligated both purchaser and seller to complete the transaction later. God's gift of the inner sanctifying power of the Spirit, received at baptism, is God's pledge that he is committed to bring the converts' salvation to completion. Meanwhile, converts have as their obligation the responsibility for bearing fruit of the Spirit. Not only the use of the word arrabon but also the word "inheritance" shows that the writer has a future consummation in mind. Arrabon is used in the New Testament elsewhere only in 2 Cor 1:22 and 5:5, where it is also used of the Spirit. The writer of Ephesians was undoubtedly influenced by those passages.

A reference to the future is clear also from the words translated as "toward the ransoming of the obtaining of it." But the meaning of the Greek words which convey that reference is not so clear. Literally, they may also be translated as "for [or "toward"] a redemption of the possession." We may assume influence on the writer from Rom 8:23, where Paul uses "redemption" with a future reference. Redemption has a future reference also in Eph 4:30, where it is the center of an intensely moral/ethical section.

Neither the author of Ephesians nor the author of Colossians uses the verb "justify" (dikaioo). In Ephesians the noun dikaiosyne is used only with the meaning righteousness (Eph 4:24; 5:9; 6:14), never with the meaning justification. The noun does not occur at all in Colossians. Neither the word "save" (sozo) nor the word "salvation" (soteria) occurs in Colossians. In fact, the author of Colossians seems to place all the emphasis on the past experience of converts, with reference only to the present, and without any anticipation of a greater experience to come in the future. Indeed, in Colossians, with reference to the experiences of converts, all seems to have been accomplished in the past. God's action is described in the past tense. The future tense is missing. Compare the following statements in Colossians with similar statements in Paul's undisputed letters: "who delivered us from the power of darkness and transferred us into the kingdom of his beloved Son" (Col 1:13) with "who delivers us from the wrath that is coming" (1 Thess 1:10) and "the unrighteous will not inherit the kingdom of God" (1 Cor 6:9; see also 1 Cor 15:50; Gal 5:21); "You were buried with him in baptism, in which you were also raised with him" (Col 2:12) with "We were buried with him by virtue of baptism into death. . . . For if we have been united with the likeness of his death, we shall also be (a likeness) of his resurrection" (Rom 6:4-5); and "He [God] made you alive together with him" (Col 2:13) with "We believe that we shall also live with him" (Rom 6:8).

Surely, these passages from Ephesians and Colossians show how different and distinctive the ideas of the real Paul are from those of the "Paul" of those disputed letters.

There is nothing in the undisputed letters of Paul like the statement in 2 Tim 3:15 that the sacred writings "can make you wise for salvation by virtue of faith, faith in [Greek, en] Christ Jesus." The Greek translated as "by virtue of faith, faith in Christ Jesus" is dia pisteos tes en Christo Iesou. Compare this with similar but distinctively different phrases of Paul himself in Gal 2:16, 20; 3:22; Rom 3:22, 26; and Phil 3:9, passages discussed later in this work. None of Paul's phrases with reference to faithfulness is the same as the phrase "by virtue of faith, faith in Christ Jesus" in 2 Tim 3:15.

Observations and Summary

Although, unlike Paul, the writer of the Jewish apocryphal work known as 2 Esdras thought of salvation as occurring on this earth in the messianic age, Paul might well have agreed with the writer about how to attain it: "It shall be that all who will be saved and will be able to escape on account of their works, or on account of the faith [in God] by which they have believed, will survive the dangers that have been predicted, and will see my salvation in my land" (2 Esdr 9:7-8; NRSV) and "[God] will protect those who fall into peril, who have works and faith toward the Almighty" (2 Esdr 13:23; NRSV).

The apocalypse of 2 Esdras, the letters of Paul, and the Epistle of James all date within a few decades of each other. And their writers all seem to agree that for the attainment of salvation, no matter how it may be conceived or expressed, works or actions befitting faithfulness were expected (scc James 1:19-25; 2:14-26 and recall the discussion of Paul and James in the Introduction to this work).

For Paul the ideas of "save" and "salvation" are sometimes synonymous with the concepts of "justify" and "justification" and thus refer to the time and the process of becoming converts. Otherwise, with one possible exception, salvation lies in the future and always depends upon the moral life of those who have begun the way to ultimate salvation. There are probably two reasons for Paul's view. First, there was the emphasis on morality/ethics in his Jewish heritage, coming, of course, from the law itself. The second reason may be the Hellenistic environment in which he lived. Paul may have wanted to avoid giving any wrong impressions to those Gentile converts who were familiar with the belief that initiation into the Graeco-Roman mystery religions conferred upon the initiates the certainty of salvation or eternal life in whatever form it was promised.

Jesus' Death and Resurrection

Paul's ideas of the justification or "righteousing" of converts and their ultimate salvation is linked with his belief in the efficacy of Jesus' death and resurrection. Paul thought of Jesus' resurrection as the confirmation of his Pharisaic belief in a general resurrection of the dead at the final judgment (1 Cor 15:20) and as the assurance that righteous converts would also rise in the general resurrection (1 Thess 4:13-17; 1

Corinthians 15; 2 Cor 4:14). But the resurrection of Jesus meant more than these things. It had theological implications for Paul. It did not just happen. God was responsible for it, and this idea is a frequently recurring theme in Paul's letters (see, for example, 1 Thess 1:10; 1 Cor 6:14; 15:4, 15; 2 Cor 4:14; 13:4; Gal 1:1; Rom 4:24; 8:11; 10:9). Jesus became the "Son of God in power . . . by his resurrection from the dead" (Rom 1:4).

Paul sometimes links Jesus' death with the resurrection, and his death also has theological implications. "Christ died on behalf of the impious" (Rom 5:6), and his death was a sign of God's love (Rom 5:8). In Rom 6:1-10, part of the classic passage on baptism, Paul writes that when persons being baptized are immersed in the water, they share symbolically in Jesus' death, so they are dead to sin. Baptized persons emerging from the water also share in Jesus' resurrection and so are alive to God in Christ. The essence of Paul's belief in the death and resurrection of Jesus is that they made the justification or forgiveness of converts' past sins by the grace of God possible: Jesus "was handed over [for death] by virtue of our trespasses and raised for our justification" (Rom 4:25). But the justification of converts does not mean that they are assured of ultimate salvation. Ultimate salvation depends upon their continuing to live by the Spirit, that is, living moral lives free from sin.

Paul uses the creative expressions "in Christ" and "Christ in" to convey his own religious experience as a Christian Jew and to try to get his readers to share his feelings. A key passage is Gal 2:20: "I have been crucified with Christ; it is no longer I who live, but Christ who lives in me; and the life I now live in the flesh I live in [Greek preposition en] the faithfulness of the Son of God, who loved me and gave himself for me" (see the discussion of Gal 2:20 in chapter 4 of this work). Another key passage is Rom 8:9-10: "But you are not in the flesh, but in the Spirit, if indeed the Spirit of God dwells in you; and if anyone does not have the Spirit of Christ, that person is not his. But if Christ is in you, although the body is dead because of sin, the Spirit is life because of righteousness."

These passages indicate that for Paul the expressions "in Christ" and "Christ in" convey a kind of mystical, spiritual experience of the spiritual or risen Christ in converts' lives. That experience will be enriched in the life after death when believers will be "with Christ," "with the Lord," or with Jesus (see 1 Thess 4:17; 5:10; 2 Cor 4:14; Rom 6:8; 8:32; Phil 1:23). According to Paul, the spiritual presence of Christ, which is experienced when living by the Spirit, informs converts about Christian morality and transforms them to live in accordance with that morality. Right here we have the clue to understanding Paul's moral/ethical teaching. The consequence of being in Christ and living by the Spirit is the demand for moral life with all its individual and social obligations. Morality is the outward manifestation in Christian life of the inner experience of the spiritual Christ.

Faithfulness and Ethics

As a Christian Jew, Paul's beliefs about Jesus did not lessen his profound faithfulness as a Jew, still, toward the only God in existence (1 Cor 8:4-6; 10:20-21; Gal 3:20; Rom 3:28-30). Faithfulness toward God was Paul's primary concern when trying to win converts. Beliefs about Jesus were, therefore, only a secondary concern. And, really, if we judge by the amount of space he gives to any one subject, Paul's main concern, along with faithfulness toward God, is the moral/ethical responsibilities of his readers, the new converts in the communities addressed in his letters.

For Paul, the right or wrong conduct of a person always puts that person in a right or wrong relationship with God. As with Judaism, Paul never separates faithfulness from morality/ethics. In every letter he is concerned with the moral lives of the people to whom he is writing. As a man of feeling and action, ethics (moral values and responsibilities, or right human character, aims, and actions) are foremost in his mind.

As a Pharisaic Jew, Paul already had a disciplined hatred of idolatry, sexual misconduct, and immoral behavior of any kind. But as a Christian Jew, the motivating force behind his ethical teachings is the experience of the Holy Spirit or Spirit of Christ in his life. Moral acts are the culmination of those who live under the influence of the Spirit and who do not, therefore, need to live by ceremonial laws. Life by the Spirit gives the freedom to be morally responsible in personal and social life. The basis of this responsibility is love as summed up in the Jewish command: "You shall love your neighbor as yourself" (Lev 19:18). For Paul, this love command is the summation of the whole law, as stated clearly in both Galatians and Romans (Gal 5:14; Rom 13:9; see also 1 Thess 5:12-22; 1 Cor 13:1-14:1; 2 Cor 8:7-8, 24; Gal 5:13-26; Rom 12:9-21; 13:8-10). For Paul love does not proceed from faithfulness. Rather, love is what makes faithfulness effective-- "faithfulness set in operation through love" (Gal 5:6).

Faithfulness, Ethics, and the Kingdom of God

What Paul writes about the kingdom of God is similar to the teaching of Jesus on that subject as regards faithfulness. Although what Jesus is reported as saying about the kingdom and what Paul writes about it are different in many respects, both Jesus and Paul were, to some extent at least, trying to prepare the people addressed for the kingdom either as it was thought to exist in their own times or as it would exist at some time in the future. But--and this is most important--any suggestion of faith as a requirement for entrance into the kingdom is entirely absent from the reported teachings of Jesus and in the letters of Paul.

Paul does not write much about the kingdom of God, and his ideas on the subject are not always consistent. But most of his references to the kingdom are in contexts of his moral/ethical teachings. "The kingdom of God is not food and drink but righteousness and peace and joy in the Holy Spirit" (Rom 14:17; see also 1 Cor 4:20). Here the kingdom is perceived as a present reality, perhaps the community of justified persons or perhaps the Christian life and religion experienced as individuals. In some passages the kingdom is a future phenomenon to be inherited by the righteous. Paul asks the Corinthian converts if they "do not know that the unrighteous will not inherit the kingdom of God" (1 Cor 6:9). In the same way, he warns the Galatians: "Those who do such things [works of the flesh; see Gal 5:16-21] shall not inherit the kingdom of God" (Gal 5:21; see also 1 Cor 6:9-10).

One thing is unmistakably clear from Paul's letters: The justification or forgiveness of the past sins of converts on the basis of the faithfulness of Jesus (see comments on Gal 2:15-21 in chapter 4 of this work) through God's grace and the reception of the Holy Spirit do not assure participation in the kingdom of God, whether perceived as a present or as a future phenomenon. That depends on right moral conduct, life worthy of the kingdom.

Paul is always more concerned with discussing concrete moral/ethical issues among the recipients of his letters than with abstract intellectual faith. Because he sometimes uses <u>pistis</u> absolutely, that is, without a stated object, as in Rom 1:17, for example, we cannot always be sure what he means. On the other hand, there is never any doubt about where Paul stands on moral issues and what he means when he talks about them.

The explanation just given represents the essence of Paul's ideas of justification by virtue of the faithfulness of Jesus, of his idea of salvation, of his morality/ethics, and of his eschatology. But Paul's moral/ethical teachings are inseparable from each of the others. Justification imposes upon persons justified a responsibility for moral/ethical behavior, and such behavior is demanded for ultimate salvation in the age to come. This is implied in the very statement, "The person who on the basis of faithfulness is righteous shall live" (Gal 3:11; Rom 1:17). The unrighteous person, even though that person has faithfulness, will not live. Faithfulness and righteousness are inseparable in Paul's thinking.

In the next chapter I discuss the probable background for the ideas of Paul that we have been considering.

Chapter 2

The Background Of Paul's Ideas

Having briefly considered Paul's ideas of justification, faithfulness, the grace of God, the law, and salvation, I want to suggest what influenced him most with respect to those ideas. In the chapters that follow I show how Paul's ideas developed under the influence of his background from his earliest letter, 1 Thessalonians, through Philippians.

It is axiomatic that Paul's thought is greatly influenced by his Jewishness and especially by the Jewish scriptures so frequently quoted and alluded to by him. In light of that fact, is the idea that God justifies the ungodly or unrighteous on the basis of their faithfulness toward him found in Judaism earlier than Paul? Certain texts from Qumran, especially the Manual of Discipline (1QS), seem to anticipate several of his ideas.

The Sect of Qumran

There are some basic differences between the Sect of Qumran and Paul on the subjects of faithfulness and justification or righteousness.

For example, whereas faithfulness toward God is the cardinal aspect of Pauline theology, it is only infrequently mentioned in the texts from Qumran, although, of course, certainly assumed. This is consistent with Judaism in general. And faithfulness in the sense of loyalty, honesty,and reliability is implicit in many passages. And an examination of the interpretation of Hab 2:4, a passage cited by both the writer of Qumran and Paul, shows how close the two writers are and also the differences between them.

1QpHab 8:1-3

The following is a passage from the Commentary on Habakkuk (1QpHab): "But the righteous shall live by his faithfulness (Hab 2:4). Its interpretation concerns all those who do the law in the house of Judah, whom God will deliver from the house of judgment because of their work and because of their faith in the Teacher of Righteousness" (8:1-3).

There is no indication in the Qumran Scrolls that the Qumran community had ascribed to the Teacher of Righteousness, the leader of the community, a work of redemption comparable to that attributed to Christ by orthodox Christianity. Yet, in the passage just cited, faithfulness of some kind and work of some sort are essential for escape from the judgment or for acquiring ultimate deliverance. But whether "faith" in the Hebrew expression "their faith" is a personal faithfulness which will bring deliverance (salvation) or simply loyalty to the teacher's interpretation of the law, there is insufficient evidence to decide. In light of the context (1QpHab 8:4-9:11), "their faith" may be trust in the leadership of the Teacher of Righteousness for their deliverance from the enemy rather than in the leadership of the Wicked Priest who sought personal gain and did not keep the precepts of God. As with Paul, however, the writer of the commentary is primarily concerned with God. God delivered the Wicked Priest into the hands of his enemies because he had acted wickedly toward God's chosen ones.

We cannot determine what is included in the Hebrew expression "their work." Perhaps it is the work of doing the law, which all members of the Qumran Sect had to pledge to keep in its entirety. Perhaps it included "good works," since members of the Sect also assumed the responsibility for doing what is good and right before God and to keep themselves apart from all wickedness. If "their work" means keeping or doing the law, the idea is not entirely unlike Paul's concept of the <u>dikaioma</u> <u>tou</u> <u>theou</u>, the "just requirement of God," and the <u>dikaiomata</u> <u>tou</u> <u>nomou</u>, the "just requirements of the law," as presented in Romans (see chapter 8 of this work). If "their work" refers to "good works," it coincides exactly with Paul's emphasis on proper moral/ethical conduct as necessary for ultimate deliverance or salvation. At any rate, there is in the passage from the Habakkuk Commentary the requirement of work of some sort and of faithfulness for escape from the judgment to come. In commenting on the first part of Hab 2:4 the writer of the Qumran commentary explains that the wicked will be severely punished and will not be shown loving kindness at the time of judgment. This is also an idea shared by Paul.

For Paul, faithfulness toward God takes precedence over everything else as the basic requirement for the justification of Gentile converts. For Jews who already had such faithfulness and for everyone, including Gentiles, in the process of becoming Christian converts certain beliefs about Jesus were also required. But in every letter Paul stresses, most of all, that works in the sense of moral/ethical behavior, to which converts pledged themselves, were required for ultimate salvation. It is interesting to observe that in the Qumran text work is listed before faith in the teacher. Yet, in spite of the differences between them, it is clear that Paul and the Sect of Qumran belong to two very similar worlds of thought.

Rom 3:21-24 and 1QS 11:2-15

Rom 3:21-24 is a key passage for Paul's view of justification (see discussion of that passage in chapters 4 and 5 of this work):

> But now the righteousness (justification) of God has been manifested apart from law, although it is borne witness to by the law and the prophets, the righteousness (justification) of God by virtue of the faithfulness of Jesus Christ for all who have faithfulness [toward God] . . . who are justified as a (free) gift by his grace by virtue of the redemption that is in Christ Jesus.

With Rom 3:21-24 compare this passage from Qumran (1QS 11:2-15):

> But for me, to God belongs my justification, and in his hand is the
> perfection of my way, with the uprightness of my heart, and in his
> righteousness my transgression will be wiped out . . . and from the
> fountain of his righteousness comes my justification, a light in my
> heart. . . . If I stumble in sin of the flesh, my justification is in the
> righteousness of God which stands forever. . . . By his compassion
> he has caused me to come near, and by his loving kindness he will
> bring my justification, by the justice of his truth he has justified me,
> and in his great goodness he will atone for all my sins, and by his
> justice he will cleanse me from all human uncleanness.

In both Rom 3:21-24 and 1QS 11:2-15 there is the idea of
justification of sinners by God's righteousness. "His loving kindness"
in 1QS corresponds to "his grace" in the Pauline passage. The phrases
"by virtue of the faithfulness of Jesus Christ" and "by virtue of the
redemption that is in Christ Jesus" are Paul's distinctive contribution to
the idea of justification of the unrighteous or sinners by God. An
examination of the passage quoted from 1QS 11:2-15 and several lines
not quoted reveals that the ideas of the righteousness of God, human
sinfulness and the association of such sinfulness with the flesh, election
or predestination, grace, and faithfulness are all present. All of these are
concepts found in Paul's letters, to say nothing about such comparable
Pauline ideas as the conflict between the flesh and the Spirit, the
prominent part given to the Spirit in the lives of the members of the
Sect of Qumran, and other ideas of Paul.

1QS 1:1-10

Exactly what was required of persons wanting to enter the
community of Qumran or a Christian community we do not know. In
the community of Qumran the Holy Spirit was associated with the
ceremonies of entrance into the Sect, just as it was with the initiation
rite of baptism of converts entering the Christian community. As with
Christianity, when persons entered the Qumran Sect they were forgiven
of all their past sins. And Qumran initiates were also expected to
"conduct their lives perfectly in all the ways of God" (1QS 3:9-10).

Paul addresses the members of communities to which he writes as
"holy one" (saints), and the same description is sometimes used with
reference to members of the Qumran community. The holy ones of

Qumran were instructed to live according to the rule of the community. I quote from the first several lines of the Manual which set forth the rules for the community (1QS 1:1-10):

> [The holy ones are] to live according to the way of the community; to seek God . . . and to do what is good and right before him, just as he commanded by the hand of Moses and by the hand of all his servants the prophets; to love all that he has chosen and hate all that he has rejected; to abstain from all evil and hold fast to all good; to practice truth and righteousness and justice upon earth; and to walk no longer in the stubbornness of a guilty heart and lustful eyes, doing all evil; to bring all who presented themselves to do the statutes of God in a covenant of loving kindness to be united in the counsel of God; to live perfectly before him . . . and to love all the sons of light . . . and to hate all the sons of darkness.

With that passage from Qumran compare these passages from letters of Paul, most of them from Romans, and notice the similarities in language and thought. "For you are all sons of light and sons of day; we are not of night or of darkness. . . . See that no one repays evil for evil to anyone but always pursue the good for another and for all. . . . Hold fast what is good, abstain from every form of evil" (1 Thess 5:5, 15, 21; see also 1 Cor 10:6; 2 Cor 5:10; 9:8; Gal 5:16-24; 6:10; Rom 2:5-10, discussed later; Rom 6:12-13; 8:28). "For the wrath of God is revealed from heaven against all ungodliness and wickedness of persons who in their wickedness suppress the truth" (Rom 1:18; see also Rom 1:24-27). "Do not be conformed to this age but be transformed by the renewing of your mind, that you may try to approve what is the will of God, what is good and well-pleasing and perfect. . . . Shrink from what is evil, adhere to what is good" (Rom 12:2, 9). "Let us put off, then, the works of darkness and clothe ourselves with the weapons of light" (Rom 13:12; see also 16:19).

As at Qumran, the holy ones (saints) at Rome had become obedient from the heart to the model of teaching to which they had pledged themselves (Rom 6:17; see also 16:17; 1 Cor 14:6; Gal 6:6). Apparently, as with Christianity, persons could decide whether or not to enter the group at Qumran (1QS 1:18). Apparently also, as converts to

Christianity made some sort of commitment to faithfulness toward God and to certain beliefs about Jesus, so, too, initiates into the Sect of Qumran made a comparable commitment of faithfulness toward God and toward the Teacher of Righteousness (1QpHab 8:1-3; 1QS 1:16-17).

1QS 1:16-17

With the passage from the Commentary on Habakkuk quoted above, compare this one from the Manual of Discipline: "All those who come into the order of the community shall enter into the covenant before God to do all his commandments and not to turn away from following him" (1QS 1:16-17). We have said that Paul never uses the phrases "faith in Jesus" or "believe in Jesus" and that the words "beliefs about Jesus" probably convey Paul's view in light of his profound monotheistic faithfulness toward God. So, if we were to substitute "beliefs about Jesus" for "faith in the Teacher of Righteousness" in the Habakkuk passage and "model of teaching" (Rom 6:17) for "all his commandments" in the passage from 1QS 1:16-17, we might have a statement of commitment on the part of the Qumran Sect very similar to that made by converts to Christianity.

The word translated "has caused me to come near" in 1QS 11:2-15, quoted above, apparently is a technical term for entrance into the community of Qumran. According to the context, God in "the justice of his truth" and "great goodness" made it possible for persons to enter the Qumran Sect. Although there is no term that should best be translated as "grace" in the sense of the Greek word charis, the Hebrew words hesed, translated as "loving kindness," and emeth, translated as "truth," are both regularly used in the Hebrew scriptures to describe the grace existing within the covenantal relationship between God and his people. And the Hebrew word sedaqah, translated as "justice," is most frequently rendered in the Septuagint with dikaiosyne, "righteousness" or "justification." It is a favorite word of Paul's in Romans where it usually has the meaning "righteousness."

Observations and Summary

The evidence from Qumran brings us rather close to Paul's concept of Jews and Gentiles coming into the Christian religion as the result of their justification or being made righteous by the grace of God. Paul has the added elements of the faithfulness of Jesus and beliefs about him, although faith of some kind in or faithfulness toward the Teacher of Righteousness seems to have been required for admission into the Sect of Qumran. After admission of members into the community of Qumran, and after admission into the Christian community, the ultimate salvation of the members of each community was dependent upon their living in accordance with stringent moral/ethical demands. For the members of the Qumran Sect those demands were the doing to the utmost the prescribed Jewish law (including, apparently, regulations of the community itself), which included first and foremost moral/ethical behavior. For Christian converts the primary demand was moral/ethical probity in accordance with the just requirements of the law of God (see chapter 8 of this work).

Yet, in spite of all the evidence presented, we probably should not look to the Sect of Qumran alone for the background of Paul's ideas of justification, grace, salvation, works of the law, and moral probity. But surely the thought worlds of Paul and Qumran are very close. Perhaps Paul was influenced indirectly by Qumran or by some phase of Judaism closely related to that of Qumran. At any rate, by the time Paul wrote, the concept of a community of people brought together through their justification (forgiveness of sins) by the grace and righteousness of God was known in Judaism. Members of Qumran and of Christianity were expected, above all else, to have faithfulness toward God. Members of both groups also held certain beliefs about a righteous teacher who was a teacher of righteousness. And both groups pledged themselves to righteous conduct in the hope of ultimate deliverance or salvation in the age to come.

For lack of completely convincing evidence, however, we must turn elsewhere than to Qumran to determine more probably the origin of the Pauline ideas of justification, grace, faithfulness, works of the law, and salvation. I suggest that Paul was most influenced by the covenantal relationship between God and his people Israel as reported in the Jewish scriptures.

The Jewish Scriptures

God's deliverance of the people of Israel from the Egyptians at the Red Sea is a frequent theme in the Jewish scriptures. The classical narratives of that experience in the book of Exodus are followed by those of the Mosaic covenant at Sinai. In a form well known in the ancient near east, the covenant expresses a relationship between two parties, one superior to the other. In such a covenant the greater party promises protection or support in exchange for obedience by the lesser party to the imposed stipulations. In the making of such covenants or agreements it was understood that failure on the part of the lesser party to obey would lead to a curse or downfall. On the other hand, obedience would bring deliverance or the fulfillment of the promises.

<u>Exodus 19-24</u>

In the Sinai narratives (Exodus 19-24), as elsewhere in the Hebrew scriptures, deliverance from the Egyptians at the Red Sea was clearly thought to be not the result of the people's obedience but of God's grace (Exod 3:7-12; see also Judg 6:8-10; 1 Sam 10:17-19; Pss (77)78;11-16; (80)81:10-11; (105)106;6-12, 21-22; (135)136:10-16; Jer 2:6; 7:22-23; 11:1-7; Ezek 20:5-8; Amos 2:10). God tells Moses: "Thus you shall tell . . . the children of Israel: you yourselves have seen what I did to the Egyptians and carried you on the wings of eagles and brought you to myself" (Exod 19:3-4). The promise of God that follows his redeeming act is conditional. Moses is instructed to tell the people: "If now you really listen to my voice [that is, "obey me"] and keep my covenant [that is, obey the laws of the Decalogue and Covenant Code in Exodus 20-23], you shall be my special treasure among all the peoples . . . and you shall be to me a kingdom of priests and a holy nation" (Exod 19:5-6). Moses then puts the proposition before the people, and they respond, "All that the Lord has spoken we will do" (Exod 19:7-8; see also 24:3-8).

Thus, the people of Israel are to enjoy a unique position with God among all the peoples of the world and be a kingdom of priests and a holy nation <u>if</u> they obey God by keeping the law (see also Lev 11:44-45; 19:1-4; 20:26; Deut 8:1-4; 9:4-5; 11). The same thing is stated in Deut 8:1: "All the commandments that I command you today you shall observe to do, in order that you may live and multiply and go in and take possession of the land which the Lord swore (to give) to your fathers." The dual ideas of deliverance only by God's grace and of the expectation of obedience to God's will required by covenant law are clear and emphatic. In the same way, God called Abraham and made him great promises (Gen 12:1-3). But God chose Abraham in order that he might charge his family "to keep the way of the Lord by doing righteousness and justice" so that the Lord might do for Abraham all that he had promised him (Gen 18:19).

In anticipation of the discussion (in chapter 3 of this work) of converts as persons who are "called" or "chosen" by God, I mention here that Paul reminds the Thessalonian converts that they were called "not for uncleanness but in holiness" (1 Thess 4:7; see also 2:12). Paul reminds the Galatian converts that they were called to freedom and exhorts them not to use their freedom for an opportunity in the flesh (that is, immorality) but through love to be slaves to one another (Gal 5:13). And Paul thanks God that the Roman converts had become obedient to the model of teaching to which they had been pledged (Rom 6:17). The parallels between these passages from Paul's letters and those from the Hebrew scriptures cited above certainly show that those scriptures helped to shape Paul's views about justification, grace, the just requirements of the law, and ultimate salvation.

There are a number of other passages in Exodus that influenced Paul's ideas. I mention only Exod 20:20: "I am the Lord your God who led you out of the land of Egypt, and out of the house of slavery; you shall have no other gods besides me . . . that reverence for God [literally, "the fear of God"] might be in you and that you do not sin." According to Paul, converts who became faithful to God were delivered from the slavery of sin from which God freed them (Rom 6:6). Paradoxically, at the same time, converts were to become slaves of righteousness, were not to let sin rule in their lives, and were to be "obedient from the heart to the model of teaching" to which they were committed (Rom 6:1-20; see also Gal 5:1).

Deut 7:6-16

Whereas in Exodus the condition of obedience is associated with Israel becoming God's special possession, in Deuteronomy it is associated with the covenant idea itself. According to Deut 7:6-16, which is another version of Exod 19:4-6, God chose Israel as his own special people, not because they were more in number but "because of the love of the Lord for you, and because he keeps the oath which he had sworn to your fathers, that the Lord brought you out with a mighty

hand, and redeemed you from the house of bondage, from the hand of
Pharaoh, king of Egypt" (Deut 7:8). The people are exhorted to know
that the Lord their God is "the faithful God who keeps covenant and
mercy with those who love him and keep his commandments [entolai] .
. . and repays those who hate him to . . . destroy them. . . . Therefore,
you shall keep his commandments [entolai] and his ordinances
[dikaiomata] and his judgments [krimata] which I command you today
to do them" (Deut 7:9-11).

In Deut 10:12-11:32 and elsewhere there are the same basic
principles. The continued covenantal relationship between God and
Israel depends upon the people's obedience to God's laws. Either the
people keep God's laws or perish. The terms of their relationship to
God are as simple and as emphatic at that! Paul's overall message is the
same and equally emphatic.

Josh 24:14-28

Joshua 24 may be a record of the renewal of the Mosaic covenant
between Joshua and Israel or that of a separate covenantal tradition from
Shechem. After recounting their earlier history, including their
deliverance from Egypt and the destruction of their enemies in Canaan,
Joshua challenges the people of Israel to choose between the Lord God
and the gods of their neighbors. They decide to serve the Lord their God
who brought them out of Egypt and saved them from their enemies.
Joshua reminds the people that such a choice is a serious matter, not
one to be made on the spur of the moment. After they reiterate their
desire to serve the Lord God, Joshua exhorts them to put away foreign
gods and to turn their hearts to the Lord, the God of Israel. The people
reply: "The Lord we will serve, and his voice we will obey. And Joshua
made a covenant with the people on that day, and he gave them a law
and a judgment [krima] in Shechem" (Josh 24:14-25).

The significant point to observe here is that the making of the
covenant and the establishing of laws are a part of the same process. It
is by keeping the laws that the people serve and obey God and thus
maintain a valid covenantal relationship with him. In this version of
Israel's covenantal relationship with God the condition is stated
negatively: "If you forsake the Lord and serve other gods, then he will

come upon you and do evil to you and consume you after he had done good to you" (Josh 24:20).

Paul's first priority for converts was that they turn from idols to faithfulness toward the Jewish God. Paul had constantly to remind converts not to return to their former ways of idolatry. If they did revert to their former ways, their justification would be of no value. Again, the parallels between the ideas expressed in the passages from the Jewish scriptures and those of Paul are obvious.

Israel's subsequent disobedience to the covenantal laws led those great reformers of Israel, the prophets, to develop a concept of judgment. Judgment must follow as the result of the people's disloyalty, idolatry, crimes, and injustices of all sorts. With the exception of a few passages, the messages of the prophets Amos, Hosea, Isaiah, and Micah are, therefore, primarily messages of doom. Judgment is always portrayed as the activity of God himself against his people and is motivated by their misdeeds (see, for example, parts of Amos 3-6; Hosea 4-13; Isaiah 1-5; 8:5-8; 9:8-10:4; Micah 1-3; 6:1-5; 6:9-7:6). As with the prophets, Paul thought that the wrath of God was motivated by the misdeeds of human beings (Rom 1:18; 2:8; 13:4-5) and that such wrath served to show the righteousness of God (Rom 3:5-6).

There are passages in the prophets that express confidence in a future deliverance. Sometimes that deliverance is to be conditioned by repentance (see, for example, Hosea 14:1-7; Amos 9:11-15; Jer 3:12-4:2), but sometimes it appears that deliverance is expected or accomplished only because of God's love and mercy (see, for example, Jer 23:5-8; 31:7-9; Isa 37:30-35; 43:1-7), not because of good deeds of the people. This is particularly true for some post-exilic passages in which it seems that the writers think Israel has suffered enough (see, for example, Isa 40:1-2; 44:21-23). For that reason God will restore the people in their homeland or deliver them (see, for example, Isa 52:1-10). After Israel's deliverance or restoration, it was understood that the faithfulness of the people toward God and obedience to his will would be renewed. As a matter of fact, after Israel's return to Jerusalem following the Exile, the law of God (Torah) became and remained the regulating feature of all Jewish life and religion.

In the same way, it was the suffering of his people in Egypt that moved God to deliver them (Exod 3:7-8, 16). Indeed, it would be accurate to say that at least by implication there was thought to be merit in the suffering itself that moved God to deliver his people from Egypt and from the Exile.

Observations and Summary

In the narratives of God's dealing with his people Israel grace on the part of God and right conduct on the part of his people, in accordance with his laws, were invariably linked together. If, indeed, God had delivered his people from Egypt or from Exile by his grace, from that point on they had to serve him in order to maintain his favor. This was true from the very beginning. Moses was reportedly told by God to speak to Pharaoh thus: "Send my people out, in order that they may serve me" (Exod 7:26 [LXX, 8:1]; see also 4:23; 7:16; 9:1, 13; 10:7-26; Joshua 24).

Paul and the Jewish People

After Jesus' coming and Paul's joining the Jesus movement, Paul did not forsake "the people of Israel" (Phil 3:5). He still spoke of Jews who put him in peril as "my own people" (2 Cor 11:26; Gal 1:14). According to Paul, God, by virtue of the faithfulness of Christ, gives fresh meaning to his covenant with Israel so that its basis is no longer what is written (the law) but the Spirit (2 Cor 3:6). All who distinguish between righteousness and iniquity, turn from idol worship to faithfulness toward God, and touch nothing unclean will be welcomed by God. The words "touch nothing unclean" (2 Cor 6:17; from Isa 52:11) mark the transition from ritual to moral purity of the people of the renewed covenant community of God. God will live among them and be their God, and they will be his people (2 Cor 6:14-17; see Lev 26:11-12; Ezek 37:27).

This new covenantal relationship with God and the Spirit is open to all people, Gentiles as well as Jews, for whom neither circumcision nor uncircumcision counts for anything but "a new creation" (Gal 6:15-16; see chapter 6 of this work). "For in one Spirit we were all baptized into one body, whether Jews or Greeks, slaves or freed persons, and all were made to drink one Spirit" (1 Cor 12:13). And Paul writes: "We are the (true) circumcision, who serve God in Spirit and boast in Christ Jesus and do not have confidence in the flesh" (Phil 3:3).

The surety behind the first covenants was the faithfulness and love of God (Deut 7:6-16). This was acknowledged by the writer of Isa 49:7 long after the time of Moses: "Because the Holy One of Israel is faithful, and I have chosen you" (LXX, whose translator had some difficulty with the Hebrew text). In the same way, Paul thinks that God who is faithful is the surety behind the renewed covenant community of God and calls converts into it (1 Thess 5:24). Paul writes in 1 Cor 1:9: "God is faithful, by virtue of whom you were called into the fellowship of his Son, Jesus Christ our Lord." And according to Paul, it was by virtue of the faithfulness of Jesus that God, by his grace, made it possible for all persons to become justified and enter into the renewed covenant community of God. The faithfulness of Christ is the only new aspect of Paul's thought.

In spite of the fact that in the renewed covenant community of God the emphasis was on the Spirit, not the law, there were still the just requirements of that law, the dikaiomata tou nomou, and the commandments of God, the entolai theou, to be followed by the members who conduct their lives according to the Spirit, not according to the flesh. The dikaiomata and the entolai are the very words of the covenantal relationship expressed in Deut 7:9-11, along with the "judgments" (krimata) of God (see chapter 8 of this work). Paul's use of the word krima (Rom 2:2-3; 3:8; 11:33) also reflects his influence from the vocabulary of the covenantal relationship as recorded in the passages mentioned.

As with the first covenants, members of the renewed ccovenant community of God were to regard their moral/ethical behavior as most sacred. And as with the first covenants also, immoral persons were to be expelled from the community of the holy ones, according to Paul (1 Cor 5:2). Paul repeats his command in 1 Cor 5:13: "Remove the wicked person from among you." This command is almost a literal quotation from the Septuagint of Deut 17:7. In the context of the Deuteronomy passage anyone who does evil in God's sight by violating his covenant is to be purged from the community (see also Deut 13:1-11; 22:23-24).

With these first chapters as background, we turn now to a more detailed consideration of Paul's ideas as they developed in his writing from one church to another.

Chapter 3

According To 1 Thessalonians And The Corinthian Letters

<u>Jews and Gentiles in the Church at Thessalonica</u>

Neither in Acts 17:1-10 nor in 1 Thessalonians is there any hint about observance of Jewish law for persons in Thessalonica who join the Jesus movement. Jews do not even raise the issue. According to Acts some Jews were upset just because Paul preached that Jesus was the Messiah and that as Messiah he had to suffer and die. In 1 Thessalonians there is evidence of a problem with some Jews, but it is not entirely clear what the problem is. At any rate, some Jews in Thessalonica are accused of killing the Lord Jesus and the prophets, driving out the missionaries, and preventing them from speaking to the Gentiles that they may be saved (1 Thess 2:14-16).

As with other communities of converts outside Jerusalem, the community in Thessalonica was comprised mostly of Gentiles. This is clear from Paul's words to the members there: "You turned to God from idols to serve a living and true God and to wait for his Son from heaven, whom he raised from the dead, Jesus who rescues us from the wrath that is coming" (1 Thess 1:9-10). These words are the essence of early mission preaching to Gentiles and are a combination of Jewish polemic against idolatry and of Jewish-Christian theology and eschatology. Converts to Christianity give up the worship of idols that, according to Paul, "are nothing in the world" because "there is no God but one" (1 Cor 8:4) to serve a God that is living and genuine. To that Jewish monotheism are added the Christian beliefs that Jesus is the Son of God, that he was raised from the dead by God, and that he would return to deliver righteous believers from the coming wrath--the final judgment.

Paul's Response to the Situation in Thessalonica

Paul defends himself and his companions from accusations by persons who were not members of the community of converts at Thessalonica (1 Thess 2:1-12). By reading Paul's statements in his defense, we can determine the accusations by his adversaries. Already in 1 Thess 1:5 Paul says that the power of God and the Holy Spirit were at work in his ministry. His hortatory appeal was not motivated by error or impurity or deceit, nor did he aim to please humans, but to please God. In other words, Paul's behavior was ethically sound in God's sight, so he was not treacherously deceiving others. His adversaries were wrong in thinking that he had acted from unethical motives.

Paul's words in 1 Thess 2:5, 9-10 indicate that some people who opposed Paul thought he did not consider others and was greedy for financial gain. He wants it to be clearly understood that he is not just another one of those ubiquitous street preachers belonging to some religious and philosophical cult who was eager to make a living, whose speech was deceiving, and for whom religion and morality were often not related. Paul concludes his defense with the words, "We exhorted and encouraged and solemnly charged you to conduct your lives worthy of God who calls you into his own kingdom and glory" (1 Thess 2:11-12). As with most references of Paul to the kingdom of God (see 1 Cor 6:9; Gal 5:19-21; Rom 14:17; and comments in chapter 1 of this work), virtuous life is required for participation in it. This is clear from what has preceded and from what follows in 1 Thessalonians 4 and 5.

It is emphatically clear that Paul defends himself on moral/ethical grounds, and they are the grounds of his main concern for the converts at Thessalonica. After expressing his exuberance at the good news brought by Timothy of the Thessalonians' faithfulness toward God and love, Paul prays that God may increase their love to one another and toward all persons so that they may attain their goal blameless in holiness before God at Jesus' second coming. Paul exhorts the converts to conduct their lives in a way that pleases God as he had instructed them, only to do so even more (1 Thess 4:1-8). Paul's use of the phrases "in the Lord Jesus" and "through the Lord Jesus" suggest that converts received ethical instruction, probably based on teachings of Jesus transmitted orally. Converts are to abstain from sexual immorality, marry "in holiness and honor," and not have illicit sexual relations "like the Gentiles who do not know God."

Paul reflects the mores of the Jewish covenantal society, where all of life was regulated by the law and disobedience was regarded as rejection of God's will. The mores of pagan society in general were not so strict as those of Jews. Pagans must have found it difficult, to say the least, to give up the practices of their former idolatrous lives for their new lives as converts. So Paul has to remind them that God called them not "for uncleanness but for holiness." God had given them his Holy Spirit, so they are responsible to him because he is "an avenger" in matters of immorality (1 Thess 4:6).

Paul's Early Theology and Ethics

The last chapter of 1 Thessalonians contains final exhortations and gives an insight into Paul's early theological development. Again, as in 1 Thess 1:3, Paul uses the triad of faithfulness, love, and hope: "Put on the breastplate of faithfulness and love and as a helmet the hope of salvation, for God has not set us apart for wrath but for the obtaining of salvation through our Lord Jesus Christ, who died on our behalf . . . that we might live with him. Therefore encourage one another and build up one another, just as you are doing" (1 Thess 5:8-11). The whole context of this passage is the return of Christ and the converts' preparation for it. Consequently, the concepts of wrath and salvation are used with reference to the final judgment.

Paul does not say that God has set the converts at Thessalonica apart for salvation. They must do their part in God's plan in order for them to obtain ultimate salvation. Paul's conception of the ultimate salvation of converts provides the framework for all the moral demands he thinks necessary for them to obtain it. Obviously, Paul's exhortations to watchfulness, sobriety, and moral/ethical behavior would not make sense if believers were destined for salvation apart from moral probity. This is positively clear from Paul's final exhortations: "Do not quench the Spirit. . . . Hold fast to what is good; abstain from every form of evil" (1 Thess 5:19-21).

Although in 1 Thessalonians Paul does not work out any theological idea in detail and support it with arguments, the letter is important for insight into the essence of Paul's early theology and of his moral/ethical teachings. "For since we believe that Jesus died and rose again . . . for God has not set us apart for wrath, but for the obtaining of salvation through our Lord Jesus Christ, who died for us" (1 Thess 4:14; 5:9-10).

The statement about the death and resurrection of Jesus, beginning with the words "We believe that," probably indicates that Paul has taken over a formula from earlier tradition with respect to Jesus' resurrection and used it here. This is true because in 1 Thess 4:14 Paul tells the converts in Thessalonica that at Jesus' second coming God will bring with Jesus those who have died (see also 2 Cor 4:14). This implies that God will raise the dead and coincides with Paul's own view elsewhere that God also raised Jesus from the dead rather than that Jesus rose from his own power. Paul writes to the converts at Corinth: "We testified about God that he raised Christ" (1 Cor 15:15) and to the Romans: "Who believe on him who raised Jesus our Lord from the dead" (Rom 4:24; see also 1 Thess 1:10; Gal 1:1; Rom 8:11; 10:9). These passages indicate that although Paul inherited from earlier Christian tradition the belief that Jesus rose from the dead (1 Thess 4:14), he himself believed that God was responsible for raising Jesus. This adds more evidence to support the argument that Paul is primarily concerned with God and only secondarily with Jesus.

If we return now to 1 Thess 4:14 and 5:9-10, we learn that Paul believes that somehow Jesus' death was effective for determining the ultimate destiny of believers, but he does not explain how this was made possible, except to say that Jesus died for them. They now have the hope of salvation (1 Thess 5:8), but that hope is still only a hope because salvation comes at the end of time. However, the converts at Thessalonica are on the right course because God gave them his Holy Spirit. But Paul exhorts them not to quench that Spirit (1 Thess 5:19). And, under the influence of the Spirit, converts must not live as they did before becoming converts. And when Paul says that the Thessalonian converts are to build one another up (1 Thess 5:11), he uses the verb "build" (oikodomeo) in a moral sense with the meaning "strengthen one another spiritually and morally." The counterpart of that statement is "Abstain from every form of evil" (1 Thess 5:22).

What Paul Does Not Say about Faithfulness in 1 Thessalonians

1 Thessalonians is important not only because of what it tells us about Paul's early beliefs, but also because of what it does not tell us.

Paul uses the noun pistis in 1 Thessalonians 8 times, the verb pisteuo ("believe") 5 times, and the adjective pistos ("faithful") 1 time. He uses pistis for the first time in 1 Thess 1:3 in his thanksgiving for the converts' "work of faithfulness," "labor of love," and "patient enduring of hope." Recall that in the Qumran passage of 1QpHab 8:1-3 the writer combines work and faithfulness as qualities because of which God will deliver persons who have those qualities from judgment. In 1 Thess 1:3 the phrase "work of faithfulness" means faithfulness toward God that is at work or active in doing something, perhaps in being imitators of the mission workers in becoming a model to all who believed in Macedonia (1 Thess 1:7). It is difficult to tell exactly what Paul does mean by pistis here, and this is true many times when he uses the same noun also in his other letters.

I have three comments about the passages in 1 Thess 1:3 and 1:7. First, Paul uses both the noun pistis and the verb pisteuo without an object of belief either stated or implied. He does not say whom or what believers have faith in. Moreover, Paul never defines pistis (contrast Heb 11:1). And many times, as here, he uses it absolutely, that is, without a stated object. He uses it the same way also in 1 Thess 3:2, 5-7, 10; 5:8. Therefore, Paul rarely, if ever, uses pistis in the sense of intellectual assent to creed or doctrine. Rather, the faith or, better, faithfulness of converts becomes a kind of inner conviction that begins with and from the experience of becoming converts.

So, then, how would I define pistis when I translate it as "faithfulness"? Overall, I believe that, according to Paul, faithfulness is a right relationship with God that includes trust and an obligation to live morally. Both elements come from Paul's understanding of the Jewish covenantal relationship with God. And how do I decide when to translate pistis as "faith" or "faithfulness"? The fact that often one cannot be completely certain what Paul means by pistis sometimes makes the choice arbitrary. However, I have tried to be guided by the context in which it occurs in light of Paul's ideas in general. Most times, therefore, I believe "faithfulness" is the better choice, and I usually translate it that way. Rarely, if ever, does pistis for Paul mean abstract, intellectual assent in the sense that we understand "faith." Sometimes, then, I simply do not translate it. But evidence presented throughout this book indicates that in most, if not all, instances the object of pistis or pisteuo, whether stated or only implied, is God.

The second comment I have with respect to 1 Thess 1:3 and 1:7 is that "those who believe" or "believers" became one of the earliest words used to designate converts (see additional comments on these words in chapter 6 of this work). The use of the term believers to refer to members of the Jesus sect of Jews is confirmed by the writer of Acts when reporting about the early Christian community in Jerusalem (see Acts 2:44; 4:32; 5:14; see also 1 Thess 2:10, 13). In its earliest usage "believers" referred to those Jews who had faithfulness toward God, were not idol worshipers, and who also believed that Jesus was the Messiah (Christ).

The third comment is that pistis in the sense of assent to or belief about something was expected of converts. But on the basis of 1 Thess 1:3 and 1:7, we do not know what that was. However, 1 Thess 1:8 gives us the answer: "Your faithfulness toward God has gone out in every place." Here the Greek of Paul is he pistis hymon he pros ton theon. The use of the article he a second time indicates that the emphasis is on what follows. So Paul's Greek means, "Your faithfulness, that is, your faithfulness toward God," not toward idols. Gentile converts were obviously required to give up the worship of idols and worship the one God of the Jews (see 1 Thess 1:9). In later letters Paul also thinks of God as the object of faithfulness, even after he develops christological ideas.

The words in 1 Thess 1:8 that I have translated as "toward God" are pros ton theon and mean that converts' faithfulness is directed toward God, not pagan gods. Paul uses the phrase pros ton elsewhere only in Phlm 5. There Paul thanks God for the pistis Philemon has "toward the Lord Jesus" (pros ton kurion Iesoun), and it means faithfulness directed toward Jesus as Lord, not toward any of the many pagan lords (see comments on Phlm 5 in chapter 5 of this work).

In 1 Thess 4:14, there is, of course, real content in Christian faith: "For since we believe that Jesus died and rose, then, through Jesus, God will bring with him those who have fallen asleep." The statement that Jesus died and rose may, indeed, be a pre-Pauline confession of Christian belief. However, it is important to observe that Paul uses the faith statement to assure the Christian converts at Thessalonica that believers who had died would not miss Jesus' return. Paul does not use it in the context of his defense of himself against the troublemakers in the church at Thessalonica. There never was a controversy over pistis in any church of Paul.

This summary of Paul's concept of pistis is intended to serve as a background for what I shall say later and especially to serve as a contrast to what Paul does not say. He never uses expressions for faith in or believing in Christ as those expressions are usually understood. When we understand what Paul says about faithfulness toward God, we can also understand that Paul speaks only of beliefs about Jesus.

There is not even a hint about justification by faith in 1 Thessalonians. The idea of "grace" as we find it later in Galatians and Romans is entirely lacking. And the word "save" (sozo) occurs only once--when Paul is accusing some Jews of preventing him and his companions "from speaking to the Gentiles that they may be saved" (1 Thess 2:16). Here the word is the equivalent of "become converts to faithfulness toward God." As converts they become eligible for future or ultimate salvation. The word "salvation" (soteria) occurs twice in 1 Thess 5:8-9, and it refers to the time of the final judgment. The implication is that Gentiles who do not become converts do not have the opportunity of becoming saved.

In 1 Thessalonians Paul does not mention the Jewish law or circumcision, nor does he refer to the baptism of converts. And he does not use the word "sin" with reference to the Thessalonian converts. Obviously, there was no problem concerning Jewish law in the community of converts at Thessalonica.

Converts at Thessalonica as Called or Chosen

In 1 Thess 1:4 Paul address the converts as "beloved by God" and says that God has chosen them (literally "God's choice [ekloge] of you"). In 1 Thess 2:12 he exhorts the converts to conduct their lives in a manner worthy of God who calls them into his own kingdom and glory. In 1 Thess 4:7 Paul gives the purpose for God's calling converts: "God has not called us for uncleanness but (to be) in holiness." The word "holiness" comes from the basic verb form hagiazo, which originally meant "set apart" by or for God for the purpose of becoming holy. Thus, converts are called by God as set apart for the purpose of becoming holy persons. Again, Paul is influenced by the Jewish scriptures (for example, Exod 13:2; 29:27-28; Deut 5:12).

Influence from the Jewish Scriptures

In his use of the terms "call" and "choose" Paul is influenced by the idea that Israel is chosen by God to be a holy people, whom God has called because he loved them, and who are to help carry out his plan for the world. Notice the similarities between the passages in 1 Thessalonians and the one in Deut 7:6-8: "For you are a people holy to the Lord your God; the Lord your God has chosen you to be a people for his own special possession above all nations on the face of the earth. It was not because you were more in number than all the peoples that the Lord chose you deliberately and picked you . . . but it is because the Lord loves you" (recall comments on these verses in chapter 2 of this work).

Paul concludes 1 Thessalonians with a prayer: "May the God of peace himself sanctify [literally "make holy"] you completely, and may your spirit and soul and body be kept sound and blameless at the arrival of our Lord Jesus Christ" (1 Thess 5:23). Paul would not have uttered this prayer if he had been convinced that the converts in Thessalonica were already saved and were not, therefore, in danger of lapsing into the previous state of their pre-Christian pagan existence. Then Paul adds: "He [that is, God] who calls you is faithful, who also will do it" (1 Thess 5:24). Paul is confident, that with God's help, his prayer will be answered and that the converts at Thessalonica will continue the moral/ethical behavior that they had been taught in the process of becoming converts. If they succeed in doing that, God, who called them not for uncleanness but for holiness (1 Thess 4:7), will be true to his promise of calling them into his own kingdom and glory (1 Thess 2:12).

When Paul says "God who is faithful," again he shows influence from Deut 7:6-11. God chose his people Israel because he loved them, and he reminds them that he kept his oath to deliver them from Egypt. We read: You will know "that the Lord your God . . . is a faithful God, who keeps covenant and mercy for those who love him and who keep his commands" (Deut 7:9; from the Greek text). Influence from both the language and thought of Deuteronomy on Paul is very clear.

Paul's Response to the Situation in the Church at Corinth

It is clear from the book of Acts and from Paul's letters that Paul had adversaries at Corinth as at Thessalonica. According to Acts 18:5-11, some Jews in Corinth opposed and reviled Paul because he was preaching to them that Jesus was the Christ (Messiah).

It is difficult to tell from Paul's letters who his adversaries were. They may have been Jewish Christians from Judea who claimed to have greater authority than Paul because they had known the earthly Jesus. Perhaps they were Hellenistic Jews who imitated prophets, astrologers, magicians, and philosophers who traveled throughout the Graeco-Roman world proclaiming various ideas. Such persons claimed they received special revelations from the gods and tried to prove it by performing miracles. Or, perhaps, the persons who opposed Paul were Gnostics who argued that gnosis ("knowledge"), not pistis, was the basic requirement for salvation, which for the Gnostics was a state of complete spiritual existence.

Divisions developed within the church at Corinth because converts tended to follow certain leaders, perhaps persons who had baptized them (1 Cor 1:10-4:21). The first women's liberation movement began in

Corinth when some women joined the Christian community, apparently without the consent of their husbands (1 Cor 7:12-16). Women began participating in prayer and prophecy in the church (1 Cor 11:2-16), obviously not conforming to what was expected of them in that time. Paul had to deal with those situations (1 Cor 7:1-40; 11:2-16; 14:33-36). Among other matters in Corinth that Paul deals with are Christians and marriage (1 Cor 7:1-16, 25-40), eating meat offered to idols (1 Cor 8:1-13; 10:14-30), behavior at meetings of worship (1 Cor 11:3-16), spiritual gifts (1 Corinthians 12-14), the certainty of Jesus' resurrection and of the resurrection of Christian converts themselves (1 Corinthians 15), and the collection of money for the holy ones (saints) in Jerusalem (1 Cor 16:1-14). Paul's response to those matters is usually moderate, without criticism of the past behavior of believers. Paul appeals to sayings of Jesus, scripture, and his own authority in responding to those problems.

Paul's response to several more serious problems in the church in Corinth, however, is not so moderate. Among those problems are the incestuous man "living with his father's wife" (1 Cor 5:1-5), the human body and immorality (1 Cor 6:12-20), and conduct at the Lord's Supper (1 Cor 11:17-34). When dealing with these problems Paul is usually uncompromising, sometimes even hostile. The incestuous man should "be expelled from among you" (1 Cor 5:2). Paul remembers the past immoral behavior of the pagan converts and bluntly reminds them of it--"And such were some of you" (1 Cor 6:11). When scolding participants in the Lord's Supper for their misbehavior, Paul speaks on his own authority, without appealing to anyone or anything else: "I do not commend you. . . . Shall I commend you? In this I do not commend you" (1 Cor 11:17, 22).

In most of 2 Corinthians Paul deals with his adversaries on a personal basis, putting his own authority against theirs. However, Paul's main concern with the Corinthian converts in general is their conduct or manner of life. Corinth was known for its revelry and immorality, especially in its seaports. There were always temptations for illicit sex at the seaports for athletes who came to Corinth for the Isthmian games. The same kind of temptation faced many residents of the city and itinerant sailors. The danger that converts would lapse into the immoral ways of their pagan past was probably greater at Corinth than in any other city to which Paul wrote. Among converts at Corinth, problems of immorality were greater and caused Paul more concern than in any other city. How Paul deals with these problems on the basis of faithfulness, justification, the law, grace, and salvation is my main concern.

Corinthian Converts and Baptism

In 1 Corinthians Paul begins by addressing his letter "to the church in Corinth" as "those sanctified (made holy) in Christ Jesus, called to be holy ones (saints) . . . who call on the name of our Lord Jesus Christ" (1 Cor 1:2). As at Thessalonica, Paul believes that converts at Corinth were called for the purpose of moral/ethical life. This is emphasized by his use of the words "sanctify" and "holy ones." Paul uses the verb sanctify again in the Corinthian letters only in 1 Cor 6:11. There it is part of a strong moral/ethical context that also refers to the time his readers became Christian converts. Paul reminds them that the unrighteous (adikoi, from the same root as "justify" [dikaioo]), male prostitutes, idolaters, adulterers, voluptuous persons, sodomites, thieves, greedy persons, drunkards, and revilers will not inherit the kingdom of God. He bluntly reminds the Corinthian converts, "And such were some of you." Then he adds: "But you were washed, but you were sanctified, but you were justified (made righteous) in the name of the Lord Jesus Christ and in the Spirit of our God" (1 Cor 6:9-11). The three verbs "washed," "sanctified," and "justified" are used synonymously and refer to the time of the converts' baptism, as the word "washed" indicates. Paul does not speak of baptism again in the same way anywhere else in the Corinthian letters, presumably because the converts at Corinth understood its meaning from their own experience of the phenomenon.

According to Acts, in the early church converts were regularly baptized "into the name of Christ" in order to acquire forgiveness of their past sins and to receive the gift of the Holy Spirit (see, for example, Acts 2:38; 8:14-17; 10:48; 19:4-6). The phrase means that baptism occurred under Christ's authority and that persons baptized became participants in the experience of the spiritual Christ and owed him their allegiance. Paul's response to Chloe's report (1 Cor 1:11) makes it clear that there should not be divisions in the church about following anyone but Christ, since converts were not baptized into the name of anyone else and therefore did not owe allegiance to any person but Christ. Paul does not forthrightly negate baptism, but he certainly does not emphasize its ceremonial aspect. He thanks God that he baptized none of the converts except Crispus (1 Cor 1:14).

Paul had not yet fully worked out his own theology of baptism when he wrote the letters to the church in Corinth. However, in 1 Cor 12:13, Paul says: "In one Spirit we were all baptized into one body." Through baptism converts experienced the Spirit. "One body" is the spiritual body of Christ and is used metaphorically of the whole renewed covenant community of God. When Paul is thinking about the subject of baptism later, he speaks of being "baptized into Christ" (Gal 3:27; Rom 6:3; see discussion of Romans 6 in chapter 6 of this work). In such a body, as with the church in Corinth, there should be no distinctions on the basis of sex, race, or social status because all alike have shared the experience of the Spirit: "For in Christ Jesus you are all sons of God through faithfulness [toward God]. For as many of you as were baptized into Christ have put on Christ. There is neither Jew nor Greek, there is neither slave nor free, there is neither male nor female; for you are all one in Christ Jesus" (Gal 3:26-28). Here we should observe that only the conviction of moral probity made the social principle of "neither Jew nor Greek," "neither slave nor free," and "neither male nor female" the only one possible. By baptism converts were not only taken into the renewed covenant community of God, but the one God became the source of their new life in Christ as moral beings.

Paul does not bring up the subject of baptism in 2 Corinthians because, apparently, baptism was not a problem when he wrote the material making up that letter.

<u>Grace in 1 and 2 Corinthians</u>

That Paul thinks God is responsible for the converts at Corinth, as elsewhere, becoming converts is clear from the words "called [by God] to be holy ones" and "for the grace of God which was given to you" (1 Cor 1:2, 4). At the same time, they are called into the spiritual fellowship of his Son (1 Cor 1:9). This means that those who become converts are not only expected to be holy persons as individuals, but also collectively as members of that fellowship. Paul surely had in mind Exod 19:5-6: "And, now, if you indeed hear my voice and keep my covenant, you shall be to me a special people of all the nations . . . and you shall be to me . . . a holy nation" (LXX). Paul believes that all Christian converts are a holy people, that is, set apart for the purpose of becoming holy, and God's own possession among all peoples. They share the same experience "with all those who call upon the name of our Lord Jesus Christ in every place" (1 Cor 1:2). Thus, besides a commitment to holy life as individuals, there was also some communal commitment to beliefs about Christ, but we are not told what that commitment was. However, the words "calling on" seem to imply prayer and reverence for Christ, perhaps expressed every time converts met for worship. But, again, Paul does not elaborate on what he means (see comments on early Christian worship in chapter 6 of this work).

From the moment converts are called, sanctified, justified, washed--words used by Paul synonymously for the idea behind the process by which converts become Christians--they are responsible for holiness of life. Paul emphasizes his belief that God is responsible for that process not only by the use of the word "called," but also by the expression "grace of God," which he introduces for the first time also in connection with the process whereby pagans become converts (1 Cor 1:4). Elsewhere in 1 and 2 Corinthians, Paul also uses the expression "grace of God" with reference to the converts becoming Christians (2 Cor 4:15; 6:1; 8:1, 9; 9:14). And he uses it also with reference to his own becoming a Christian and to his work as an apostle. He writes that by the grace of God he is what he is and that by the grace of God that is with him, he worked harder than all his adversaries (1 Cor 15:10; see also 1 Cor 1:1; 3:10; 2 Cor 12:9). By the grace of God Paul, in contrast to his adversaries, was able to act toward the Corinthians with sincerity and purity (2 Cor 1:12).

Besides the grace of God, with which Paul is primarily concerned, he occasionally mentions the grace of Christ. He speaks about it in two ways. First, he mentions the grace of Christ in the salutations and endings of his letters (for example, 1 Thess 5:28; 1 Cor 1:3; 16:23; Gal 1:3; 6:18; Rom 1:7; Phil 4:23; Phlm 3). Second, Paul speaks about the grace of Christ in its relationship to converts in their lives as Christians (2 Cor 8:9; Gal 1:6; Rom 5:15). In the former instance Paul's word for grace is probably derived from the usual Greek word for greeting (chairo) in Greek letters of his time and which meant "rejoice." In both instances, but especially in the latter, we see that Paul gives the word a distinctively Christian meaning, and the usage in both instances may have originated with him. At any rate, the grace of God and the grace of Christ were intended by Paul to have a positive effect on converts' lives. For example, their experience of the grace of Christ should make them feel the obligation to contribute liberally to the collection for the poor Christians in Jerusalem (2 Cor 8:9).

Pistis and Pisteuo in 1 and 2 Corinthians

In 1 Cor 1:21 Paul mentions "those who believe," and the natural object of believing would be "in him," that is, God. God is the subject of the sentence: God was pleased through the foolishness of the preaching to save those who believe [in him]. Moreover, in the context, the preaching is about Christ, not faith in Christ. And Paul thanks God for the Corinthians because of the grace of God given them in Christ Jesus (1 Cor 1:4). As with the Thessalonian converts (1 Thess 1:2-4), Paul is grateful that God has chosen them, so it is clear that they would be converted, above all else, to faithfulness toward God. The same thing is meant also in 1 Cor 14:22.

Paul first introduces pistis in the Corinthian letters in his discussion of the wisdom of God and human wisdom (1 Cor 2:4-5). He says that he first spoke to the Corinthians under the influence of the Spirit and the power of God, which for Paul probably mean the same thing, that is, the power of God is the Spirit. That phenomenon was responsible for the response of the Corinthian converts to Paul's preaching of "Jesus Christ and him crucified" (1 Cor 2:2). Therefore, the converts at Corinth should place their pistis in the power of God responsible for their conversion and not in the kind of wisdom advocated by Paul's adversaries.

Paul refers to Apollos and himself as servants through whom the Corinthians believed (1 Cor 3:5). "Believed" is the same as being converted to faithfulness toward God, as we know from 1 Thess 1:8. In 1 Cor 12:9, in the words "faith in the same Spirit" (pistis en to auto pneumati), we cannot be sure what Paul means by pistis, but perhaps it is the kind needed to work miracles referred to in the next verse. Pistis has the same meaning in 1 Cor 13:2.

In 1 Cor 13:7, "Love believes all things," we do not know what Paul really means here, but perhaps he means that love is constant in faithfulness. If that is true, then it is as sound to think that God is the object of such believing as anything or anyone else. It probably has the same meaning also in 1 Cor 13:13.

In the words "unless you believed in vain" (1 Cor 15:2) "believed" refers to the phenomenon of becoming Christians: "unless you became Christian converts to no purpose." So God is to be assumed as the object of believing, and what converts were taught to believe about Christ as part of the gospel Paul preached (see 1 Cor 15:1) is given in the next verse: Christ died for the Corinthian converts' sins, was buried, and was raised (1 Cor 15:3). God is to be understood as the implied object of believing in the sense of becoming converts to faithfulness toward him also in 1 Cor 15:11.

In his discussion of the resurrection in 1 Cor 15:14-17 Paul says that if Christ has not been raised, his preaching is worthless and the Corinthians' faithfulness is worthless (1 Cor 15:14). Faithfulness toward God came as the result of Paul's preaching of Jesus' resurrection, and faithfulness included the belief that God raised Jesus from the dead. 1 Cor 15:14, then, is a key passage, and it confirms all I have said thus far about converts having faithfulness toward God and believing certain things about Christ. Paul continues: "We are found (to be) false witnesses of God [that is, if it is true, as some Corinthians say, that there is no resurrection from the dead], because we have testified of God that he raised Christ. . . . If Christ has not been raised your faithfulness [toward God] is ineffectual, and you are still in your sins" (1 Cor 15:15-17). Paul is saying that if Christ had not been raised, then the converts at Corinth would still be in the same immoral state ("in your sins") as they had been before their conversion, of which Paul had earlier reminded them--"and such were some of you" (1 Cor 6:11). But they were washed, sanctified, justified, that is, their past sins were forgiven when they were baptized. At the same time, apparently, in addition to their faithfulness toward God, converts began to receive instruction in

moral/ethical life and in certain beliefs about Jesus, in this instance that
God raised him from the dead. The faithfulness of the Corinthian
converts, however, was not yet complete or mature because Paul hopes
that it will increase (2 Cor 10:15; see also 1 Thess 3:2, 10). When their
faithfulness is more mature, then Paul will be able to extend his
mission outreach to others and not have to consider only their needs for
his attention.

In the clauses "Stand firm in your faithfulness" (1 Cor 16:13) and
"Not that we lord it over your faithfulness . . . for you stand firm in
your faithfulness" (2 Cor 1:24), God is the object to be understood in
both passages, as 1 Cor 16:7-10 and 2 Cor 1:23 make clear (so also in
2 Cor 10:15).

Paul and his fellow converts have the same spirit of faithfulness as
the psalmist: "Because we have the same spirit of faithfulness in accord
with what is written, 'I believed, therefore I spoke' [Ps 115(116):1], we
also believe and therefore speak" (2 Cor 4:13). The following clause
makes clear that faithfulness toward God is meant: "Knowing that the
one [that is, God] who raised the Lord Jesus will also raise us with
Jesus" (2 Cor 4:14; see also 1 Thess 4:14).

In 2 Cor 5:7, "For we conduct our lives by virtue of faithfulness,
not by virtue of appearance," Paul is writing about the experience of
being "at home with the Lord" (Jesus) after death. Before that Paul had
said: "The one who has worked out this very thing for us is God who
has given us the down payment of the Spirit" (2 Cor 5:5). This verse,
then, indicates that faithfulness toward God is meant in 2 Cor 5:7.

Paul encourages the Corinthian converts to give liberally to the
collection for the poor converts in Jerusalem: "Just as you exceed in
everything, in faithfulnes . . . [I pray that] you may also excel in this
gracious [endeavor] (2 Cor 8:7). Here, as elsewhere, faithfulness toward
God is to be understood and is one of the qualities that leads Paul to
expect an excellent response to the collection.

In 2 Cor 13:5 Paul writes: "Test yourselves to see if you are in the
pistis." That faithfulness toward God is meant is clear from the
preceding verse, which gives an essential element of faithful assent as
part of the Christian religion: faithfulness toward God makes possible
the belief that he raised Jesus from the dead. As Paul says, "For he was

crucified from weakness, but he lives from the power of God. For we are weak in him, but we shall live with him as a result of the power of God" (2 Cor 13:4). Moreover, the verses that follow in 2 Cor 13:5-9 indicate that pistis (faithfulness) includes the moral/ethical life of the converts. Paul asks them if they do not perceive that Jesus Christ is in them. Paul has not failed in his mission activity, even though it may appear that he has. He prays that the converts may not do evil but do what is ethically good (to kalon) and that their ethical sensitivity may be strengthened (see comments on these verses in chapter 7 of this work). Converts are to test their own moral existence as compared with what it ought to be.

Faithfulness Toward God and Ultimate Salvation

The question is: Do converts automatically retain the status of forgiveness received at the time of their baptism so that their ultimate salvation is assured? Only one passage in Paul's letters to Corinth seems to indicate that is the case--1 Cor 1:4-9 (see also Phil 1:6).

Despite all the moral/ethical problems in the church at Corinth, Paul says that as converts wait for the return of Christ, God will confirm them to the end, blameless (1 Cor 1:8). If this means that because God has called them to be holy ones, that is, set apart for the purpose of holiness, they have already obtained salvation unconditionally, it contradicts what Paul says elsewhere in 1 and 2 Corinthians and other letters, where ultimate salvation is dependent upon converts' continuing faithfulness toward God and their moral probity. Paul goes on to say that "God is faithful by whom you were called into the fellowship of his Son" (1 Cor 1:9). The reference to God as faithful is the same expression Paul had used in 1 Thess 5:24 which, as we said, shows influence from Deut 7:6-11. This means, then, that God, who called persons as converts, will also confirm them at the end. Paul's words in 1 Cor 1:7-9 hark back to verse 2 where he says that God called the Corinthian Christians to be holy ones. Paul's confidence in God's faithfulness gives him the hope that the converts will receive ultimate salvation. But their continuing moral probity is to be understood, with the sustaining power of the Spirit made possible by the gracious gift of God.

Paul never says elsewhere that Christian converts are free from the responsibility for moral life, so does he say that in 1 Cor 1:8? In 1 Cor 10:12 he says: "Therefore, let anyone who thinks he stands take care lest he fall." In the context of this statement Paul is warning converts at Corinth against idolatry and reminds them that they could revert to idol worship just as the ancient Israelites did (see, for example, Exod 32:1-10). But, again, the same confidence of Paul in God's faithfulness is clear: "God, who is faithful, will not let you be tempted beyond what you are able to endure, but with the temptation he will also provide the way out so that you will be able to endure it" (1 Cor 10:13). However, the context, both before and after the sentence quoted, makes it also clear that Paul believes the converts themselves must resist the temptation. They must not be immoral or put the Lord to the test as some ancient Israelites did (1 Cor 10:8-9). If converts yield to the evils of idolatry by ignoring "the way out," they will "fall" as the Israelites did. Furthermore, Paul exhorts his readers: "Therefore, my beloved, flee from the worship of idols" (1 Cor 10:14). And Paul has written in 1 Cor 6:9-11 that idolaters are among those who will not inherit the kingdom of God. All of these things help to confirm the view that Paul's primary concern for his converts was for them to come to faithfulness toward God and reject the worship of idols. And not only that! They were to continue in that faithfulness and not revert to idolatry and its accompanying immorality.

If my interpretation of the passage in 1 Cor 1:8 is not correct, and if 1 Cor 1:8 really does indicate that Paul believed that by becoming Christians converts were assured of ultimate salvation, it is the only one of its kind in Paul's letters (but recall comments on Rom 5:9-10 in chapter 1). And we should not draw any conclusion from Paul's inconsistent writing based on only a passage or two. We must consider all of his letters in order to determine his basic ideas on any subject.

Faithfulness, Circumcision, and the Law in 1 and 2 Corinthians

How, according to 1 and 2 Corinthians, did Paul believe circumcision and the law relate to Christian faithfulness and life? My study is confined to 1 Corinthians because neither circumcision nor the law enters into Paul's discussion in 2 Corinthians.

In 1 Corinthians Paul refers to circumcision only once, but the passage in which it occurs is very crucial for considering his views on circumcision and the law later in Galatians. In 1 Cor 7:17-20 Paul writes:

> Let every one conduct one's life just as God has called each one . . . just as I also command in all the churches. If anyone called was circumcised, let him not undo his circumcision; if anyone called was uncircumcised, let him not be circumcised. Circumcision is nothing, and uncircumcision is nothing, but keeping the commandments of God. Each person should remain in the calling in which that person was called.

Here the principle is simple: Being either Jew (circumcised) or Gentile (uncircumcised) is not important when a convert is called. Ethnic differences, as well as social distinctions (see 1 Cor 7:21-24), count for nothing. Paul elaborates this principle later in Galatians and Romans when he brings faithfulness into his discussion of circumcision and life in Christ or life as a new creation (see, for example, Gal 5:6; 6:15; Rom 4:9-12). The most significant thing in the quotation is the words "but keeping the commandments of God." That is what makes converts realize that there are no ethnic or social differences in the community to which they belong (see the discussion of this subject in chapter 8 of this work).

Paul first brings in the subject of Jewish law in 1 Corinthians 9 when he is defending his rights as an apostle. He is really concerned with only one theme: his right to monetary support from the converts at Corinth. He supports his argument with an appeal to the law of Moses: "You shall not muzzle an ox tramping out grain" (1 Cor 9:9; Deut 25:4). This means that as the farmer gains benefits from the harvest, so Paul is entitled to get pay for his work.

In 1 Cor 14:21 Paul loosely quotes a passage from Isaiah 28:11-12 introduced by the formula "in the law it is written." Here "law" (Greek, nomos) is used for the Hebrew scriptures as a whole, not just for the Pentateuch as with the quotation from Deut 25:4 above. Paul is arguing for his preference for prophecy to speaking in tongues in early Christian worship. When God speaks to people in a strange language, they do not listen. Therefore, speaking in tongues is ineffective because it misses the point of worship--to edify believers (1 Cor 14:1-5, 19; see discussion of this point in chapter 6 of this work).

Paul appeals to the law, without actually quoting any particular passage--"even as the law says"-- to support his view of the subordination of women (1 Cor 14:34). Because elsewhere when appealing to the law (as in 1 Cor 9:8; 14:21, for example), he cites a specific text but does not do so here, and for other reasons this passage may be a later non-Pauline interpolation.

According to 1 Cor 9:20, Paul was not an observant Jew in the strictest sense--"though myself not being under the law." As a Christian Jew he came to realize that observances such as circumcision (1 Cor 7:17-20; Gal 6:15) and dietary laws (1 Cor 8:8; Gal 2:11-14) count for nothing in Christian life. Nevertheless, Paul was more of a practical man than a consistent theologian, so he admits that in order to win as many converts as possible, he fluctuated in his observance. To the Jews he became as a Jew, to those under the law he became as one under the law to win those under the law, to those without the law he became as one without the law to win those without the law (1 Cor 9:20; see also 1 Cor 6:12). But be sure to notice that Paul says he was "not without the law of God yet obedient to the law of Christ" (1 Cor 9:21). I shall have more to say about Paul's obedience to the law and his expectations for converts with respect to the law in chapter 8 of this work.

The guiding principle for Paul with respect to converts and the law is stated in 2 Cor 3:6, even though he does not mention the word law: "God has made us sufficient ministers of a new covenant, not of the letter but of the Spirit, for the letter kills, but the Spirit gives life." Living by the Spirit, as all converts, both Jews and Gentiles, were expected to live, makes the ceremonial aspects of the law count for nothing. The law must not interfere with life by the Spirit, and that, as Paul sees it, is the real danger of the law among converts who do not properly understand its requirements.

In 1 Cor 15:56 Paul says: "The power of sin is the law." Here Paul is concerned with the subjects of death and the resurrection. The sting of death is gone for Christian converts because of the resurrection. Jews believed that because of sin death gained control over humans. In the same way, only when there is law to be broken is sin possible. In the resurrection there is not only immortality but also no law to be broken. Both of these conditions--immortality and freedom from transgression of the law--were made possible by God by virtue of the Lord Jesus Christ (1 Cor 15:55-57). Paul elaborates a bit on sin and the law in the introduction to his discussion of Adam and Christ in Rom 5:12-13: "Just as sin came into the world by virtue of one man and death by virtue of sin, thus also death came to all humans because all humans sinned. Sin was in the world before the law, but sin is not reckoned where there is no law." (On this point see discussion of Romans 7 in chapter 6 of this work.)

Except for the passages mentioned, elsewhere in the Corinthian letters the relationship of sin to the law is not a concern of Paul's. The issue of justification on the basis of faithfulness and its relationship to the law simply did not arise in his discussion with the church in Corinth. However, faithfulness toward God and beliefs about Jesus and their relationship to the law and his life by the Spirit as a Christian Jew are beginning to become a theological problem for Paul. He develops his theological position on those matters in his response to the problem in the churches of Galatia and then in considerably more detail in Romans, letters to which we turn in the next chapter.

Chapter 4

According To Galatians And Romans

Jews and Gentiles in the Churches of Galatia

For information about the makeup of the churches in Galatia we must depend almost entirely on the book of Acts, but Galatians also reflects that makeup. In Antioch of Pisidia Paul addresses the people in the synagogue as "sons of the family of Abraham and those among you who reverence God" (Acts 13:26). The first group addressed, of course, were Jews; the second group were Gentiles who attended the synagogue and worshiped the God of the Jews without becoming fully converted to Judaism. Besides these two groups there may also have been some former pagans who had become converts to Judaism. Such persons had to be circumcised, if males, of course, and obey Jewish law. They would have been taught that they also were now a part of the family of Abraham, God's special people. From these groups came most of the converts, the majority of whom were probably Gentiles, in the churches of Galatia. Among these groups there were undoubtedly discussions about Jewish law. There would also be questions concerning circumcision and dietary laws as requirements for themselves and for newer converts (see Gal 2:3-14), as well as discussions about the function of the law as a religious institution.

The Problem in Galatia

In Galatia some converts were being persuaded by persons outside the Christian community there (Gal 1:6-9) that Gentile converts to Christianity should be circumcised (Gal 5:2; 6:12-13) and obey Jewish law (Gal 2:11-14; 3:2-5, 21; 5:4). Although Paul does not specifically name his adversaries, he refers to James, Cephas (Peter), and John, who were leaders in the Jewish Christian church in Jerusalem (Gal 2:9). This may indicate that those men or their associates were at least somewhat responsible for the problem in Galatia.

Because of their zeal for Jewish law, the troublemakers in Galatia are usually referred to as Judaizers, Jewish Christians who wanted Gentile converts first to become Jews before becoming Christians. It is possible that those causing the trouble were Gentile Christians who were following some Jewish laws and wanted others to do the same thing. However, evidence seems to support the view that Jewish Christian Judaizers were responsible for the problem in the churches of Galatia, perhaps instigated by one or more of the Jewish Christians named by Paul in Gal 2:9.

There seems to be a single major problem in the churches of Galatia with which Paul is concerned. He is not arguing most against Gnostics or spiritualists, sometimes thought to be adversaries of Paul in Galatia, but against those who want Gentile converts to be circumcised and to obey Jewish dietary regulations. Throughout the letter to the Galatians Paul responds to such Judaizers and their persuasive influence. Converts have received the Spirit on the basis of faithfulness toward God, not on the basis of works of the law (Gal 3:1-9). They "desire to be under law" (Gal 4:21). And if they "become circumcised, Christ will be of no benefit to" them (Gal 5:2). Paul accuses the Judaizers of being zealous for the Galatians but "not honorably" (Gal 4:17), of not keeping the law themselves (Gal 2:14; 6:13), and even says that "they ought to be castrated" (a literal translation of the Greek word apokopto, in the Greek middle but probably with passive meaning in Gal 5:12).

Requirements for Gentile converts to the Jesus movement with respect to Jewish legal observances were not a problem for Paul before the Judaizers at Galatia insisted that such converts had to be circumcised and obey Jewish dietary laws. The trouble at Galatia forced Paul, as a Christian Jew, to work out his own views with respect to requiring circumcision and other Jewish legal observances, especially dietary regulations, for Gentile converts. Later Paul wrote and elaborated his views in a letter to the Romans.

A number of affinities between Galatians and Romans indicate that in Romans Paul is elaborating themes that arose from his dealing with the situation in Galatia. The summary of Paul's thought in Gal 2:15-21 provides the outline from which he develops his views about justification on the basis of faithfulness, not by works of the law, in Romans 1-8. In Galatians 2-4 and Rom 3:21-8:11 Paul deals with these main subjects: justification and works of the law, the faithfulness of Abraham used to support Paul's argument, the law and its function, union with Christ, slavery and freedom, flesh and spirit, and the sending of God's Son to deliver those under the law to freedom under the Spirit.

Other striking similarities occur in Galatians and Romans. In both Paul quotes Hab 2:4 to support his argument of justification on the basis of faithfulness (Gal 3:11; Rom 1:17), quotes Lev 18:5 to show that those under the law are to live by the law (Gal 3:12; Rom 10:5), maintains that converts belong to descendants reckoned through Sarah and Isaac (Gal 4:27-31; Rom 9:6-11), and quotes Lev 19:18 as a summary of the whole law for converts (Gal 4:28-31; Rom 13:9).

If the crisis concerning requirements of Jewish law for Gentile converts had not developed at Galatia, we might not have Paul's views on faithfulness and the law, especially as argued in Romans. Romans is Paul's effort to find himself as a Christian Jew after he had to deal with the problem at Galatia. In Romans Paul is concerned with two basic subjects: the faithfulness of God and the relationship between Christian converts and the Jewish law, with the implications of that relationship for Christian life that faithfulness toward God demanded. In Romans, then, we can find an honest evaluation of how Paul was trying to work out beliefs of his own even though the letter is inconsistent and probably even incomplete with respect to the views discussed there.

Paul's Response to the Problem in Galatia

Jews who became Christian converts had been taught that they alone were God's special people and that they would inherit his promises to Abraham to make them a great nation (Gen 12:1-3, 7; 13:14-17; 17:1-19; Acts 3:25). Such Jewish Christians also believed that their Jewish Christianity was only for Jews and no others. Obviously, then, if Gentiles wanted to become Christians, they first had to become converts to Judaism by submitting to circumcision and agreeing to follow Jewish law. This was the sincere conviction behind the insistence of the Judaizers that Gentile converts to Christianity had to be circumcised and obey the law of the Jews. Paul writes to the Galatian converts emphatically to deny that position.

Justification on the Basis of Faithfulness

Paul's ideas about justification and the law, ideas that originated when he had to deal with the problem in Galatia, were polemical. They arose out of the conflict with Judaism, but the basic problem was one with reference to Gentiles, not Jews, and to paganism, not Judaism.

Gal 2:15-21

Gal 2:15-21 gives Paul's main argument of Galatians and Romans in a paragraph:

We are Jews by nature (birth) and not sinners descended from Gentiles. But knowing that a person is not made righteous (justified) on the basis of works of the law but by virtue of the faithfulness of Jesus Christ, even we believed toward [eis] Christ Jesus in order that we might be made righteous (justified) on the basis of the faithfulness of Christ and not on the basis of works of the law, because on the basis of works of the law, no one [Greek, "all flesh"] shall be made righteous (justified). But if when seeking to be made righteous in Christ, we ourselves also were found to be sinners, is Christ, then, a minister of sin? By no means. For if the things that I broke down, I build those things up again, I show myself a transgressor. For by virtue of the law, I died to the law in order that I might live to God. I have been crucified with Christ; and it is no longer I that live, but Christ lives in me; and what I now live in the flesh, I live in faithfulness, the faithfulness of the Son of God who loved me and gave himself up [to death] for my sake. I do not make of no effect the grace of God; for if righteousness is by virtue of the law, then Christ died to no purpose.

This translation differs from the way these sentences have been universally translated. Translators have generally been committed to the Reformation doctrine--not to Paul's ideas--that Christians are justified by faith in Christ, not by good works. However, a study of the Greek text and the use of a good Greek lexicon will prove that the translation of every word can be justified, to use an expression of Paul. So let me make several comments about the translation and then show how the ideas expressed there coincide with those of Paul elsewhere.

The words "descended from" translate the Greek preposition ek, which signifies origin, and they are almost the antithesis of "by nature," that is, by birth. Paul, speaking as a Jew, reflects the idea that Gentiles were greater sinners than Jews, presumably because they did not have the law. In the Jewish apocryphal works of 1 Maccabees and Tobit, Gentiles are described as "a sinful people" (1 Macc 1:34) and as "a nation of sinners" (Tob 13:6). But Paul says that when Jews seek to be made righteous in Christ, they realize that they are also sinners.

The words "made righteous" translate Paul's special verb dikaioo, for which there is no word in English that conveys the full meaning as Paul uses it. In the passive, as in Gal 2:15-21, it would have to be translated by a word such as "is righteoused," but that would be awkward, to say the least. So I chose "made righteous," since, according to Paul, God was responsible for converts obtaining the state of righteousness. In fact, Paul most often uses the word in its noun form "righteousness" (Greek, dikaiosyne) or "justification." It occurs most frequently in Romans 1-10.

The phrases "on the basis of" and "by virtue of" represent the Greek prepositions ek and dia, respectively. Both prepositions clearly indicate the ground for or the basis of the resulting state of righteousness, and there is little, if any, difference in meaning.

Faith or Faithfulness?

I have translated the Greek noun pistis, almost universally translated as "faith," as "faithfulness." It is a perfectly good translation of the word many times, especially in the Septuagint, and even in Paul's letters. For Paul, pistis certainly included intellectual assent to certain beliefs, such as "We believe that Jesus died and rose again" (1 Thess 4:14) and "Christ died for our sins according to the scriptures" (1 Cor 15:3). For Paul, however, pistis is more than intellectual assent to certain propositions. Many times it is more akin to the Hebrew noun emunah, meaning loyalty or fidelity to the facts in one's behavior or to one's promises and, thus, faithfulness. The psalmist writes: "The word of the Lord is upright (or righteous), and all his works are [done] in faithfulness" (Ps 32(33):4, Hebrew). Recall the discussion about "God is faithful" to his promises (see 1 Thess 5:24; 1 Cor 1:9; 10:13; 2 Cor 1:18). In Isa 11:5 (Hebrew) we read: "And righteousness shall be the girdle of his loins and faithfulness the girdle of his hips." In the first passage (Ps 32(33):4) uprightness or righteousness and faithfulness are attributes ascribed to God. In the second (Isa 11:5), the same attributes are ascribed to the messianic figure predicted by the prophet Isaiah.

In Ps 32(33):4 the Septuagint translates the Hebrew word for faithfulness with pistis, the same word Paul uses in Gal 2:15-21. In Isa 11:5 the Greek word for righteousness is dikaiosyne, the noun from the verb dikaioo, and means "righteousness" or "justification." And for "faithfulness" the Septuagint has "truth" (Greek, aletheia, the equivalent of the Hebrew emunah, "faithfulness"). The basic root of the Hebrew noun emunah, "faithfulness," regularly translated in the Septuagint with pistis, is the Hebrew verb aman. It is usually translated in the Septuagint with pisteuo, the Greek verb used by Paul for "believe."

In the Septuagint passages just cited, the ideas of righteousness and faithfulness are in parallel. This means that the ideas they represent are inseparably linked together, with reference to God in the first passage and with respect to the Messiah in the second passage. The same attributes are linked together also in a very popular Pauline passage: "The righteous person shall live on the basis of faithfulness" (Gal 3:11; Rom 1:17), a quotation from Hab 2:4. These observations become important as we continue with our examination of Gal 2:15-21.

Faith or Faithfulness of Jesus?

Paul's phrase dia pisteos Iesou Christou I have translated as "by virtue of the faithfulness of Jesus Christ." The words after the preposition dia are in the genitive case and may be taken either as subjective or objective. If taken as subjective, the words after the preposition should be translated as "the faithfulness of [my emphasis] Jesus Christ" in order to show that Jesus is the subject and has the faithfulness. If taken as objective, the same words should be translated as "faith in [my emphasis] Jesus Christ" in order to indicate that Jesus is the object of the faith on the part of the one who believes. Until recently the phrase has usually been taken to mean "faith in Jesus Christ" because of the Reformation doctrine of justification by faith and not by works. No matter how one should translate the phrase, we should translate it the same way also in Gal 2:20; 3:22; Rom 3:22, 26; and Phil 3:9. The arguments for one interpretation over the other on the basis of Greek grammar are inconclusive, and sometimes they are as ambiguous as Paul's Greek. So, we cannot settle the matter on the basis of Greek grammar.

There are probably two main arguments why there has been a hesitancy to attribute the faithfulness Paul talks about to Jesus. First, it seems unfitting to ascribe a mundane quality such as faithfulness to the Christ of Christian theological understanding. Second, it is impossible for Christians to have the same kind of faithfulness as that of Christ. Here it is important to remember again that we are trying to deal with Paul in his time and with his ideas, not ours, and that Paul had in mind only recent converts, not Christians of later times.

Finally, one more comment on my translation of Gal 2:15-21. Where Paul says "Christ lives in [Greek, en] me, and what I am now living in [Greek, en] the flesh, I live in [Greek, en] faithfulness, the faithfulness of the Son of God," I have translated the Greek preposition en as "in" every time. Instead of "in faithfulness" translators generally translate the Greek as "by faith," whereby "by" translates the preposition en, but they do not translate it that way anywhere else in the sentence. Paul believes he shares in the faithfulness of Jesus, so the translation as "in" brings out Paul's feeling precisely. It is a part of Paul's mystical experience of the risen Christ, as with the phrases "in Christ" and "Christ in."

Moreover, the second time Paul mentions faithfulness in connection with Christ he states it in a different way. His Greek words en pistei zo te tou huiou tou theou I have translated as "I live in faithfulness, the faithfulness of the Son of God." I do so because the adjective te emphasizes the faithfulness, and the genitive after it in this case clearly indicates that the faithfulness is that of the Son of God, not that of Paul.

The Faithfulness of Abraham (Gal 3:6-4:22; Rom 4:1-16)

In Gal 3:6-4:22 and Rom 4:1-16 Paul writes about the faithfulness of Abraham. Abraham was the first person who became righteous (was justified) on the basis of faithfulness toward God. In Galatians Paul quotes Gen 15:5-6 to show that Abraham, the father of many nations, "believed God and it was reckoned to him for righteousness" (Gal 3:6). Since Abraham lived long before Moses, to whom the Jews believed God gave the law, Abraham's faithfulness was an example of the gospel coming before the law in order to show that God would make the Gentiles righteous on the basis of their faithfulness toward God (Gal 3:8, 14). So all persons, including Paul's adversaries the Judaizers, who share in the promise that in Abraham all the nations would be blessed must also share his faithfulness toward God (Gal 3:6-9). Paul never gave up his belief that the Jews were God's special people. He simply broadened the concept to include all persons who by virtue of their faithfulness toward God are sons of God in Christ Jesus (Gal 3:26).

In Romans, which represents a later stage in Paul's thinking about faithfulness and righteousness, Paul also discusses the faithfulness of Abraham (Rom 4:1-16). As in Galatians, Paul uses the faithfulness of Abraham to prove that converts are made righteous on the basis of faithfulness, not works of the law. But before discussing Romans 4 I want to comment on Rom 3:22, 26, verses that present a problem, as with the ones in Gal 2:15-16, about whether faithfulness is used with reference to Christ or to believers.

Rom 3:22, 26

According to Rom 3:22, 26, God's righteousness has been manifested apart from the law,

> the righteousness of God by virtue of the faithfulness of Jesus Christ for all who believe [in God]. For there is no distinction . . . in the forbearance of God, to show his righteousness in the present time, that he [God] himself is righteous [that is, by keeping his promises

to Israel through Abraham] and makes righteous (justifies) the human being on the basis of the faithfulness of Jesus.

It is very difficult to translate these verses, and I surely do not do so with complete confidence. To understand what I mean just compare several of the most recent translations, including the RSV and the NRSV.

Several times in Galatians and Romans Paul says that Abraham's faithfulness was reckoned to him as righteousness (Gal 3:6; Rom 4:3, 9, 22; see Gen 15:6). It was reckoned to him as righteousness because he believed God before he was circumcised. Circumcision was only a sign of God's covenant with Abraham because his righteousness came by virtue of his faithfulness while still uncircumcised and long before there was law. All Paul's discussion, of course, is to support his argument that converts are made righteous (justified) on the basis of faithfulness, not works of the law. But faithfulness of whom or in whom?

The Faithfulness of Jesus

Notice that in Romans 4 Jesus is not brought into any of Paul's discussion about Abraham. Obviously, Paul would not say Christ's faithfulness was only "reckoned" to him for righteousness because he believed Jesus actually was righteous. In 1 Cor 1:30, a passage we have already considered, Paul says God is responsible for converts being in Christ who became righteousness for them. In 2 Cor 5:21 Paul says that God made Christ who knew no sin to be sin for the sake of converts in order that they might become the righteousness of God. In Rom 5:12-21, a later stage in Paul's thinking, Paul compares the sinfulness of Adam and its effect on humanity to the righteousness of Christ and its effect. Paul says that "by virtue of the obedience of one man [Christ] the many will be made righteous" (Rom 5:19). And, according to Paul, Christ became obedient to God unto death (Phil 2:8). Since Paul attributes the qualities of righteousness and obedience to Christ, and since he also attributes righteousness to converts, would it not be natural for him to think also of the faithfulness of Christ? This is the more likely in view of the quotation from Isa 11:5 where righteousness and faithfulness are attributes of the messianic figure predicted by the prophet. That Paul knew Isaiah 11 is clear from the fact that in Rom 15:12 he quotes Isa 11:10 as part of his proof from the scriptures that Christ became a minister to the circumcised (Jews) to confirm the promises of God to the patriarchs and for the hope of Gentiles.

If, for the moment, it may be granted that in the passages we are considering Paul has in mind the faithfulness of Jesus and not that of believers, what can we discover in those passages about the faithfulness of those who believe? But first let us return to Paul's discussion of Abraham in Romans 4.

In Romans 4 God, naturally, is the object of Abraham's faithfulness throughout. God reckoned Abraham's faithfulness toward him as righteousness on the basis of that faithfulness, not on the basis of works of the law (Rom 4:3, 17-20). In the same way, Paul says: "And to the person who does not work but believes on him [God] who makes the impious righteous, his faithfulness is reckoned for righteousness" (Rom 4:5). Through his grace, God's promise was made not only to the person who observes the law, but also to the person who shares the faithfulness of Abraham (Rom 4:16). Again, in Rom 4:23-25 we read: "[The words] 'It was reckoned to him' were written not for the sake of him alone, but also for the sake of us to whom it will be reckoned to those who believe on the one [God] who raised Jesus our Lord from the dead."

From the texts of Rom 4:5, 17-20, 23-25 it is clear that the object of the believer's faithfulness is God, not Jesus. Romans 4 ends with the words, "[Jesus] who was handed over for death for our trespasses and raised for our justification." The effectiveness of Jesus' death for sinful persons becomes the main subject of Romans 5, which begins: "Therefore, because we are made righteous (justified) on the basis of faithfulness [toward God], we have peace with God, by virtue of our Lord Jesus Christ" (Rom 5:1). Here the object of faithfulness is still God because what follows the word "faithfulness" in the sentence would make no sense if we understood "in Christ" as the object of that faithfulness. The meaning clearly is: "Because we are made righteous on the basis of faithfulness toward God, we have peace with God by virtue of our Lord Jesus Christ."

Perhaps we can now consider the passages that raise the problem of the faithfulness of Jesus or of the believer in a more enlightened way by working backwards. Every place in Romans 4 where the word faithfulness is used with reference to believers and without an object, we should understand God as the object (Rom 4:5, 11, 12, 14, 16). Moreover, the phrase to ek pisteos Abraam in Rom 4:16 cannot be translated in any other way than as "the faithfulness of Abraham," as it is, of course, universally translated. The phrase is exactly parallel to the one in Rom 3:26 (ton ek pisteos Iesou) and very close to the ones in Rom 3:22; Gal 2:16, 20; 3:22; and Phil 3:9. This is substantial linguistic evidence that in the passages just listed the phrases pisteos Iesou Christou (Rom 3:22) and pisteos Iesou (Rom 3:26) should be translated as "faithfulness of Jesus Christ" and "faithfulness of Jesus," not as "faith in Jesus."

Rom 3:22 and 3:26 are part of a context in which Paul deals with the efficacy of Jesus' death for the forgiveness of sins by God (Rom 3:21-26). Paul says, "The righteousness of God has been manifested apart from (the) law . . . the righteousness of God by virtue of the faithfulness of Jesus Christ for all those who believe [in God]" (Rom 3:21-22). In light of the related passages in Romans 4, this seems to be the appropriate translation. And here, as in the passages in Romans 4 and Rom 5:1, we should understand God as the object of those who believe. By virtue of Christ's faithfulness, God by his grace makes all converts, both Jews and Gentiles, righteous (justifies them) or forgives their past sins. The past tenses are significant: "all who have sinned" (Rom 2:12; see also 3:9, 23), "sins previously committed" (Rom 3:25; see slso 5:12). Through Christ God acted in response to the fact that all persons were under the influence of sin: "Whom [Christ Jesus] God set forth as a propitiation by virtue of faith in his blood to show his righteousness" (Rom 3:25). Belief in God, who sent Christ as a propitiation for past sins as a sign of God's righteousness, is still assumed. Believers have faith in Jesus' blood, that is, believe in the efficacy of his death by virtue of which propitiation was made possible by God. Perhaps the NRSV conveys Paul's idea well: "Whom God put forward as a sacrifice of atonement by his blood, effective through faith" (that is, faithfulness toward God).

Again, the faithfulness of believers is something <u>about</u> Jesus, not <u>in</u> the person of Christ. We should not overlook Paul's reference to "God is One" (Gal 3:30), the universal Jewish declaration of their monotheistic belief (Deut 6:4). For Paul, "there is no God but One" (1 Cor 8:4). And there is one God, the Father, compared with the many gods of the Gentiles, and one Lord, Jesus Christ, compared with the Gentiles' many lords (1 Cor 8:5-6). To profess faith <u>in</u> Christ would fly in the face of all Paul, still a Jew, although recently become a Christian one, believed about the one God.

Paul ends his discussion in Rom 3:21-26 by saying that God makes righteous (justifies) the person who shares the faithfulness of Jesus (Rom 3:26). It is interesting to observe that in Rom 4:16 the <u>NRSV</u> translates the comparable Greek phrase <u>ek pisteos Abraam</u> as "faith <u>of</u> Abraham" (emphasis mine). But in Rom 3:26 the phrase <u>ek pisteos Iesou</u> is translated as "faith <u>in</u> Jesus" (so also the <u>REB</u>; emphasis mine). However, unlike in the <u>RSV</u>, the <u>NRSV</u> has "faith of Jesus" in a footnote.

Paul believed that Jesus was the personification of the righteousness and faithfulness of God. By virtue of and on the basis of that faithfulness and righteousness, God made it possible for all converts to share in that faithfulness and righteousness. Of course, Paul writes all of these passages to argue that converts are made righteous (justified), that is, have the sins of their past existences forgiven on the basis of faithfulness toward God and certain beliefs about Jesus, especially that his death was somehow effective for such forgiveness. This same theological theme is the larger context for the passage in Gal 3:22, another passage that raises the question concerning faithfulness of Jesus or faith in Jesus.

Gal 3:22

In Galatians 3, as in Romans 4, Paul has used the example of Abraham's faithfulness to support his argument of justification ("righteousing") by faithfulness, not works of the law. Paul says that the law is not against God's promises. "But the scripture has confined all things under (the influence of) sin in order that the promise might be given to those who believe [in God] on the basis of the faithfulness of Jesus Christ" (Gal 3:22). This translation of a very difficult passage conveys the language and thought of Paul and coincides with passages elsewhere with which we have been concerned.

In the verses that follow Gal 3:22 there is the clearest evidence that the faithfulness in the passages we have been considering is that of Christ, not that of the believer. Paul uses these phrases: "before faithfulness came"--"until faithfulness should be revealed"--"until Christ came"--"faithfulness has come" (Gal 3:23-25). These phrases are a perfect example of a literary device in Hebrew poetry known as synonymous parallelism, whereby an idea in the first line is repeated with equivalent but different words in one or more lines that follow. This indicates that Paul clearly identifies Christ with faithfulness. The sentence in Gal 3:22 means, then, that Christ is the personification of God's faithfulness to his promises and that Christ's faithfulness makes it possible for all ("for there is no distinction" [Rom 3:22; 10:12]) who share Christ's faithfulness toward God to become the beneficiaries of God's promises.

Paul says that the law was a paidagogos (Greek literally is "boy-leader," usually translated as "custodian") for the Jews until Christ came in order that they might be made righteous (justified) on the basis of their faithfulness toward God, not on the basis of their law (Gal 3:24). Jews, as well as Gentiles, have been sinful, so the faithfulness of Christ, according to Paul, makes it possible for Jews who already have faithfulness toward God to have their past sins forgiven. Thus, Jews and those Gentiles who have only recently acquired faithfulness toward God are now eligible to share equally as beneficiaries of God's promises.

Paul's use of the word paidagogos indicates that he had the moral/ethical aspects of the Jewish law in mind. In Greek society the paidagogos, usually a trusty slave of the family, took boys to school, provided them with writing materials, including ink. But the paidagogos was also responsible for teaching the boys moral/ethical instruction in accordance with the society in which they lived.

According to Rom 5:18-19, God made the forgiveness of past sins of converts possible on the basis of the righteous action and obedience of Christ. Thus, Paul came to think of the faithfulness, righteousness, and obedience of Christ as one and the same thing. He also believed that faithfulness toward God, righteous life, and obedience to the just requirements of the law, along with certain beliefs about Christ, especially that his death was effective for the forgiveness of past sins of both Jews and Gentiles, were inseparably linked together for those converts who were undergoing preparation for entrance into the renewed covenant community of God. (On these points see chapters 7 and 8 of this work.)

Gal 2:15-21, Again

We return now to Gal 2:15-21, the passage with which we began this chapter. In retrospect, we can see that these verses, in which Paul argues against his adversaries who insisted that Gentile converts had to be circumcised and obey Jewish law, are a rudimentary outline of his theology and his convictions about Christian life. Both aspects of his thinking become clearer as he proceeds with his arguments in Galatians and then later in Romans. And both are summed up in Gal 2:19-20: "By virtue of the law I have died to the law, in order that I might live to God; I have been crucified with Christ; and it is no longer I who live, but Christ lives in me; and what I now live in the flesh, I live in faithfulness, the faithfulness of the Son of God who loved me and handed himself over [to death] for me." These verses contain the distinctive Pauline phrase in me which, along with the more frequent in Christ, represent Paul's attempt to describe his religious experience of the spiritual Christ in his life.

There can be little doubt that the Greek phrase en pistei zo te tou huiou tou theou is correctly translated as "I live in faithfulness, the faithfulness of the Son of God." Yet, in Gal 2:16 Paul writes, "Even we have believed toward [Greek preposition eis] Christ Jesus." This may appear to be a clear contradiction of what I have been saying. But the formula of eis plus the accusative with reference to faithfulness is literally "believed into Christ Jesus." It could also be translated as "with a view toward Christ Jesus." Either of these two translations is meant to convey the converts' experience of committing themselves to loyalty to Jesus as the Christ and Lord (see chapter 5 of this work). It does not mean the same thing as the formulas "believe in" or "believe on" Christ (with the Greek prepositions en or epi), phrases that Paul never uses with reference to faithfulness and Christ.

Observations and Summary

In Gal 2:15-21 Paul is arguing strongly against the Judaizers by saying that God made possible the justification (righteousing) of Gentile converts by virtue of Christ's faithfulness and not on the basis of works of the law. Paul's commitment to the Christian life and religion came about because he became convinced that he shared Christ's faithfulness toward God. The "we" in the clause from Gal 2:15, quoted above, represents Paul and others, including Peter, who may well have shared Paul's ideas with respect to justification and the law. This is true because Paul reprimands Peter for being hypocritical (Gal 2:11-14). Paul's reprimand would be pointless if Peter had not at least partly shared his ideas, especially about food laws. Paul's words in Gal 2:12 that Peter feared the circumcision party may indicate that Peter himself was not fully committed to the position of the Judaizers. There is no indication that when Peter was entrusted with a mission to the Jews and Paul to the Gentiles (see Gal 2:7-9) that the content of their mission preaching was different. In fact, Paul says that God was working through both of them (Gal 2:8). Only in retrospect does Paul say that he and other Jews, especially Peter, became converts in the first place in order to be made righteous (justified) by virtue of the faithfulness of Christ and not on the basis of the law. This coincides precisely with his statement, also made only in retrospect, that God had set him apart for mission work to the Gentiles even before he was born (Gal 1:15-16).

In light of Paul's comments in Galatians 2, I believe that the words "believed in [literally, "with a view toward"] Christ Jesus" are to be understood in the sense of becoming converts to the belief that Jesus was the Christ and to the Jesus movement. Paul is reminding his opponents, then, that "even <u>we</u>" became Christian Jews in order that we might be made righteous (justified) by virtue of the faithfulness of Jesus as the Christ and not on the basis of works of the law.

Chapter 5

Further Comments On Faithfulness And Believing According To Galatians, Romans, And Philippians

I have already discussed faithfulness and believing in 1 Thessalonians, the Corinthian letters, and in some passages in Galatians, Romans, and Philippians. With that discussion as background, we are better able to understand the same ideas as they appear elsewhere in the last three letters mentioned.

Gal 1:23. Paul says that the churches of Christ in Judea had heard that "he [Paul] who formerly persecuted us is now preaching the pistis that he formerly was devastating." Here pistis is not faithfulness toward God because Paul would never have tried to destroy such faithfulness. But the next verse indicates that the faithfulness of the Jewish Christians in Jerusalem was faithfulness toward God because Paul says that "they glorified God for me." So, by "the faith" in Gal 1:23 Paul is referring to the beliefs of Jewish Christians in Jerusalem about Jesus that certainly included a belief that he was the Messiah. The

99

messiahship of Jesus was the primary ingredient of much early Christian preaching among Jews: "And every day in the temple and at home they did not stop preaching Jesus as the Christ" (Acts 5:42; see also 8:4-5). But this belief certainly did not replace the basic faithfulness of early Jewish Christians toward their God.

Gal 3:2. "Did you receive the Spirit on the basis of works of the law or on the basis of a hearing of faithfulness?" Here Paul refers to the receiving of the Spirit by the Galatian converts, probably when they were baptized. Then they also heard the preaching about Christ evident in the faithfulness of the preachers. This is a testimony of Paul's own faithfulness toward God and the expectation of the same faithfulness on the part of the converts.

Gal 3:8. In his discussion of Abraham's faithfulness, Paul says: "The scripture foreseeing that God would make righteous (justify) the Gentiles on the basis of pistis." Obviously, the natural object to be supplied is "in him," that is, God, whom Paul has just mentioned. This interpretation is confirmed in Gal 3:6-7: "Just as Abraham 'believed God and it was reckoned to him for righteousness,' so, you know, that it is the persons of faith [in God] that are the sons of Abraham."

Gal 3:11. "'The righteous person shall live on the basis of faithfulness.'" Paul uses the quotation from Hab 2:4 to support his statement "That no one is made righteous (justified) by [Greek preposition en] the law before God is evident." Paul cites Hab 2:4 in a way that corresponds neither to the Hebrew nor to the Greek text. The Hebrew reads, "The righteous [man] lives by (in) his [own] faithfulness" (toward God); the Greek reads, "The righteous man shall live by my [God's] faithfulness." By omitting the pronouns "my" and "his" Paul does not cite either text exactly. Perhaps he wants his readers to think of the faithfulness of God. This view would correspond to his idea that "God is faithful" (1 Cor 1:9; 10:13; 2 Cor 1:18; 1 Thess 5:24). Paul writes to the converts at Rome that the unfaithfulness of some Jews does not annul the faithfulness of God (Rom 3:3). And in the same context he uses the terms "faithfulness," "righteousness," and "truth of God" synonymously (Rom 3:3, 5, 7).

The author of Hebrews also quotes Hab 2:4 and transfers the pronoun "my" (Greek, mou) of the LXX text from after faithfulness to after righteous. So the text of Hebrews reads, "My righteous one shall live by faithfulness." In this way the author attributes the faithfulness to the Christian believer.

In Gal 3:11 the quotation from Hab 2:4 is part of a context that comes at the end of Paul's discussion of the faithfulness of Abraham. This may indicate that faithfulness in the quotation from Hab 2:4 is that of believers in God, as with the faithfulness of Abraham. Or if the interpretation of Gal 2:15-16, 26, and 3:22 given above is correct, then the faithfulness is that of Christ and not of the believer. The meaning of the quotation would then be: "The righteous person shall live by virtue of the faithfulness of Christ." And "shall live" probably means "obtain eternal life" as in 1 Thess 5:10 and Rom 8:13. Nothing in the context indicates that Paul means "faith in Christ." However, a belief that Christ ransomed the Galatian converts from the curse of the law (Gal 3:13) may be included in the faithfulness of the believer if such faithfulness is intended. But there is no reason why Paul would not have in mind faithfulness toward God, as with Abraham and as with the Hebrew text of Hab 2:4.

Gal 3:14. "That we might receive the promise of the Spirit by virtue of faithfulness." Immediately before this Paul says that the death of Christ ransomed the converts in Galatia from the curse of the law "in order that in Christ Jesus the blessing of Abraham might come upon the Gentiles." God is the object of the faithfulness here as in the example of Abraham's faithfulness. God is to be understood as the implied object of pistis also in Gal 3:12.

Gal 5:5. "We, by the Spirit, on the basis of faithfulness, wait for the hope of righteousness." Here the Spirit is the Spirit of God, so God is probably intended as the object of faithfulness. Or, perhaps, the faithfulness of Christ is intended by Paul.

Gal 5:6. "For in Christ Jesus neither circumcision has any validity nor uncircumcision but faithfulness working through love." Faithfulness toward God is to be understood because to understand Christ as the object of faithfulness would make no sense in view of Paul's use of "in Christ" earlier in the sentence.

Gal 5:22. Paul includes faithfulness as a fruit of the Spirit. Again, faithfulness toward God is to be understood because Paul has just said that persons who do the works of the flesh will not inherit the kingdom of God.

Gal 6:10. "Let us do what is good toward all, but especially to those of the household of the faith." "Household of the faith" is to be understood as "fellow converts" or "fellow believers," who share a common faithfulness toward the same God.

Romans 1 and Elsewhere in Romans. Romans 1 contains key verses for understanding what Paul means by pistis. He begins Romans by saying: "Paul, a slave of Jesus Christ, called [to be] an apostle, set apart for the gospel of God . . . through whom we have received grace and apostleship for obedience of pistis among all the Gentiles for the sake of his name" (Rom 1:1, 5). The antecedent of "through whom" is "Jesus Christ our Lord" of the preceding verse, so it would not make sense to understand Christ as the object of faithfulness. Paul means, then, "for obedience of faithfulness toward God among all the Gentiles for the sake of Christ's name."

Paul addresses Romans "to all those in Rome beloved by God" (Rom 1:7) and thanks his God through Jesus Christ for all the converts there because their faithfulness (toward God) is announced in the whole world (Rom 1:8). Recall 1 Thess 1:8, "Your faithfulness toward God has gone out to every place." As with 1 Thessalonians, Paul begins the letter to Rome with an emphasis on God that continues throughout. He is not ashamed of the gospel, "for it is the power of God for salvation to everyone who believes ["in him," that is, God, obviously the natural object], to the Jew first, and also the Greek. For the righteousness of God is revealed in it [that is, the gospel] from (one) faith to (another) faith, just as it is written, 'The righteous person shall live on the basis of faithfulness' [toward God]" (Rom 1:16-17; recall comments on Gal 3:11 above).

The words enclosed in parentheses and brackets are not in the Greek text. I have inserted them to bring out the meaning that Paul probably intended. I do so for several reasons. First of all, in the context Paul is talking about God and why the Gentiles do not have the righteousness that comes from faithfulness toward God. Even though Gentiles knew better, they continued in their idolatrous ways through all kinds of immoral behavior: "Although knowing God, they did not glorify him as God or give thanks to him. . . . They transformed the truth of God for falsehood and reverenced and worshiped the created thing instead of the one who created it" (Rom 1:21, 25). And a few verses later Paul says: "And since they did not think it fitting to have God in their knowledge [that is, to acknowledge God], God gave them up to an unfitting mind, to do the things that are not fitting" (Rom 1:28).

The Jews addressed by Paul in Romans 2 already have faithfulness toward the one true God. Paul is not castigating them because they do not have such faithfulness. Indeed, he assumes it. Rather, he criticizes them because they did not behave as the law required but misbehaved. Even if some were unfaithful in that respect, their unfaithfulness would by no means annul the faithfulness of God (Rom 3:1-4).

The faithfulness of God becomes a main theme of Paul in Romans in dealing with both Jews and Gentiles. God did not reject his people (Rom 11:1). "The gifts and call of God are not to be repented of" (Rom 11:29). Paul's summary conclusion as regards God's faithfulness with respect to both Jews and Gentiles is stated in Rom 15:8-9: "For I tell you that Christ became a servant to the circumcised as an agent of the truthfulness of God to confirm his promises to the fathers and that the Gentiles might glorify God on behalf of his mercy."

The passages from Romans 1 clearly show that Paul is thinking about the idol worship of Gentiles and their refusal to come to faithfulness toward the one true God of the Jews and Christians. Paul thinks of Gentiles as refusing to be converted from their belief in idols to faithfulness toward God. On the basis of these passages, I have translated Paul's Greek ek pisteos eis pistin as "from one faith to another faith." The righteousness of God is revealed when the Gentiles convert from their idolatrous religion to the religion of the Christian Jews with its faithfulness toward the true God. Thus, they become converts from one faith to another faith.

The second reason why I translate Rom 1:16-17 as I do is that there, as with some passages previously discussed, Paul's language and thought show influence from the Septuagint. In Psalm 83(84) the psalmist writes about his anticipation of experiencing the presence of God in the temple in Jerusalem as he was going up to that place: "Blessed are all who dwell in your house . . . who go from one power to (another) power; the God of gods shall be experienced in Zion" (Ps 83(84):5, 8). Here the Greek phrase that I have translated as "from one power to another power" is ek dynameos eis dynamin and corresponds exactly to Paul's ek pisteos eis pistin, "from one faith to another faith." The psalmist is writing about going from the power of the pagan world around him on the way to God's presence in the temple in Jerusalem.

This interpretation is confirmed by the reference to "the living God" (verse 2 of the Psalm) and the second part of verse 7: "The God of gods shall be seen in Zion." Both expressions, "the living God" and "the God of gods" were generally used in contrast to the lifeless idols of pagan gods. In the same way, Paul writes about converts going, or refusing to go, from the pagan world of idolatry to faithfulness toward the living God, the God of gods of the psalmist's faithfulness. The parallel is obvious. Moreover, the Greek word for "power" is dynamis, the same word Paul uses when he says that the gospel is "the power of God for salvation to everyone who believes" (in God). Psalm 83 ends with the statement: "Blessed is the person who sets his hope on you" (God).

Finally, we need only turn to a passage Paul had written earlier to clinch my understanding of his language and thought in Rom 1:16-17. In 2 Cor 3:18 there is a comparable phrase: metamorphoumetha apo doxes eis doxan. It may well be translated as "transformed from one glory to another" (NRSV, "from one degree of glory to another"). The converse of this is, "They exchanged the glory of the immortal God for images resembling a mortal human being or birds or four-footed animals or reptiles" (Rom 1:23, NRSV). These passages confirm my translation of "from one faith to another faith" in Rom 1:17.

In Rom 1:5 Paul writes that his apostleship is for the purpose of bringing about the obedience of faithfulness among all the Gentiles for the sake of Christ's name. Obviously, here faithfulness toward God is meant. According to Paul, obedience includes a moral element, and in this respect it is closely related to faithfulness. Because of Adam's disobedience to God many persons became sinners, but by virtue of Christ's obedience many were made righteous (Rom 5:19). In Rom 6:15-23 Paul thanks God that the Roman converts, who were slaves of sin, have become obedient from the heart to the model of teaching to which they were pledged. Such obedience is for the purpose of righteousness (<u>eis</u> dikaiosynen). On the basis of their obedience the Roman converts have become "slaves of righteousness." Righteousness is the goal of Paul's mission in trying to bring about the obedience of faithfulness among all the Gentiles (Rom 1:5). And this is the kind of obedience Paul wants to win on the part of the Gentiles (Rom 15:18) and of the Jews who have not yet all obeyed the gospel (Rom 10:16).

When Paul speaks about <u>pistis</u> he means faithfulness toward God, not faith in the person of Christ. This is true especially when he is speaking with reference to Gentiles. But what about the nature of <u>pistis</u> with respect to Jews who already have faithfulness toward God and who might become Christian converts? The starting point for understanding Paul as a Christian Jew and his understanding of Jews with respect to faithfulness and the law is Rom 2:28-29: "The Jew is not one outwardly, nor is circumcision (one) outwardly in the flesh. But the Jew is one inwardly, and circumcision is of the heart, in spirit, not literal, whose praise is not from humans but from God." Here, again, and into the next chapter (Romans 3) Paul shows influence from his Jewish scriptures (see Lev 26:41-42; Deut 10:16; 30:6; Jer 9:25-26; <u>Jub</u>. 1:23).

Jews have the advantage because they have been entrusted with the law. If some were unfaithful, their unfaithfulness does not nullify the faithfulness of God. Yet Jews are no better than Gentiles because all have sinned, and Paul quotes from Pss 13(14):1-3 and 52(53):2-4 to prove his point. Paul's point is that "no human being will be made righteous (justified) before God on the basis of works of the law, for by virtue of the law is the knowledge of sin" (Rom 3:20). This is an important point. It is not that the Jews do not have faithfulness toward God. It is that through the law they became aware of sin. "But now," says Paul, "the righteousness of God has been manifested apart from the law . . . the righteousness of God by virtue of the faithfulness of Jesus Christ for all who believe" (in God; Rom 3:21-22). All persons, Jews and Gentiles, are made righteous (justified), that is, have their past sins forgiven by God's grace as a gift, by the redemption that is in Christ Jesus made possible by virtue of his faithfulness. Before the faithfulness of Christ came this would have been impossible. So Paul stresses his main point again: "We reckon that a human being is made righteous (justified) by faithfulness [toward God] apart from works of the law" (Rom 3:28). God is the God of the Gentiles as well as of the Jews, "since God is one, who will make righteous (justify) the circumcision [Jews] on the basis of faithfulness and the uncircumcision [Gentiles] by virtue of the faithfulness" of Christ (Rom 3:28-30). But, then, leave it to Paul, he asks: "Do we, then, make the law of no effect by virtue of this faithfulness?" And then he answers: "By no means. Rather, we make the law valid" (Rom 3:31). I shall have more to say about this apparent contradiction in a later chapter of this work.

Observations

At this point let me make another observation that helps to support my thesis. Not only is God, not Christ, the object of <u>pisteuo</u>, <u>pistis</u>, and <u>pistos</u> for Paul, but his use of their negative counterparts <u>apisteo</u> ("be unfaithful," "disbelieve"), <u>apistia</u> ("disbelief"), and <u>apistos</u> ("unbelieving") indicates that God, not Christ, is also the object of disbelief. In Rom 3:1-4 Paul speaks about the advantages of the Jews and then asks: "What does it matter? If some disbelieved (<u>epistesan</u>), does their unfaithfulness <u>(apistia)</u> annul the faithfulness of God? By no means!" (see also Rom 4:20; 11:20, 23). In his discussion about believers and unbelievers in the Corinthian letters God is always the object to be understood. Here are two examples: "If any of the unbelievers (<u>ton apiston</u>) invites you" (1 Cor 10:27) and "So that tongues are a sign not to those who believe (<u>tois pisteuousin</u>) but to the unbelieving (<u>tois apistois</u>; 1 Cor 14:22; see also 1 Cor 6:6; 7:12-15; 2 Cor 4:4; 6:14-15).

I return now to the discussion of faithfulness in Romans.

Rom 9:30-10:13. Romans 9 and 10 are key chapters in the latest development of Paul's thought with respect to righteousness (justification) on the basis of faithfulness, not works of the law. Paul discusses the quest for righteousness on the part of Jews first and then of Gentiles. He wrestles with the problem of the Jews being God's special people who received his promises and yet did not have the righteousness of God. The reason is that the Jews did not pursue righteousness on the basis of faithfulness but on the basis of works of the law. Then Paul says that the Jews have stumbled over the stone of stumbling and quotes a combination of Isa 28:16 and Isa 8:14: "Behold,

I am placing in Zion a stone of stumbling and a rock to cause stumbling, and the person who believes on him shall not be put to shame" (Rom 9:32-33). In this compound quotation from the Septuagint the Greek words translated as "a stone of stumbling" (lithon proskommatos) and as "a rock to cause stumbling" (petran skandalou; literally, "rock of stumbling") are synonymous and, therefore, mean the same thing. But the question is to whom or to what did Paul intend them to refer?

In spite of the fact that in the later New Testament writing of 1 Peter (2:4-8) the stone of stumbling is used with reference to Christ, there is nothing in the immediate context in Romans to support that view. This is in sharp contrast to the passage in 1 Pet 2:4-8, where the writer also quotes from or alludes to several passages from the Scptuagint, including Isa 28:16. There, however, the writer's introductory comment makes it clear that the quotation is used with reference to Christ: "Come to him, a living stone, rejected by humans but in the judgment of God chosen and precious" (1 Pet 2:4).

The quotation in Rom 9:32-33 follows after the statement that the Jews pursue righteousness not on the basis of faithfulness but on the basis of works. Paul's whole point is that the Jews have misplaced the emphasis: they have put the emphasis on the law and not on their faithfulness toward God. They have failed to recognize God as the basis and end of the law, so they have rejected him. The stone of stumbling, therefore, probably refers to the law. Paul uses similar expressions elsewhere with reference to a cause of stumbling for converts, perhaps even to the law itself in Rom 11:9-12. But the Jews still have a chance because Isaiah says, "The person who believes on him [that is, God] will not be put to shame."

The words "on him" in the sentence quoted in Rom 9:33 are not in the Hebrew or Greek text of Isa 28:16, so the Jews whom Paul was addressing would naturally have understood God as the object of believing. However, the words "on him" could be an insertion into the text of Isa 28:16 from the Greek text of Isa 8:14 where the object of believing is clearly God. And, indeed, Paul probably means the "on him" in Rom 9:33 to refer to God rather than to Christ. He has not mentioned Christ anywhere in the context of his long discussion since the beginning of the chapter (Rom 9:1-5). His discussion centers on God and the Jews' relationship to him and to the law. But Paul assures the Jews that the person who believes in God will not be put to shame. Because of their faithfulness toward God, God, by his grace, will make it possible for them to come into the renewed covenant community of God and, therefore, ultimately for them to be saved. But they must pursue righteousness on the basis of their faithfulness toward God and not on the basis of the law. And, just as importantly, the Jews must believe certain things about Jesus. Indeed, these things are the whole point of Paul's discussion in Romans 10 and 11.

If the cause of stumbling does refer to Jesus, then the "on him" refers to Jesus as the Christ (Messiah) crucified. This earliest and most important belief about Jesus was very hard for most Jews to accept, because they could not conceive of a Messiah who died on a cross. The best reason for this interpretation is that Paul refers to the crucified Christ as a cause of stumbling for the Jews in 1 Cor 1:23. There the Greek word meaning "a cause of stumbling" is skandalon, the same word as in the second part of the quotation from Isa 28:16, quoted by Paul in Rom 9:32-33. He uses the same word in Gal 5:11 in the discussion with his adversaries: "But I, fellow converts, if I still preach circumcision, why am I still persecuted? Then the cause of stumbling has been abolished." Here Paul seems to be saying that if circumcision were still maintained as law then there would not be any concern about Christ crucified. However, in Galatians 5 the cause of stumbling for the Jews is not so much the crucified Christ as the freedom those persons have who conduct their lives by the Spirit, not by the law (Gal 5:13-26). Gal 5:11 and its context help to enlighten and confirm my interpretation of Rom 9:32-33.

In Rom 9:5 Paul lists the things that originate with the Jews, and then he adds that from them also originates "the Christ [Messiah] according to the flesh." Although not in the Hebrew text of Isa 28:16, the words "on him" are inserted after "believes" in some manuscripts of the Septuagint. They were inserted by Jewish translators of the passage with reference to the Messiah, as we know from later Judaism. Since in the context Paul is talking only to Jews, he may have in mind Jesus as the Messiah as the object of their believing. But in light of the whole context in Romans 9, and in light of Paul's discussion in Gal 5:11 and its context, the best interpretation is that the cause of stumbling in Rom 9:32-33, according to Paul, is the law. In Rom 10:1-4 Paul continues with his concern about the Jews' relationship to God. He prays that they may be saved, that is, come into the Christian religion, and testifies to their zeal for God. But he also says that their zeal is not according to knowledge. The Jews are ignorant of the righteousness of God, seek to establish their own righteousness, and do not submit to the righteousness of God, that is, righteousness on the basis of faithfulness toward God, not on the basis of the law. "For Christ [as the Messiah] is the end of the law for the purpose of righteousness to every one who believes" (that is, has faithfulness toward God).

Acceptance of Jesus as the Messiah was the basic belief about Jesus necessary for Jews who wanted to become Christian converts, as we learn from the first apostolic preaching reported in Acts. The writer of Acts reports that after his religious experience on the road to Damascus Paul himself "confounded the Jews who lived in Damascus by deducing [from the scriptures] that Jesus was the Christ" (Acts 9:22). Sometimes suffering is associated with Jesus as the Christ (see Acts 3:17-26; 17:1-4). These things may help to support the argument that in the quotation from Isaiah in Rom 9:33 Paul had Jesus as the (crucified ?) Christ in mind.

In Rom 10:5-13 Paul discusses the matters of righteousness and salvation for all persons, Gentiles as well as Jews. Here we come to the ultimate of Paul's views of beliefs about Christ for all persons who are in the process of becoming converts. Paul says that "the word" in a quotation from Deut 30:14 is "the word of the pistis that we preach." Then he continues:

> If you confess Jesus as Lord with your mouth and believe in your heart that God raised him from the dead, you will be saved. For a person believes with the heart with a view toward righteousness and confesses with the mouth with a view toward salvation. The scripture says, 'No one who believes on him will be put to shame.' For there is no distinction between Jews and Greeks, for the same Lord is over all and gives his riches upon all who call upon him. 'For every one who calls upon the name of the Lord will be saved' (Rom 10:9-13).

Here there is no doubt that a condition for ultimate salvation of converts is belief about Jesus as well as faithfulness toward God--"if you confess" and "if you believe" (emphasis mine). Here Paul also goes beyond the belief that God raised Jesus from the dead, expressed in earlier letters, and includes the confession that Jesus is Lord (see also Phil 2:11). But salvation still lies in the future, as the future tense of the verb in Rom 10:9 indicates--"you will be saved." That the future is intended is also clear from Paul's Greek in Rom 10:10. That is why I have translated the phrases eis dikaiosynen and eis soterian as "with a view toward righteousness" and "with a view toward salvation," respectively. Here the Greek preposition eis with the accusative means that the action is not yet complete but is still moving toward the goal specified. The translations of the RSV and the NRSV, "is justified" and "is saved" are misleading. The REB version is better here: "leads to righteousness" and "leads to salvation." Faithfulness toward God is the first step for the righteousing or forgiveness of converts' past sins and for ultimate salvation. And now Paul also adds as another step toward ultimate salvation the confession that Jesus is Lord.

At first glance, it appears that in Rom 10:5-13 Paul identifies Jesus with God; but that is not true, even though the line Paul draws between the two is very fine. Up to verse 10 Paul is speaking about Christ, but beginning with verse 10 his thought returns to God. So believing on him in verse 11 refers to God, not Jesus, and the Lord in verse 13 is the Lord God as in the Greek text of Joel 3:5 that Paul quotes, not Jesus as Lord of verse 9. This is true for two reasons. First, according to Paul elsewhere, it is the one God who is the God of Gentiles as well as Jews (Rom 3:29-30). And in Rom 9:5 Paul specifically says, "God who is over all be blessed forever, amen." Second, in Rom 11:33 Paul speaks of the riches of God (compare Rom 10:12), and in Phil 4:19 the distinction between God and Christ is quite clear: "God will fill every need of yours according to his riches in glory in Christ Jesus."

Belief that Jesus is Lord

We must remember that Paul is always writing to persons who are in the process of becoming or have recently become converts. He is also concerned that converts have faithfulness toward the one God of the Jews and that they believe that Jesus is the Christ (Messiah) and acknowledge him as the only Lord, as over against the many lords of the pagan world. In that world humans, especially kings, rulers, and persons who had authority over others, were sometimes given the title "Lord." For example, Herod the Great, who ruled Palestine from 37-4 B.C., was referred to as "king Herod lord." In the West, Roman emperors did not accept the title "Lord" (kurios) until after the time of Paul. In the East, however, people from Egypt and Syria applied the title to the emperors Augustus, Claudius, and often to Nero. For example, an Egyptian papyrus from the year A.D. 1 mentions sacrifices and libations "on behalf of the god and lord Emperor" (Augustus).

At first glance, Paul's views with respect to Jesus as Lord seem to coincide with early Christian mission preaching, according to Acts: "God has made him both Lord and Christ" (Acts 2:36). In such preaching the two titles are sometimes combined--"the Lord Jesus Christ" (Acts 11:17; see also 15:26; 20:21). Paul uses the same combination in every letter either as "the Lord Jesus Christ" (1 Thess 1:1; 1 Cor 1:3; 6:11; 2 Cor 1:2; Rom 1:7; 13:14; Phil 1:2; 3:20) or as "our Lord Jesus Christ" (1 Thess 1:3; 5:9; 1 Cor 1:7,; 2 Cor 1:3; 8:9; Gal 1:3; 6:14; Rom 5:1, 11; 15:6) or as "Jesus Christ our Lord" (1 Cor 1:8). Upon closer scrutiny, there is one fundamental difference between the writer of Acts and Paul, to which I now turn.

<u>What Paul Does Not Say</u>

Perhaps, again, we can best understand Paul's thought from what he does not say. In early mission preaching according to Acts, the preachers use expressions such as believing "on [epi] the Lord Jesus" (Acts 16:31) or "on [epi] the Lord" (Acts 9:42) or "on [epi] the Lord Jesus Christ" (Acts 11:17). "Crispus, the ruler of the synagogue, believed on the Lord" (dative, without a preposition; Acts 18:8). Paul is reported as speaking to the elders of Ephesus about "faith in [eis] our Lord Jesus" (Acts 20:21). In the same way, Felix heard Paul speak "concerning faith in [eis] Christ Jesus" (Acts 24:24). When telling Agrippa about his visionary religious experience, it is reported that Paul says that the voice of the risen Jesus spoke about his mission to work "among those who are sanctified by faith in me" (dative, without a preposition; Acts 26:18).

Those expressions concerning faith in Jesus are in sharp contrast to what Paul himself writes concerning beliefs about Jesus. And they especially help us to realize what Paul does not say. The phrases in Acts correspond to the expressions of Paul's epitomizers in Ephesians and Colossians. In Ephesians the author writes: "I have heard of your faith in [Greek preposition en] the Lord Jesus" (Eph 1:15). Similarly, the writer of Colossians says that he has heard of the readers' "faith in [en] Christ Jesus" (Col 1:4) and speaks of "the bulwark" of their "faith in [eis] Christ" (Col 2:5; see also 1 Tim 1:14; 3:13; 2 Tim 1:13). Paul never writes about faith in or believing in Christ in the same way as the writers of Acts, Ephesians, Colossians, and the Pastoral Epistles do (see, for example, 1 Tim 1:16; 2 Tim 3:15). Nor, on the other hand, do those writers speak of the faithfulness of Jesus as Paul does.

There is, however, a single exception in Eph 3:1-13, where the writer conveys Paul's thought about the faithfulness of Jesus exactly. Writing in the name of Paul ("I, Paul"; 3:1) and speaking biographically, he speaks about the grace of God given to him to preach the good news of the inexplorable riches of the Messiah. Then the writer continues: "In whom ["the Messiah, Jesus our Lord," the antecedent] we have the boldness and access [to God] with confidence by virtue of his faithfulness" (dia tes pisteos autou; Eph 3:12). Here the epitomizer of Paul's letters has conveyed Paul's idea of the faithfulness of Jesus precisely.

Lest it be objected that in saying Paul does not speak about faith in Jesus I am content with an argument from silence, let me reply in the words of the Greek epigrammatist Palladas (fl. c. A.D. 400): "Silence is man's chief learning." Although we may not always understand what Paul says, sometimes what he does not say helps us to better understand what he does say, as well as what some other writers of the New Testament say. The silence of Paul has been too long ignored in trying to understand his basic ideas. (I return to the silence of Paul in chapter 7 of this work.)

In the Hebrew scriptures one of the expressions for God is "the Lord God," and it is used in the Greek equivalent kurios ho theos or ho kurios theos many times in the Septuagint and sometimes in the New Testament (for example, Rev 1:8; 4:8; 19:6). But the expression is never used that way of Jesus. And Paul is careful to distinguish between God and Jesus. Apparently his Jewish monotheism made it important that in the world of polytheism where he preached he make the distinction clear. The basic text for understanding Paul on this point is 1 Cor 8:4-6. In contrast to the many gods and lords of polytheism, there is "one God, the Father, and one Lord, Jesus Christ." Paul makes the distinction clear, especially in the salutations of his letters: "To the church of the Thessalonians in God the Father and the Lord Jesus Christ" (1 Thess 1:1; see also 1 Cor 1:3; 2 Cor 1:2; Gal 1:1, 3); and "God and Father of our Lord Jesus Christ" (2 Cor 1:3). Yet, believing that Jesus was Lord was next to having faithfulness toward God and was the highest expression of belief about Jesus. But according to Paul, Christ himself did not count equality with God a thing to be snatched at (Phil 2:6). And, also according to Paul, the confession of Jesus as Lord was to be done for the purpose of glorifying God the Father (Phil 2:11).

Although Paul always distinguishes between God and Jesus, in his own mind he does not make a similar distinction between Jesus as Christ and Jesus as Lord. So he can speak of "Jesus Christ our Lord" and "our Lord Jesus Christ." Although Paul never identifies Jesus as Lord with God, after he came to believe in Jesus as Lord, it was quite natural for him to read the title "Lord" back into his Jewish scriptures and connect it with the title Lord used as a name for God. The Pauline distinction between Lord and God with reference to Jesus disappeared in later Christian theology. Specific examples of this are to be found in the gospel of John where the writer says that when Thomas saw the resurrected Jesus he said, "My Lord and my God" (John 20:28). Thomas's words reflect the author of John's own theology as stated in the prologue to the gospel: "The Word [Jesus] was with God, and the Word was God" (John 1:1; see also 1 Tim 1:11; Titus 2:13). There is nothing comparable to these passages in Paul's letters. This observation may not help us to better understand what Paul says, but it certainly helps us to perceive what he does not say. Here his silence is our chief learning.

Observations and Summary

It is difficult to explain exactly what Paul means by Jesus as Lord, although Lord certainly was an exalted title for the risen or spiritual

Christ. Perhaps for Paul there was little difference between Jesus as Lord and the Lord God of the Jews. This is evident in those passages (for example, 1 Cor 1:31; 2:16; 2 Cor 10:17; Rom 10:13; 14:11) where, apparently, he reads the title Lord used of Jesus back into texts of the Jewish scriptures and connects it with the title Lord used as a name for God. But in most, if not all, of those passages that are quotations from or allusions to the Jewish scriptures Paul really speaks of the Lord God, not the Lord Jesus. Moreover--and this is important-- Paul never explicitly makes the identification of Jesus as Lord with God. Again, it is very important to note what Paul does not say.

In sum, "Lord" (kurios), when applied to Jesus by Paul, even in its highest sense, does not imply deity or identification in essence or substance with the distinctive God of the Jews. The closest Paul comes to making such an identification is in 2 Cor 4:4. There he writes that "the god of this world has blinded the minds of unbelievers, so that the light of the gospel of the glory of Christ, who is an (the) image (likeness) of God." That "image" or "likeness" here does not mean the same as God is clear from the fact that Paul speaks of man (aner) as "the image and glory of God" (1 Cor 11:7; see also 1 Cor 15:49). Paul would not say that man is the same as God. According to Paul, God had also predestined some persons to share the image of his Son (Rom 8:29; see also 2 Cor 3:18). In all of these passages Paul was probably influenced by the story of man's creation in Genesis (see 2 Cor 4:6).

For Paul, Jesus as Lord symbolizes a relationship with those converts who believe Jesus is the Lord, as against all other lords of the polytheistic world. The significance of the title is not theological but experiential. Paul says that "the Lord is the Spirit" and "where the Spirit of the Lord is, there is freedom" (2 Cor 3:17; see also 1 Cor 12:4; 2 Cor 13:14). He also says, "No one can say Jesus is Lord except in (by) the Holy Spirit" (1 Cor 12:3). Elsewhere Paul uses the phrases "in the Holy Spirit" (1 Thess 1:5; Rom 14:17), "in the Spirit of our God" (1 Cor 6:11), "in the Spirit" (1 Cor 14:2; 2 Cor 3:6; Phil 2:1), or "the Spirit in" (1 Cor 3:16; Rom 8:9, 11) with reference to the Christian converts' experience of the Spirit. He also uses the phrases "in the Lord" (1 Thess 3:8; 5:12; 1 Cor 4:17; 7:39; 9:1, 2; 15:58; Gal 5:10; Rom 16:2, 12-13; Phil 1:14; 4:1, 2, 4) and "in Christ Jesus our

Lord" (1 Cor 15:31; Rom 8:39) in the same way. All of these expressions are synonymous and closely related to the phrases "in Christ," "Christ in," and "with Christ," Paul's most creative attempt to convey the experience of the spiritual Christ effective in the lives of Christian converts. And in his mission work Paul's personal experience of the risen or spiritual Jesus as Lord convinced him that he had greater authority than any of his rivals, even those who had known the earthly Jesus.

The bottom line, then, is that the title Lord is used by Paul not only to invoke the belief of converts who were familiar with the many lords of the polytheistic world, but equally to inspire the new life in Christ lived by the Spirit required of all converts. The spirit of paganism was polytheism, with its many gods <u>and</u> lords. It was that spirit with which Paul was contending when he taught faithfulness toward God and belief about Jesus as Lord that were best experienced when living under the influence of the Spirit.

Having discussed faithfulness in Galatians and Romans, I turn now to several passages on the subject in Philippians.

<u>Phil 1:25, 27</u>. In Phil 1:25 Paul writes that he is convinced that he should remain alive and continue with all the Philippian converts "for their progress and joy of their faithfulness" so that when he returns to them he may share in their "boasting in Christ Jesus." The phrase "boasting in Christ Jesus" in Phil 1:26 indicates that faithfulness toward God is meant in what precedes it. The phrase would make no sense if faithfulness toward God were not meant. In Phil 1:27 the statement about the converts living their lives in a manner worthy of the gospel of Christ indicates a moral context. So the statement about "struggling together with one mind for the faithfulness of the gospel" is a call from Paul for a united moral front against immoral forces (recall the discussion of this verse in chapter 1 of this work).

<u>Phil 1:29</u>. Paul reminds the Philippian converts that their salvation is from God. Then he says: "It has been graciously granted to you for the sake of Christ, not only to believe in him [eis <u>auton</u>] but also to suffer for his sake." The object of both believing and suffering here is God to whom the converts owe their salvation, so the "in him" refers to

God, in whom converts believe and for whom they suffer for the sake of Christ.

Phil 2:17. Here pistis is used in the sense of loyalty. Paul expresses his gratitude for the Philippian converts' sacrificial financial support while he was in prison by virtue of their loyalty to him. Through their action toward Paul the converts showed their true religious faithfulness.

Phlm 5. Paul thanks God for the faithfulness that Philemon has toward the Lord Jesus (ten pistin, hen echeis pros ton kurion Iesoun). This is the closest Paul comes to the idea of faith in Jesus as Lord. However, we must interpret Paul's words here in light of 1 Thess 1:8, where Paul compliments the Thessalonian converts for their faithfulness, faithfulness toward God (pros ton theon), not toward idols. Paul's Greek in Phlm 5 shows the same kind of emphasis, "faithfullness, faithfulness which you have toward the Lord Jesus."

Philemon lived in the city of Colossae where religious syncretism was the main problem in the church there (see, for example, Col 1:15-20; 2:16-23). There was a lot of competition with the Lordship of Christ. Obviously, Christianity faced a great challenge under such circumstances. So, Paul thanks God for Philemon's faithfulness or loyalty to Jesus as Lord and not toward any of the many lords of paganism at Colossae. That pistis should be taken in this way is clear from the fact that the same faithfulness is directed also "to all the holy ones" (saints), that is, fellow believers in God. Moreover, Paul goes on to say: "I (pray) that the sharing of your faithfulness [toward God] may become effective in perceiving all the good in us for Christ" (that is, all we can do for Christ). In light of these words it would not make sense to understand "faith in" the Lord Jesus in Phlm 5-6.

Relationship among Faithfulness, the Law, and Christian Life

Now let me return once again to Galatians in which Paul's ideas about faithfulness, justification, and the Jewish law appear together for the first time. We must not assume that all pagans were immoral. In light of the moral/ethical teachings of the Stoics and other moral philosophers of Paul's time, we know that was not true. Yet, because of the moral demands made upon converts, there was always the temptation for Gentile converts to forget their new God and new Lord and to revert to the worship of idols and to their former pagan ways of life. Paul writes about this emphatically to the Galatians: "But, then, not knowing God, you were slaves to beings that by nature are no gods; but, now, having come to know God, or rather having been known by God, how can you turn back again to the weak and miserable elements, to which again you want to be slaves over again?" (Gal 4:8-9). This literal translation of Paul's Greek shows the emphasis on his question about why the Galatian converts would want to revert to their former pagan status. This is the point of Galatians 5 and 6 which begin: "For freedom Christ has set us free; stand firm, therefore, and do not again submit to a yoke of slavery" (Gal 5:1).

In other communities of converts Gentiles faced the same temptation to revert to their former modes of behavior. If they really have given up their former ways, they must not in some critical moment revert to their former modes of behavior (see 1 Cor 6:9-11; 15:1-2; 2 Cor 12:19-21; 13:1-10; Rom 6:19-22; Phil 1:27-30; see also Col 1:21-23). Paul offered all converts, not only in Galatia but everywhere, a monotheism and an impeccable morality without circumcision, dietary regulations, and other ritualistic demands of Jewish law.

At this point it may be instructive to call attention to the structure of the letter to the Galatians, in which for the first time Paul's ideas about justification, faithfulness, and the law appear together. The letter divides naturally into three parts. After the autobiographical account and the defense of his position in chapters 1 and 2, Paul becomes concerned with two threats to the Christian converts in Galatia. First, he argues against the threat to the gospel of Christ by those who stress works of the law (Galatians 3-4). Then he argues against the idea that, if freedom under the Spirit has degenerated into license, being circumcised and obeying the law can replace life by the Spirit (Galatians 5-6). The Christian community at Galatia was endangered as much by the second threat as by the first. But whereas the threat of legalism was brought into the community from the outside, the misunderstanding of freedom under the Spirit had been indigenous to the converts at Galatia. This is clear from the fact that Paul had to "warn them before" that those who do the works of the flesh will not inherit the kingdom of God (Gal 5:19-21; see also 1 Thess 2:11-12).

Paul was equally concerned with both threats to genuine Christian life in the churches of Galatia. Sometimes in admonishing those who misunderstood their new freedom he alludes to discussion raised by the legalistic argument. "All the law is fulfilled in one word, 'You shall love your neighbor as yourself'" (Gal 5:14). At the same time, Paul says that there is no law against the works that are the fruit of the Spirit (Gal 5:22-25). Such works fulfill the law of Christ (Gal 6:2). Thus, Paul believed that at Galatia moral/ethical behavior, the fruit of those who really live by the Spirit, was actually a replacement for much of the law of Moses, especially the ritualistic requirements of circumcision and dietary laws.

The Galatian converts did not understand that the gift of the Spirit imposed the obligation of a transformed way of life. They were still unable to make proper moral/ethical decisions, just as formerly when they did not know God (Gal 4:8). So Paul had to remind them of the coming judgment when each person would be responsible for what that person had done. This is clear from the future tenses in the concluding sentences to the last part of the letter (Gal 6:4-9):

> Let all persons individually examine their own work, and then in themselves alone they will have reason to boast. . . . For all persons will have to bear their own burdens. . . . Do not be deceived, God is not mocked. For whatever each person sows, that will each also reap; for the persons who sow to their own flesh from the flesh will reap corruption, but the person who sows to the Spirit from the Spirit will reap eternal life. Let us not become tired of doing good, for at the proper time we will reap if we do not give out (Gal 6:4-9).

Thus, Paul repeatedly insists that becoming Christian converts means that their lives are changed. Before the problem developed at Galatia, the moral/ethical lives of new converts in his churches was Paul's main concern. He encourages the Christian converts at Thessalonica in their affliction and reminds them that when present he had charged them "to conduct their lives worthy of God, who calls you into his own kingdom" (1 Thess 2:11-12). He begs and exhorts them "that as you learned from us how you ought to conduct your lives and to please God, just as you are conducting your lives, you do so more and more" (1 Thess 4:1; see also 4:2-12). Anxiety over the second coming of Jesus was no excuse for moral laxity, according to Paul (1 Thess 4:13-5:23). Before the problem in Galatia concerning circumcision and the law for Gentile converts, faithfulness and works of the law were never placed in antithesis to each other, nor were they afterward except in Romans (see also Phil 3:8-9).

There is little or no evidence to indicate that until the time of Galatians Paul himself had not followed Jewish law. In fact, the word "law" (nomos) is not even mentioned in 1 Thessalonians or 2 Corinthians. In 1 Corinthians Paul appeals to the law to support his own position on various matters (1 Cor 9:8-9, 20; 14:21, 34; but see 15:56). After Galatians, besides Romans, the word law appears only in Phil 3:5-9, where Paul boasts of his training in the law as a Pharisee. In Acts it is reported that Paul believes "all things according to the law and written in the prophets" (Acts 24:14) and that he has not done any wrong "against the law of the Jews" (Acts 25:8; see also 13:38-39; 21:20-28; 22:3; 23:3; 28:23). Although the passages in Acts may be somewhat redactional on the part of the author to minimize the conflict between Jewish and Gentile Christianity, they do represent the view that Paul, as a Christian Jew, almost certainly did observe some Jewish law. And I suspect that, in spite of all Paul says about the law, if he had been the father of sons, even after he became a Christian Jew, he would have had them circumcised.

Perhaps the best evidence that Paul did not, indeed could not, put the law, the very heart of his Judaism, out of his existence as a Christian Jew, and that some aspects of the law continued to have validity for him, is the frequency with which he cites the law to support a variety of his arguments.

Paul and the Jewish Scriptures

For the Jews the interpretation of their scriptures was the means by which those scriptures were transformed into a useful tool for faithfulness and moral life. Interpreters in Paul's time, who lived long after the Jewish scriptures were composed, frequently read into the scriptures what they hoped was written in them. Sometimes unwittingly, then, when using the scriptures, interpreters sincerely

The Apostle Paul

thought they were reading out of them what, in fact, they were actually reading into them. Paul was, to be sure, no exception.

As we might expect, the most remarkable and distinctive feature of Paul's Greek is influence from the Septuagint. The Greek Paul writes is not highly literary, nor, on the other hand, is it careless like that found in the nonliterary papyri of the first century. Influence from the Septuagint is evident by direct quotations, especially in 1 and 2 Corinthians, Galatians, and Romans, which serve to support his arguments against his adversaries by appealing to the scriptures, the very authority his adversaries apparently so strongly emphasized. But most importantly for understanding Paul as a Christian Jew, there is scarcely a paragraph in his letters that does not reveal allusions to the Septuagint that flow naturally from mind to words expressed in his somewhat peculiar style of expression.

In contrast to Paul's frequent quotations from and allusions to the Jewish scriptures, he cites only one sentence from Greek literature, and that was probably a popular proverb (1 Cor 15:33). But in 1 and 2 Corinthians, Galatians, and Romans their are about 88 direct quotations from about 15 different writings of the Septuagint. Fifty-three of Paul's quotations--about two thirds--are in Romans. In addition to direct quotations, in the same letters plus Philippians there are many allusions to passages from many different books of the Septuagint (for example, 1 Cor 13:5 to Zech 8:17; 2 Cor 7:6 to Isa 49:13; Gal 4:22-27 to Gen 16:15-16; Rom 9:18 to Exod 4:21; Phil 1:19 to Job 13:16).

For Paul, as for all Jews, their scriptures were the basis of authority for belief and practice. The words "it is written" and "scripture says" were common authoritative formulae for introducing an appeal to scripture. Paul sets forth his principle in 1 Cor 4:6: "that you may learn from us not (to go) beyond what is written" (in scripture). Naturally, Paul's beliefs as a Christian Jew shaped his interpretation of the scriptures, but the scriptures retained the same authority for him as a Christian Jew that they had before he became a Christian. In 1 Cor 15:3-4 he writes: "Christ died for our sins according to the scriptures . . . he was raised the third day according to the scriptures."

Almost every chapter of Romans, the so-called classical statement of the Christian faith, contains a direct quotation from or an allusion to some Septuagint text. I mention only a few examples. The idea that "God shows no partiality" in his dealing with those, both Jews and Greeks (that is, Gentiles), who do evil or good (Rom 2:9-11) is an allusion to Deut 10:17. For other allusions in the Romans passage see also LXX Isa 28:22 and Deut 28:53. Paul quotes from several Psalms (13[14]; 5; 139[140]; 10; 35[36]) and Isaiah (59) to support his charge that "both Jews and Greeks are under sin" and need God's grace for righteousness (Rom 3:9-18). His arguments in Rom 9-11 that God can save some or all Jews and Gentiles are supported by quotations from the Pentateuch, Hosea, Isaiah, the Psalms, and other books from the Jewish scriptures. Paul gives a series of quotations from Psalms, Deuteronomy, and Isaiah to support his view that Christ became a slave to the circumcised in order to confirm God's promises made to the Patriarchs and that the Gentiles might glorify God for his mercy.

These few passages from Romans show how important and authoritative the Jewish scriptures were for Paul. For him the Pentateuch was thought to have been written by Moses. Paul cites it as a work of Moses (1 Cor 9:9; Rom 10:5, 19), and he does so with the authority which those writings characteristically had among Jews. As a matter of fact, in Galatians 3-4, where Paul argues about the law, almost all his quotations from the Jewish scriptures are from the Torah. Thus, Paul actually uses the law when writing about the law to the Galatian and Roman converts.

Summary

The evidence of Paul's familiarity with the Jewish scriptures gives us the best insight into the depth of his Jewishness, even as a Christian Jew. At the same time, his experience as a Christian Jew made him think of those scriptures in a new way. The righteousness of God was no longer made available through the scriptures but by virtue of the faithfulness of Christ. Paul used the scriptures to help clarify and confirm what he believed God had done because of Christ's faithfulness.

At Galatia for the first time Paul the Jew by birth had to take a position as a Christian Jew on the relationship of the law to his newly acquired beliefs about Christ. Paul's answer to the problem of the relationship of beliefs about Christ to works of the law is that converts, Gentiles and Jews alike, are justified (made righteous) only on the basis of faithfulness toward God, not on the basis of works of the law. Subsequently, converts were taught a minimum of beliefs about Christ. All this was made possible by the grace of God by virtue of the faithfulness of Christ.

As a Christian Jew Paul could not give up his conviction that ultimate salvation came through obedience to the will of God, of which the basic requirement was the comprehensive term righteousness. This righteousness is the same thing as the justification (same word in Greek, dikaiosyne) converts received as the result of their baptism. However, whereas grace entered in with their justification or being placed in a state of righteousness, that grace was not available to them in the future for their ultimate salvation unless they continued in their righteousness. For Paul, faithfulness always presumes righteousness. Righteousness, then, became the basic requirement upon which ultimate salvation depended for Gentile and Jewish converts alike. "For in Christ Jesus neither circumcision nor uncircumcision has any validity but faithfulness made effective through love" (Gal 5:6). "For neither circumcision nor uncircumcision means anything, but a new creation" (Gal 6:15).

In the next chapter we consider what faithfulness toward God made effective through love and being new creations meant for Christian converts, according to Paul.

Chapter 6

Christian Converts As New Creations

What kinds of persons did Paul think converts whose justification by the grace of God was made possible by virtue of Christ's faithfulness and their own faithfulness toward God should be?

Christians

Since neither Paul nor any gospel writer mentions the word Christian, perhaps they were unaware of or purposely avoided using it. In the New Testament the word occurs for the first time in Acts (11:26; 26:28), and it is used in 1 Pet 4:14-16 as a term of reproach. It is used among several pagan writers as a term of scorn, ridicule, or disdain, as also in Acts 26:28, so it may have originated among those authors (see Tacitus, Annals 15:44:2; Suetonius, Nero 16).

The word Christian literally means "partisan of Christ," and it may have been used to distinguish the Jesus sect of Jews from other Jews in order to designate them as a unique group in the Roman Empire. At any rate, writers of the New Testament do not use the term Christians when referring to their readers, nor did Christians generally use the term with reference to themselves before the second century. If early Christians were aware of the term, they must purposely have avoided using it. There is, however, a variety of other terms used with reference to persons we call "Christians."

Called or Chosen

Paul reminded the Thessalonian converts that God had chosen them (1 Thess 1:4) and exhorted them to conduct their lives in a manner worthy of God who calls them into his own kingdom and glory (1 Thess 2:12). And he makes quite clear the purpose for which they were called: "God has not called us for uncleanness but (to be) in holiness" (1 Thess 4:7). Converts at Corinth are called by God into the fellowship of his Son (1 Cor 1:9) and for peaceful relationships between husbands and wives (1 Cor 7:15). Converts should not be concerned about being called as slaves, for all who are called in the Lord (God) as slaves are freed persons of the Lord (God) and slaves of Christ (1 Cor 7:21-23) Galatian converts are called for freedom that is not to be mistaken for license (Gal 5:13; see also 1:6; 5:8). In Rom 8:30 being called is synonymous with being justified, and God calls Gentiles as well as Jews (Rom 9:24-25). These passages make it clear that Paul believed converts were called by God for a moral purpose in life.

Brothers

The first term Paul uses to refer to his fellow converts is "brothers" (adelphoi), and he uses it in every letter. Because the writer of Acts, when reporting about the earliest community of Jesus' followers in Jerusalem, says that members referred to other members as brothers (for example, 1:15-16; 2:29, 37), the term may have been in use before Paul's time to designate followers of Jesus. Paul, then, simply would have adopted it. He uses it already in 1 Thess 1:4 where he addresses his readers as "brothers beloved by God," whom God has chosen (see also 1 Thess 2:1; 4:1; Gal 1:11; 4:28, 31). Paul refers to Timothy, his associate, as "our brother and God's fellow worker in the gospel of Christ" (1 Thess 3:2; see also Gal 1:2). The recipients of 1 Corinthians are addressed as "brothers" when Paul appeals to them not to have any dissensions among themselves (1 Cor 1:10-11).

From the beginning, Paul refers to his fellow converts as brothers in moral/ethical contexts. In 1 Thess 4:1-5 he begs and exhorts "the brothers" that just as they received (instruction) from him and his fellow workers how they ought to conduct their lives and to please God to do so even more. "For this is the will of God, your sanctification, for you to abstain from illicit sexual relations . . . and that no one take advantage of his brother in this matter" (see also 1 Thess 4:9-12; 5:12-22). Paul wrote to the converts at Corinth "not to associate intimately with any one given the name of brother if he indulges in illicit sex or is greedy . . . or a drunkard, or a robber, not even to eat with such a person" (1 Cor 5:9-11). Paul says that those who sin against their brothers sin against Christ (1 Cor 8:11-12; see also Rom 8:12-13; 12:1-2; Phil 3:17-18; 4:8-9). In a deeply personal address he reminds the Galatian "brothers" that they were called to freedom and then exhorts them not to use that freedom as an excuse for sexual misconduct, but rather to serve as slaves to one another through love (Gal 5:13).

These passages indicate that Paul thought of the churches to which he wrote as communities of morally regenerated persons, including women, of course. For that reason I usually translate Paul's Greek word <u>adelphoi</u> as "fellow converts," perhaps occasionally as "fellow Christians." Pauline Christianity, then, viewed as individual churches or as a whole, was a kind of brotherhood or fellowship. (See suggestions on this point in the next chapter of this work.)

Baptism into the Brotherhood?

According to Acts, converts were baptized (2:38-41; 16:15, 33) and Paul also was baptized when he became a Christian (Acts 9:18). However, Paul never mentions his own baptism and does not emphasize the rite in his earliest letters. By the time he wrote Galatians, and especially Romans, he came to place the emphasis on the significance of baptism for moral life in the renewed covenant community of God.

The moral implications of baptism are described by Paul symbolically. The Greek word <u>baptizo</u> means to "dip" or to "submerge." So for baptism converts took off their clothes to be baptized naked and then put them on again when they came up out of the water. Therefore, in Gal 3:27 Paul aptly says: "For as many of you as were baptized into Christ have been clothed with Christ." By being submerged into the water converts share a kind of spiritual experience or union with the spiritual Christ, and that experience starts them on the way to a new kind of moral existence under the influence of the Spirit, individually and socially. This existence is expressed metaphorically as clothing that covers the body. Paul is influenced by Hebrew thought whereby putting on clothes was a metaphor for assuming inward or spiritual qualities or some different status is life. See, for example, Job 29:14 (LXX): "I put on righteousness and clothed myself with judgment." Here are other examples: "Let them be clothed with shame" (Ps (34)35:26) and "Your priests shall clothe themselves with righteousness" (Ps (131)132:9).

In Rom 6:1-11 Paul also describes baptism symbolically. Being submerged into the water represents converts as sharing in Christ's death and thus dying to sin. Coming up out of the water means sharing in Christ's resurrection and thus rising to newness of life under the power of the Spirit. In light of these observations I suggest that converts to faithfulness toward God were not baptized when they became members of a church or brotherhood. Converts in the brotherhood were baptized when they were sufficiently prepared morally/ethically to enter the renewed covenant community of God, the highest status or rank within the brotherhood. (See the discussion of Romans 6 below and the suggestions concerning brotherhoods of converts and the renewed covenant community of God in chapter 7 of this work.)

Those Who Believe or Believers

Another term Paul uses to refer to Christian converts is "those who believe," usually translated as "believers." It was also probably used in early Christianity before Paul to designate persons who were believing Jews or pagans as Christian converts from those who were not (see, for example, Acts 2:44; 4:32). Paul addresses converts at Thessalonica as "you who believe" (1 Thess 2:10, 13) and says that they were "an example to all who believe in Macedonia" (1 Thess 1:7). Sometimes "believe" is the equivalent of being converted to faithfulness toward God, as, for example, in 1 Cor 3:5: "What then is Apollos? What is Paul? Servants through whom you believed" (see also Rom 13:11).

One thing is certain. When Paul refers to converts as persons who believe they must have been taught something to believe. Their believing is a reaction or response to what they had been taught. But what was included in the teaching of Paul and other early Christian teachers and missionaries is largely a matter of conjecture. Those who believed were committed, above all else, to faithfulness toward God and also to certain beliefs about Jesus, the most significant of which was that Jesus was Lord. But faithfulness toward God was Paul's primary concern for believers, and that faithfulness was to motivate moral/ethical behavior. This is emphatically clear from Paul's exhortations to the Corinthian converts:

> Do not be unequally joined with unbelievers. For what partnership have righteousness and wickedness, or what fellowship has light with darkness? Or what harmony has Christ with Belial? Or what share has a believer with an unbeliever? And what agreement has the temple of God with idols? For we are the temple of the living God (2 Cor 6:14-16).

The parallels effectively bring out the contrast between what is expected of those who believe and those who do not, as does Paul's exhortation in 2 Cor 7:1: "Let us cleanse ourselves from every contamination of flesh and spirit, making holiness perfect in the fear (reverence) of God." These passages show again that Paul is most concerned with converts' faithfulness toward God, including the moral/ethical imperative, and that such faithfulness is set in contrast to the idolatry of the converts' past.

<u>Holy Ones</u>

Paul also uses the term "holy ones" (<u>hagioi</u>) to refer to converts. Although it, too, may have come to him from earlier Christian tradition (see Acts 9:13, 32, 41; 26:10), it became his characteristic form of address when referring to the recipients of his letters, except in 1 Thessalonians, of course, and Galatians (see 1 Cor 1:2; 2 Cor 1:1; Rom 1:7; Phil 1:1; Phlm 5). Apparently Paul was too angry with the Galatian converts for deserting him in order to follow other Christian leaders so that he thought they were not worthy of the designation.

Paul first uses the term "holy ones," but with a different meaning, in 1 Thessalonians. He prays for the converts' growth in love and holiness so that God might establish their hearts blameless at the second coming of Jesus "with all his holy ones" (1 Thess 3:13) Here holy ones refers to believers who had died, and its usage was probably influenced by Zech 14:5: "My Lord will come and all his holy ones (saints) with him" (see also 1 Thess 4:13-18). Compare Matt 27:52 (the only place where the term occurs in the gospels), where the author says that at the death of Jesus "many bodies of the holy ones (saints) who had fallen asleep were raised."

By the time Paul wrote 1 Corinthians he used the word "holy ones" to refer to living Christian converts, members of the churches to which he wrote. In 1 Cor 1:2 Paul identifies the holy ones with the church in Corinth: "To the church of God that is in Corinth, to those sanctified (hagiazo) in Christ Jesus, called to be holy ones, with all those in every place who call on the name of our Lord Jesus Christ" (see also 1 Cor 14:33). It was no accident that "believers" and "holy ones" were among the first words used to designate Christian converts from others in the social world of early Christianity. From the very beginning faithfulness toward God, beliefs about Jesus, and holiness of life were inseparably linked together.

Now look at 1 Cor 6:1-2: "If one of you has some matter against another, does he dare to be judged before the unrighteous and not before the holy ones? Or do you not know that the holy ones will judge the world? And if the world is judged by you, are you not worthy of making very little judgments?" Here Paul thinks of the Christian converts at Corinth as a community of holy or righteous people who are expected to settle disputes among themselves rather than have them judged by outsiders who, by contrast, are "unrighteous." (See suggestions on this subject in the next chapter of this work.)

The "holy ones," then, were persons set apart not only for the purpose of becoming holy themselves, but they were also set apart from Jews who did not accept certain beliefs about Jesus expected of those becoming converts. The designation also set believers apart from Gentiles because of their idolatry and unholy manner of life. These ideas are conveyed by the translation of hagioi sometimes as "God's people" in the REB (for example, 1 Cor 14:33; 2 Cor 1:1).

New Creations

Although the term "new creation" does not appear in 1 Thessalonians, the basis for Paul's later ideas is clearly present. On the surface, it appears that the main purpose for writing 1 Thessalonians was to assure the converts at Thessalonica that their faithful companions who had died would not miss Jesus' second coming. But the converts were suffering at the hands of hostile Jews and fellow Gentiles, and Paul also wrote to encourage them, through his own example of moral conduct (1 Thess 1:5-7; 2:3-12), to be moral persons among themselves in order to win the respect of Gentiles. The basis for Paul's exhortation is not his apostolic authority but his own moral example in accordance with his understanding of the gospel, with God's approval. IIis aim was not to please humans but to please God (1 Thess 2:3-8). The moral demand, as part of being a new creation of human existence, was included in the gospel as Paul understood it from the beginning (1 Thess 2:3).

The earliest known context of Paul's key theological statement-- "God did not appoint us for wrath but for gaining salvation by virtue of our Lord Jesus Christ who died on behalf of us" (1 Thess 5:9-10; see also 4:14)--is one of moral/ethical exhortation. The concomitant to that theological statement is the next sentence: "Therefore exhort one another and edify one another, just as you are doing" (1 Thess 5:11), along with the following verses. So, already in Paul's earliest letter faithfulness toward God, theological beliefs about Jesus, and moral/ethical life are inseparably bound together.

Paul thinks of persons who come up out of the water at baptism as rising to conduct their lives in newness of life (Rom 6:4). In 2 Cor 5:17 he writes: "If any one is in Christ, he is a new creation; the old things have passed away, behold, the new have come. All things are from God." Moffatt's translation of this passage brings out the thought of Paul very well: "There is a new creation whenever a man [or a woman] comes to be in Christ." Paul tells the Galatian converts that neither circumcision nor uncircumcision is anything, but "a new creation" (Gal 6:15).

Although the expression "new creation" by itself does not tell us very much, we can discern Paul's attempts to describe the unique life of members of the renewed covenant community of God as new creations. He uses a variety of phrases that give insight into his inner feelings and convictions. Converts "have been clothed with Christ" (Gal 3:27). "All are one in Christ Jesus" so that "there is neither Jew nor Greek . . . neither slave nor free . . . neither male nor female" (Gal 3:28). "God has sent the Spirit of his Son into our hearts" (Gal 4:6). As new creations Christian converts conduct their lives by the Spirit and do not gratify the desires of the flesh (Gal 5:16). Persons who are justified on the basis of faithfulness toward God have "peace with God by virtue of our Lord Jesus Christ" and have God's love poured into their hearts by virtue of the Holy Spirit that has been given to them (Rom 5:1, 5). Those who were reconciled to God by virtue of the death of his Son shall be saved by (Greek en) his life (Rom 5:10).

Because Paul's ideas of converts becoming new creations is largely a matter of his own personal experience, it is impossible for us to completely understand them. He seems to speak of Christ as a kind of medium in which Christian converts live. Perhaps we can think of it as with the atmosphere around us. Just as we need air for life, Christian converts have no life without Christ. We breathe air, and the air is in us and is part of us. So it is with Paul's experience of Christ. Christ is in him, and he is in Christ. In Gal 2:19-20 Paul uses a combination of expressions to convey his mystical experience with reference both to God and Christ. Through the law Paul died to the law that he might live to God. Then he says: "With Christ I have been crucified. It is no longer I who live, but Christ lives in me; and what [the life] I am now living in the flesh, I live in faithfulness, the faithfulness of the Son of God."

To be in Christ is also to be in the Spirit because "The Lord is the Spirit" (2 Cor 3:17). How, according to Paul, does this experience happen? According to the hints we get from him speaking of his own experience, God is responsible for it. "God is faithful, through whom you were called into the fellowship of his Son, Jesus Christ our Lord" (1 Cor 1:9). Because of God the Corinthian converts were "in Christ Jesus" (1 Cor 1:30). "It is God who confirms us with you [the Corinthian converts] in Christ . . . and gives us his Spirit in our hearts" (2 Cor 1:21-22). According to 2 Cor 5:17-21, the transformation comes about by action of God through Christ: "All these things are from God who, by virtue of Christ, reconciled us to himself." Persons reconciled to God have a new personal relationship with God, one no longer hostile but friendly. Moreover, as the result of converts' reconciliation to God, the righteousness of God, which makes converts' reconciliation possible as a free gift, also becomes the converts' righteousness. Thus, the essence of converts' reconciliation to God and of their changed existences as new creations is moral as well as spiritual.

Observations and Summary

It is God who acts in the converts' becoming new creations. Converts react. Paul seems to have thought that every convert should be able to say with him, "By the grace of God I am what I am" (1 Cor 15:10). Yet--and this is very important--Christian converts were responsible for maintaining their status as new creations.

Writing as one who had been reared a Pharisaic Jew, Paul would naturally reflect, in his thought and language, many aspects of contemporary Judaism, examples of which have already been noted. Quite naturally, too, Paul's writing was influenced by his recent experience as a converted Christian Jew, including his changed conception of Jesus.

The expression "new creation," with others similar to it, was used later among Rabbis to describe converts to Judaism. The following Rabbinic sayings from the Talmud and Midrashim illustrate the point. "If any one brings near [to God] an idolater and converts him, it is as if he had created him." "He who brings a person under the wings of the Shechinah [God's presence] is regarded as if he had created him." "A proselyte who embraces Judaism is like a newborn child." The thought behind all these sayings is that God would not punish converts for sins committed before their conversion to Judaism. Such views are obviously foreshadowed in Paul's words: "If anyone is in Christ, that person is a new creation, the old things have passed away, behold, the new have come" (2 Cor 5:17) and "In Christ, God was reconciling the world to himself, not counting their transgressions against them" (2 Cor 5:19; see also Rom 3:25).

It is obvious that Paul tries in various ways to convey his convictions that converts are changed persons and live different lives. To be sure, Paul takes for granted faithfulness toward God and certain beliefs about Jesus. But one thing is certain from every context: the emphasis is on God and on the lives converts live in relationship to him, not on faith in Christ or even on beliefs about him.

Again, we must remember that Paul was writing to persons, mostly Gentiles, who had only recently become converts. Such converts, living in pagan environments, literally had to start life all over again. Instead of the nothingness of idols and idol worship (1 Cor 8:4-6; 10:19-20; Gal 4:8), Christianity, like Judaism, demanded worship of a righteous God, and, in turn, that righteous God demanded righteousness of his worshipers, precisely as with the first Hebrew covenant communities of God. Although, in the process of becoming members of such communities, converts certainly had to agree to worship God and not idols and probably also assent to certain beliefs about Jesus, it is emphatically clear from every letter of Paul that there were also stringent moral/ethical requirements. But there was always the temptation for Gentile converts to revert to their former pagan ways of worship and life, so Paul had constantly to remind them of their new existence. I cannot stress too much the fact that this is Paul's main concern.

Becoming a Christian convert, then, meant a complete break in the continuity between a convert's old and new existence. This is clear from passages already examined, but there are many others that lead to the same conclusions.

New Creations and Early Christian Worship

In 1 Cor 5:1-13 Paul writes about problems in the church at Corinth and uses an analogy from the Jewish Passover, with the festival of unleavened bread as part of it. This passage provides one of the few insights into early Christian worship. Notice, first of all, that Paul deals with the Passover theme in the context of his discussion of the immoral behavior of some converts. "It is actually reported that there is illicit sexual behavior among you, illicit sexual behavior of such a kind that is not even [found] among pagans" (1 Cor 5:1). Notice also that Paul contrasts the behavior of the Christian converts with that of their pagan neighbors and that for emphasis he repeats the word porneia, which means, specifically, "illicit sexual behavior," usually translated as "immorality."

Paul writes: "Cleanse out the old leaven that you may be fresh dough, just as you are unleavened; for Christ, our paschal lamb, has been sacrificed. Let us, therefore, celebrate the festival, not with the old leaven, with the leaven of wickedness and evil, but with the unleavened bread of sincerity and truth" (1 Cor 5:7-8). Those verses are followed with Paul's exhortation to the Corinthian converts "not to associate with male prostitutes" or "with any one who bears the name of fellow convert if he is a prostitute, or greedy or is an idolater, reviler, drunkard, or robber" (1 Cor 5:9-13). Here there is evidence of Christian belief in the words "Christ, our paschal lamb, has been sacrificed." Paul may regard the deliverance of the Hebrews in the Exodus as the prototype of God's action in Christ. But the important thing is that Paul gives the festival of unleavened bread a new interpretation in light of his own experience as a Christian Jew. In Christian worship it has become symbolic of the forgiveness of converts' past sins, a part of the experience of their moral regeneration into new creations and effective for both Jewish and Gentile converts. They now celebrate the Passover as a festival of Christian life. Instead of living in wickedness and evil, all Christian converts should live by sincerity and truth (1 Cor 5:7-8).

Although Paul never worked out a theoretical view of Jesus' death as a sacrifice, his reference to Christ as a Passover sacrifice (1 Cor 5:7) indicates that in some early Christian worship Jesus was regarded as the counterpart of the Passover lamb in the story of converts' ultimate salvation. This gives Paul the opportunity to apply the regulations concerning leaven in the Hebrew scriptures analogically to the situation in the Christian community in Corinth. And the whole context (1 Cor 5:1-21) is Paul's condemnation of immoral behavior in that community and elsewhere. And after exhorting the converts not to associate with immoral persons, Paul charges them to "drive out the evil person from among you."

We simply cannot discern the full nature and meaning of early Christian worship. The few insights we get from Paul's undisputed letters indicate that worship was intimately associated with the moral/ethical lives of Christian worshipers, individually and socially, in the communities of which they were a part. In 1 Thess 5:11 Paul exhorts the converts, who were living with the expectation of the imminent end of the world, to "comfort one another and build one another up, just as you are doing." Here "build up" (oikodomeo) is used in the metaphorical sense of "edify," which means to grow or improve in moral and spiritual life. Converts accomplish this preeminently through love. "Love builds up," according to Paul (1 Cor 8:1). At the same time, converts are to avoid the things that do not edify them (1 Cor 10:23).

When the Corinthian converts met in assembly to celebrate the Lord's Supper, social divisions among them resulted in some persons eating and drinking to excess and others being hungry. Paul could not praise them for such behavior and exhorted them to be spiritually and morally prepared for proper participation in the Supper (1 Cor 11:17-34).

In the clearest passage in the undisputed letters of Paul that deals with Christian worship (1 Cor 14:1-26) it becomes evident, as with the passage dealing with the Lord's Supper, that the Corinthian converts were as confused in their worship as they were in their morals. It was even possible that if they were all speaking in tongues and an outsider or unbeliever should enter, that person might think the worshipers mad (1 Cor 14:23). So Paul stresses that "all things," including a psalm, a teaching, a revelation, speaking in tongues (ecstasy), and prophesying, should "be done for edification" (1 Cor 14:1-26). Indeed, for the purpose of such edification, that is, growth in moral and spiritual life, the Lord gave authority to genuine apostles: "For even if I boast about anything too much concerning our authority that the Lord gave for the purpose of building up and not for your destruction, I shall not be put to shame" (2 Cor 10:8). Paul writes to the Corinthian converts angrily in order that when he visits them again he may not have to be severe in using the authority that the Lord gave him "for the purpose of building up and not for destruction" (2 Cor 13:10; see also 2 Cor 12:19).

Paul exhorts the converts at Rome to pursue the things making for peaceful life and for the upbuilding of one another. Converts ought not eat or drink what they want if such action offends fellow converts who may be sensitive about eating foods they regard as improper. "If your fellow convert [Greek, "brother"] is caused grief through your food, you are no longer conducting your lives according to love" (Rom 14:15-21; see also 1 Cor 8:11-13). In this context, as elsewhere, Paul speaks of upbuilding or edification of Christian converts in their relationships with each other. His words, especially in Rom 15:2, make this clear: "Let each of us please our neighbors for good, for the purpose of edifying them." The word translated as "please" is <u>aresko</u>, which means "please" with the idea of service given willingly to others, a part of early Christian worship in the truest sense of the term.

In contexts where either a Greek verb or noun meaning "worship" is used there is also a distinctive blending of the idea of worship and moral life. Words for worship occur first in the letter to the Romans. The basic meaning of the Greek words sometimes translated as "worship" is service. In the New Testament such service is always used with reference to God, not to humans. Paul uses the verb <u>latreuo</u> that way in Rom 1:9 where, in writing to prepare the church at Rome for his visit, he says that he serves God with his spirit in the gospel of his Son. He uses it in a similar way in defence of himself against some Jews at Philippi: "For we are the circumcision, who worship in the Spirit of God and glory in Christ Jesus and put no confidence in the flesh" (Phil 3:3). Do not fail to observe again that Paul links worship inseparably with morality, as the words "put no confidence in the flesh" indicate. Worship (<u>latreia</u>; noun) is one of the things that belong to the Jews (Rom 9:4).

In Rom 1:25 Paul uses the verb <u>latreuo</u> ("serve") and a word for worship (<u>sebazomai</u>) together. Paul is reproving the Gentiles because they did not become Christian converts. "They worshiped and served the creation rather than the Creator." Notice especially that Paul says they worshiped idols because of their immoral lives (see especially Rom 1:18, 26-32). In strong contrast, Paul describes Christian worship in Rom 12:1: "I exhort you . . . by the mercies of God to present your bodies a living sacrifice, holy and pleasing to God which is your reasonable worship." This passage is part of Paul's description of the new life in Christ (Romans 12-14). The word translated as "reasonable" (<u>logikos</u>) is sometimes translated as "spiritual." Christian converts' worship of, or service to, God means that their inner spiritual lives and their outward behavior conform to God's will.

The passages on worship show that it was the blending of worship and moral life that first distinguished early Christian converts in their worship from that of the pagans in the world in which they lived. In the religions of the Graeco-Roman world of Paul's time emotional rapture was a chief feature of worship. In the worship of Dionysus, god of wine, ecstasy caused by excessive consumption of the beverage was the usual and accepted norm. While emotional expressions, such as speaking in tongues and other modes of joy and enthusiasm, were a part of early Christian worship, excesses were discouraged, and drunkenness was considered debauchery. Instead of being saturated with wine, Christian converts were to be filled with the Spirit.

The fact that Paul linked early Christian worship and morality inseparably together was clearly perceived by the writers of Ephesians and Colossians, who were greatly influenced by him. Ephesian Christians are to be "imitators of God . . . and to conduct their lives in love" (Eph 5:1-2). They are not even to think of immorality and other vices in which they had participated previously when they were pagans and lived in moral darkness, not light (Eph 5:3-14). The author exhorts the Christians to whom he writes:

> Look carefully, then, how you conduct your lives, not as unwise persons but as wise. . . . Therefore do not be foolish, but understand what the will of the Lord is. And do not get drunk with wine, for that is debauchery; but be filled with the Spirit, addressing one another with psalms and hymns and spiritual songs, singing and playing the harp to the Lord in your heart, giving thanks always and for all things in the name of our Lord Jesus Christ to God the Father (Eph 5:15-20).

The writer of Colossians refers to worship in the context of his moral exhortations. Colossian Christians are to put an end to illicit sexual behavior, impurity, passion, evil desire, greediness, wrath, anger, malice, slander, foul speech, and lying. Before becoming Christian converts the Colossians had been practicing such things (Col 3:5-7). But as Christians they "have taken off (as a piece of clothing) the old person with its practices and have clothed themselves with the new nature" (Col 3:5-10). And as God's chosen ones, holy and beloved, Christians at Colossae are to clothe themselves with compassion, pity, kindness, lowliness, patient endurance, forgiveness, and, above all, love, "which binds everything together in perfect harmony" (Col 3:12-14). The author of Colossians continues: "Let the word of Christ dwell in you richly, as you teach and admonish one another in all wisdom, as you sing songs and hymns and spiritual songs to God with thankfulness in your hearts." And then the writer concludes: "And whatever you do, in word or in deed, do everything in the name of the Lord Jesus, giving thanks to God the Father through him" (Col 3:16-17). Thus, with the writers of Colossians and Ephesians, as with Paul, Christian worship and moral probity are inseparably linked together. The model for what constituted Christian worship in the truest sense is quite clear.

New Creations and the Expulsion of Nonconforming Members

Nowhere in Paul's letters is there any evidence that a person should be dismissed from a Christian community of newly created human beings on the basis of differences concerning beliefs about Jesus or because of confused procedures in worship. However, Paul is very emphatic about the removal of persons who do not conform to the moral standards of such a community. When the man at Corinth committed a sexual offense worse than that found among pagans, some members of the community were rather arrogant and apparently thought it was all right for him to assert his Christian freedom in that way. But Paul writes that rather than be arrogant they ought to mourn. Then he adds: "Let him who has done this deed be removed from your midst" (1 Cor 5:1-2). And not only are members of the renewed covenant community of God not to associate with any person who bears the name of fellow convert if that person is guilty of immorality or other evils, but the members are to expel the evil person from among them (1 Cor 5:13). This is very strong language and indicates that persons were expelled from Christian communities on the grounds of immoral behavior, not on the basis of differences in beliefs about Jesus or confused worship practices.

In Gal 5:22-23 Paul lists the fruits of the Spirit, one of which is gentleness (<u>prautes</u>). Perhaps that is why, a few verses later, he is gentler in giving advice about a transgression: "Fellow converts, if a person is caught in a certain transgression, you who have the characteristics of the Spirit should bring such a person into the proper condition in a spirit of gentleness" (Gal 6:1). Again, I have translated Paul's Greek very literally in order to show precisely what he says, even though we may not know exactly what he means. What the transgression (<u>paraptoma</u>) was, or what Paul meant by it, is not stated, but his use of "a certain" (<u>tis</u>) with it means that the wrongdoing was not so specific or so flagrant as with the offender in the community at Corinth. Because the nature of the transgression is not known, I have used the phrase "bring into the proper condition" to translate Paul's verb <u>katartizo</u>. Paul does use the same verb, though, in an ethical sense when he exhorts the Corinthian converts to be brought into unity of mind (1 Cor 1:10). And Paul uses it also in 2 Cor 13:11 by itself with the more general meaning of "Behave yourselves properly."

In Rom 11:17-24 Paul writes about some Jews who were broken from the vine, God's people Israel, "because of their unbelief." "Unbelief" here, as always with Paul, is to be understood as lack of faithfulness toward God on the part of the Jews about whom Paul is concerned and who did not come to obey the gospel (Rom 10:14-21). They are the Jews who misplaced their emphasis by putting their trust in the law, not in God, and about whom Paul writes so much earlier in Romans. Then he speaks about wild olive branches, that is, Gentiles, who, because of their faithfulness toward God, were grafted into the vine in place of the unfaithful Jews (see Rom 10:14-21). Gentiles, on the other hand, though not equal to the Jews in morality and religion, were admitted because they accepted the gospel on the basis of faithfulness toward God.

Romans 6

Romans 6 is a passage crucial to our understanding of Christian converts as new creations and of the whole spectrum of Paul's ideas. Before their conversion to Christianity both Jewish and Gentile converts were under the power of sin (Rom 3:9, 22-23). The effect of converts' becoming Christians, as symbolized in baptism, was moral and spiritual, namely, the forgiveness of past sins, with the obligation not to continue sinning. But according to Rom 3:8, some persons of Paul's own time did not understand that his teaching about justification by God's grace and their baptism meant continuing to live without sin. So Paul writes: "And why not (say), just as some persons slander and say that we say, 'Let us do evil in order that good may come'?" (Rom 3:8). Such misunderstanding led Paul to begin his discussion of baptism in Rom 6:1 by asking, "What shall we say then? Are we to continue in sin that grace may abound?" His answer to that question is emphatic and absolutely clear:

> By no means! How can we who died to sin still live in it? Do you not know that as many as were baptized into Christ Jesus were baptized into his death? We were buried, then, with him by virtue of baptism into his death in order that, just as Christ was raised from the dead . . . we too might conduct our lives in newness of life. . . . We know that our old person was crucified with him in order that the body of sin might be destroyed, and we might no longer be slaves to sin. For the person who has died [in baptism] has been acquitted (justified) from sin. . . . So you also must consider yourselves dead to sin but living to God in Christ Jesus (Rom 6:1-11).

Paul continues by exhorting his readers: "Do not, therefore, let sin rule in your mortal body to make you obey its desires. Do not offer your members as weapons of wickedness for sin, but offer yourselves to God as living from the dead and your members to God as weapons of righteousness" (Rom 6:12-13).

Crucial words in Rom 6:7 are "has been acquitted from sin." The Greek verb for "has been acquitted" is dikaioo and is the same word translated as "justified" in Paul's expression "justified on the basis of faithfulness." He clearly thinks of the converts' forgiveness of past sins, symbolized in the rite of baptism, as their justification. In other words, converts became justified, that is, were acquitted of or forgiven of their past sins by God, at the time of their baptism. And it is clear from Romans and elsewhere that Paul expected baptized converts to remain sinless.

After having been taught that the human race is inevitably and hopelessly sinful, many Christians today may be surprised by the notion of human sinlessness. They might argue, therefore, that there is nothing in Paul's letters which even implies such an idea. But Paul did not think as Christians may think today or even think he thought. We must not water down what Paul says when considering any passage. In Rom 6:7 Paul clearly says: "The person who has died [symbolically in baptism] has been acquitted (justified) from sin." The translation "acquitted (justified) from sin" may also be translated as "is freed from sin," as in the NRSV, for example. Since in Rom 6:7 dikaioo clearly has the meaning "acquit," both translations mean the same thing. But converts have not only been forgiven of their past sins. They are also expected to remain sinless: "Do not let sin, therefore, rule in your mortal body to make you obey its desires. . . . Are we to sin because we are not under law but under grace? By no means!" (Rom 6:12, 15).

According to Romans 6, Paul would completely reject Luther's doctrine simul iustus et peccator, "at the same time righteous and sinner." To think of a person who had become justified or made righteous by God being at the same time a sinner would have been unthinkable to Paul. He had already exhorted the Corinthian converts: "Be thoroughly sober in mind righteously (dikaios, adv.) and do not sin" (1 Cor 15:34).

Romans 7

On the surface, Romans 7 may give the impression that Paul would not even think of human sinlessness. Therefore, some comments on that chapter are necessary to confirm the point I have made with respect to Romans 6. We must remember that Paul always writes with a view to making more converts, especially Gentiles (see Rom 1:5-6), to the Jesus movement and to reassure present converts of the validity of living under the power of the Spirit. It is even more important to realize this when he is talking about the law and the behavior of converts. "Whenever Gentiles who do not have the law do by nature the things required of the law, even though they do not have the law, they are a law to themselves, who show (in that way) the work of the law written in their hearts" (Rom 2:14-15). In the same way, "The Jew is not one outwardly, nor is circumcision outward in the flesh; but the

Jew is one inwardly, and circumcision is of the heart, spiritual, not written" (Rom 2:28-29). The words "flesh," "spiritual" (en pneumati), and "written" (grammati), that is, the law, provide some of the clues for understanding Romans 7.

Romans 7 may be divided into two basic parts: 7:1-5 and 7:6-25. The clue to the first section, in which Paul speaks to Jews ("to those who know the law"), is Rom 7:4. Converts (referred to as "brothers" and "you") "have died to the law by virtue of the body of Christ," that is, through his death, symbolically shared in baptism. The purpose of belonging to Christ, the Christ raised from the dead, is "to bear fruit to God." When living in the flesh, the experiences of sin brought on by the law were working in pre-converts "to bear fruit for death."

Rom 7:6 closes the first section of the chapter and makes the transition to the next section: "But now we have been discharged from the law, having died to that which held us fast, so that we serve [God] with the newness of the Spirit and not by the old written code." In verse 6 "discharged from the law" is the same thing as "died to the law" in verse 4. And what held pre-converts fast was life in the flesh. The old way of living in or by the flesh is the opposite of the new way of living in or by the Spirit. Up to this point Paul has only implied that the law was responsible for sin in the lives of Jewish pre-converts. In verse 6 the law is called a written code (gramma) and is contrasted with life by the Spirit.

Rom 7:6, then, harks back to Rom 2:14-15 and 2:27-29 and looks forward to what follows. Rom 7:6 is the first verse of an inclusio, of which the last part is Rom 8:1-4: "There is therefore, now, no condemnation for those who are in Christ Jesus. For the law of the Spirit of life in Christ Jesus has set you free from the law of sin and death. For God has done what is impossible through the law in that it is weakened by the flesh. . . . He condemned sin in the flesh in order that the just requirement of the law might be fulfilled in us who conduct our lives not according to the flesh but according to the Spirit."

The "now" of Rom 7:6 reappears in Rom 8:1 where Paul resumes the discussion of the newness of life in Christ or life by the Spirit that extends from Rom 6:1-7:6. Rom 7:7-25 have intruded into the discussion of the present life of converts and must, therefore, refer to the past. Romans 7 and 8 cannot, then, be taken as expressing simultaneous experiences of converts. Rather, they deal with successive experiences, first that of pre-converts and second that of converts.

For the reasons given it is useless to waste words arguing whether the "I" represents Paul writing autobiographically or merely using a literary device or describing converts' experiences before or after joining the Jesus movement. Several passages elsewhere show Paul's tendency to use "I" when commenting on basic religious experiences (1 Cor 6:15; 10:29-30; 13:1-3, 11-12; 14;11, 14, 15; Gal 2:18-21; 6:14; Rom 3:7). Although Rom 7:7-25 are written from Paul's perspective as a convert, he never mentions the kind of struggle described there when alluding to his own special religious experience or his life as a pre-convert. Moreover, it is incredible that Paul would think the same persons living in the newness of the Spirit (Romans 6 and 7:1-6) would sink so dismally from it (Rom 7:7-25) and then say: "For the law of the Spirit of life in Christ Jesus has set you free from the law of sin and death" (Rom 8:2; see also 6:14). The "I," then, represents no person in particular but every person in general who does not live in Christ and share in the experience of the Spirit. Paul does not mention the Spirit anywhere in Rom 7:7-25.

Rom 7:25b is a summary of life without the Spirit and of life not lived in Christ: "So, then, I myself [autos ego, that is, the person not "in Christ" (Rom 8:1) and without the Spirit], with my mind, serve the law of God but with my flesh, the law of sin." Rom 7:25b is not the answer to the rhetorical question of Rom 7:24, the answer of which is implied in Rom 7:25a. Rom 7:25b anticipates the answer that follows in Romans 8.

In Rom 7:7-25 the point is not the antithesis between the Spirit and the flesh and their desires and works, as it is in Gal 5:16-25. Rather, the flesh is opposed by the mind (nous) or the inner person (ho eso anthropos). For the convert, on the other hand, the Spirit is to overpower the flesh (Rom 8:5-13; Gal 5:16). The "body of sin" and the "body of death" (Rom 6:6; 7:24; 8:10) have been destroyed.

The "now" of Rom 7:6 and 8:1 will, according to Paul, be fully realized only in the future. Converts who continue to live according to the flesh will die, but if by the Spirit they put to death the deeds of the body, they will live (Rom 8:13). They have the first fruits of the Spirit and groan within themselves, awaiting the redemption of their bodies (Rom 8:23). However, this groaning is not to be equated with the exclamation of the wretched man in Rom 7:24. That is a cry out of the past--before the "now" of Rom 7:6 and 8:1--a groaning that, according to Rom 8:18-30, looks to the future. All of this accords with Paul's ideas about morality/ethics and salvation as expressed elsewhere.

In describing the human struggle to do what is right while not under the influence of the Spirit, Paul writes in a way that would be comprehensible to both Jews and Gentiles in the Roman community of converts. Throughout the discussion the basic portrayal of the inner struggle is clear, but it is made more complicated by the varying phraseology used by Paul to describe it.

In Rom 7:7-13 Paul is still addressing primarily Jews. They would understand that the law makes them aware of wrongdoing and of their struggle to do what the law requires. The law itself is not evil (sin), but without the Spirit persons who try to follow it are powerless and subject to death, not life. In reality, "The law is holy and the commandment is holy and just and good" (Rom 7:12). Every Jew would acknowledge that. The trouble is not the law but the impulse to do evil in spite of what the law says.

Rom 7:14 is a transitional verse. The law is spiritual (pneumatikos), that is, it comes from God, not humans. The person without the Spirit is "fleshly" (sarkinos), "sold under sin." Jews, of course, believed that their law was given by God, and most Greeks and Romans believed that all laws had their origin with the gods (or God). Heraclitus of Ephesus (c. 500 B. C.) had said that all human laws were nourished by one divine law. Plato begins his Laws by having the Athenian ask the Cretan Kleinias: "To whom do you attribute the reason for your laws, to (a) god or to some human [anthropos]?" The Cretan replies: "To a god, most rightfully to a god. We Cretans call Zeus our lawgiver, and in Lacedaemon . . . people claim Apollo as theirs." (See discussion of "the law of God" below.)

The expression "sold under sin" harks back to Romans 6, where Paul says that those who are baptized live in newness of life and are no longer enslaved to sin; they are freed from sin. The expression also looks forward to Romans 8 and the idea that life in Christ or life by the Spirit has freed converts from the law of sin and death.

In Rom 7:15-20 Paul speaks with reference particularly to Gentiles, so in Rom 7:15 "law" no longer refers only to the Jewish law, as in Rom 7:7-14, but slips into the meaning it sometimes has in Rom 7:21-23. There sometimes it is any influence or motive that leads to the control of a person's will. Even though it fails, Paul can agree that the law is good because it makes persons aware that they are doing what they know they should not do.

The struggle of the human being to do what ought to be done, or what is right, but does not do it is a recurring theme in Graeco-Roman literature, including some from the time of Paul. Plato had written that in all the things we do and say "the inner man should be the most powerful (part) of the man " (tou anthropou ho entos anthropos estai egkratestatos; Republic 9:589A; see also Euripides, Medea 1070-1073; Plato, Laws 5:1). Compare Rom 7:22: "according to the inner man" (kata ton eso anthropon).

From Paul's own time Ovid (43 B. C. - A. D. 18) writes: "I perceive and approve the better things; I give way to the worse" (Metamorphoses 7:19-20; see also Diodorus of Sicily 1:71:1-4; Plutarch, On Moral Virtue). Tied in with this inner struggle is the Greek concept of error or fault. Words used to express that concept are translated as "sin" in the New Testament. The Greek verb Paul uses is hamartano, which originally meant "miss the mark," especially of a spear thrown. In general it came to mean "fail in one's purpose," "go wrong," and then "do wrong," "err," or "sin." The nouns Paul uses for "sin" are hamartema and hamartia, which originally meant "failure," "fault," "error," and then "sin."

In discussing the peculiar characteristics of error Epictetus (c. A.D. 55-135) writes:

> Every error involves an inconsistency. For since he who errs does not want to err, but to do right, it is clear that what he wants he does not do. . . . And every rational soul is by nature set against inconsistency; and so long as he does not understand that he is facing inconsistency, there is nothing to prevent him from doing inconsistent things; but when he has come to understand that an

inconsistency exists, there is great necessity for him to reject and avoid it. . . . what he wants he does not do and what he does not want he does (Discourses 2:26:1-4; see also Plato, Republic 336E).

In this passage the noun translated as "error" is hamartema, a word Paul uses for "sin" in 1 Cor 6:18 and Rom 3:25, a synonym for hamartia, which is used in Romans 7. And the verb translated as "errs" is Paul's verb for "sin" (hamartano). So many Gentiles in the community of converts in Rome would even have understood Paul when he was talking about sin and sinning.

Although the phrase "the law of God" (Rom 7:22, 25; 8:7) occurs occasionally in the Jewish scriptures and would, therefore, be understood by Jews as referring to their law, Paul never uses that phrase anywhere else to refer to the Jewish law in all that he says about it. He uses it only in the context of describing the inner struggle of the person without the Spirit to do what is right (Rom 7:15-8:8). The significance of the phrase "the law of God," then, is that it provides a clue that Paul is writing specifically with Gentiles in mind. It is a Stoic expression. With Paul's discussion of the person's inner struggle and the law of God as opposed to another law compare the following passages from Epictetus's Discourses.

Epictetus can speak about the gods and about God. He speaks about "the wretched laws of ours" in contrast to "the laws of the gods" (1:13:5). "This is the law that God has established" is stated in the context of a discussion of the good and evil and of moral purpose (1:29:1-5).

"Nothing else is able to conquer the choice (of what is moral), but it conquers itself. For this reason also the law of God [ho tou theou nomos] is most excellent and most just. . . . For this is a law of nature and of God: 'Let the better always prevail over the worse'" (1:29:13-21).

"What is the divine law?" (2:16:28; see also 3:24:42).

"Am I not wholly directed toward God and his commands and ordinances?" ([ouchi d' holos pros ton theon tetami kai tas ekeinou entolas kai ta prostagmata;] 3:24:114; see discussion of words for commands and ordinances in chapter 8 of this work).

"These are the laws sent to you from him [God], these are his ordinances; you ought to become an interpreter of them, to these you ought to subject yourself, not to the laws of Masurius and Cassius" (prominent Roman lawyers of Paul's time; 4:3:12).

"Almost all men admit that the good and the evil are in ourselves, and not in the things outside" (3:20:1).

"The principal task in life is this: separate matters and distinguish them (from one another) and say to myself, 'Things outside are not under my (power); choosing [what is moral] is under my (power). Where shall I seek the good and the evil? Within, in the things that are mine" (2:5:4-5).

In spite of obvious differences between Paul and Epictetus because of Paul's unique thought as a Christian Jew, the similarities are striking. This does not mean that Paul had read from Stoic philosophers. However, certain well-known ideas were prevalent in the air of the Graeco-Roman world, and Paul had breathed in that air deeply. He used those ideas in composing his discussion of the person without the Spirit and not living in Christ for the benefit of his Roman Gentile readers. Uniquely for Paul, "the law of God" stood in sharp contrast to "the law of sin and death" from which "the law of the Spirit of life in Christ Jesus" sets converts free. For by sending his Son God did what any law or laws, Jewish or Graeco-Roman, could not do, "in order that the just requirement of the law might be fulfilled in us who live not according to the flesh but according to the Spirit" (Rom 8:3-4). Thus, for converts the law and the Spirit are actually brought together in Rom 8:4. This has resolved the inner conflict for all converts who previously had lived without the Spirit and would do so for all persons who might want to become converts.

Observations and Summary

Paul does not think any aspect of religion or theology should be separate from the lives of converts lived as new creations. The difference between right and wrong is quite explicit. They are as different as this age and the next. Good conduct is the work of God or the fruit of the Spirit; wrong conduct is the work of the Devil or the works of the flesh. The kingdom of God consists of righteousness, peace, and joy in the Holy Spirit, not food and drink (Rom 14:17). Whatever else was a part of God's plan for members of God's renewed covenant community, it embraced simple goodness in human beings, goodness not delayed to the next life, but genuine moral character in this life.

It is no accident for Paul that the same root of <u>dikaioo</u> in Greek means legal acquittal or innocence and moral goodness (righteousness). Paul uses it with one meaning and then the other, apparently without being aware of it. Naturally, Paul ties his ideas of forgiveness and goodness to Christ. Although he never tries to explain how, the faithfulness of Jesus and his death and resurrection made possible the transition from the old sinful existences of converts to the new creations. In baptism converts die with Christ to sin and rise to righteousness (<u>dikaiosyne</u>), pass from slavery to freedom and from the works of the flesh to the fruit of the Spirit and from the control of the Devil to the power of God. If we attempt to explain how the transition takes place, we do an injustice to the concretism and objectivity of Paul's descriptions. It is enough to acknowledge the emphatic demands of Paul that converts maintain the new creations they have become.

The idea that persons who had faithfulness toward God should be free from sin was present in Judaism during the time of Paul. The wisdom of God "will not dwell in a body involved in sin" (Wis 1:4). The writer of Sirach says that those who work with the wisdom of God "will not sin" (Sir 24:22). Judas Maccabaeus exhorted his fellow Jews to "keep themselves free from sin" (2 Macc 12:42). And Sirach advises his readers: "Flee from sin as from the presence of a snake, for if you go to it, it will bite you" (21:2; see also 17:25; 18:20-21; 26:28; 38:10; 2 Esdr 15:24).

Paul thinks of persons who are new creations in Christ in a moral and spiritual sense. The righteousness of God becomes the righteousness of those persons as well. In Jewish writings an emphasis on righteousness was a regular part of Jewish eschatological belief, especially in the thought of Isaiah. In the following passages, translated from the Septuagint, the language is similar to that of Paul in 2 Cor 5:17-21 and elsewhere. "Do not remember the former things, and the ancient things do not consider. Behold, I shall do new things" (Isa 43:18-19). "By myself I swear, righteousness shall surely go out of my mouth; my words shall not be turned aside. . . . Righteousness and glory shall come to him. . . . By the Lord they shall be justified" (Isa 45:23-26). "Listen to me, you who are perishing, who are far from righteousness. I have brought near my righteousness, and I will not delay the salvation which is from me" (Isa 46:12-13). "I will not relax until her [that is, Jerusalem's] righteousness go out as light, and my salvation burn as a lamp. And the Gentiles shall see your righteousness and kings, your glory" (Isa 62:1-2). "And they shall be called generations of righteousness . . . so shall the Lord cause righteousness to spring up and exultation before all the Gentiles" (Isa 61:3, 11). "And you shall be righteous for me, says the Lord" (Isa 54:17; see also 51:6-8).

The three passages below are from Jubilees and reveal interesting parallels to the language and thought of Paul.

> After this they will turn to me in all righteousness and with all (their) heart and soul . . . and I shall create a holy spirit in them, and I shall cleanse them so that they will not turn away from me from that day and forever (Jub. 1:23).

> Mount Zion will be sanctified in the new creation for a sanctification of the earth; through it will the earth be sanctified from all sin and from uncleanness throughout the generations of the world (Jub. 4:26).

> And he made for all his works a new and righteous nature, so that they should not sin in all their nature forever, but should always be all righteous, each in his kind (Jub. 5:12).

The ideas of Paul anticipate those of Rabbis after his time who taught that humans should imitate God in holiness and righteousness. The text that served as the basis for rabbinic discussions is Lev 19:2: "You shall be holy, for I the Lord your God am holy." The following is a quotation from the Talmud:

> Holiness, according to Abba Saul, is identical with imitation of God. The nature of this imitation is defined by him thus: 'I and he, that is like unto him (God). As he is merciful and gracious, so be you

(humans) merciful and gracious.' The Scriptural phrases 'walking in the ways of God' (Deut 11:22) and 'being called by the name of God' (Joel 2:26, 32), are again explained to mean, 'As God is called merciful and gracious, so be thou merciful and gracious; as God is called righteous, so be thou righteous; as God is called holy, so be thou holy.'

In Gal 5:25 Paul reminds the Galatian converts: "If we live by the Spirit, let us also be in line with the Spirit." Here the verb I have translated as "be in line with" is <u>stoicheo</u> and is usually translated as "walk." It really means walk in a straight line or stay in rank or, also, metaphorically, "be in line with," "agree with," or "submit to." At any rate, it has a hortative meaning, and this is in line with the context, which is emphatically moral/ethical. The statement in Gal 5:25 is preceded with the passage on the works of the flesh contrasted with the fruit of the Spirit. Gal 5:25 is followed by the exhortation, "Let us not be conceited, not provoking of one another, not envying one another" (Gal 5:26). And Paul tells the Galatian converts that in light of being new creations neither circumcision nor uncircumcision counts for anything (Gal 6:15). All baptized converts, whether Jewish or Gentile, "serve in newness of the Spirit" (Rom 7:6). They are new creations.

Chapter 7

Some Observations And Suggestions

<u>Is Justification or Salvation the Greater Thing for Converts?</u>

Two passages in Romans may give the impression Paul believed that in God's justification of converts he had done the greater thing for them. How much more, then, converts could be certain that God would grant them final salvation. In light of the overall evidence, this impression is as mistaken as the view that the central message of Paul is justification by faith in Christ.

It appears that the impression is correct if we take the passages in Rom 5:8-10 and Rom 5:21 by themselves. At first glance, it seems as though in those passages there is no tension between the "now," the present status of the justified person, and the "shall be," the future salvation of the convert. Taken by themselves those passages seem to indicate that justification is effective for all time. But we should not take them by themselves without carefully examining the contexts in which they occur. Converts not only had to come to faithfulness toward God and subsequently also to assent to certain beliefs about Jesus. They

151

also had to remain obedient to the model of teaching they had been presented and to which they had pledged themselves.

As with Rom 5:8-10, so with Rom 5:21 the justification of converts seems eternal: "So that, just as sin ruled in death, grace also might rule through righteousness for eternal life through Jesus Christ our Lord." But then comes Romans 6, Paul's classic discussion of baptism, which not only signifies the forgiveness of past sins, but also imposes the obligation to remain free from sin. "What shall we say then? Are we to continue in sin that grace may abound? By no means! How can we who died to sin still live in it? . . . Let not sin therefore rule in your mortal body. . . . Are we to sin because we are not under law but under grace? By no means!" (Rom 6:1-2, 12, 15).

In Rom 8:11-13 the promise of eternal life for the justified person made in earlier passages becomes conditional: "If the Spirit of him who raised Jesus from the dead dwells in you, he who raised Christ from the dead will give life also to your mortal bodies by virtue of his Spirit dwelling in you . . . for if you live according to the flesh, you will die; but if by the Spirit you put to death the deeds of the body, you will live" (my emphases bring out Paul's meaning). Here both death and life are conditional upon the behavior of the converts.

There is not enough evidence to say that Paul really does come to the conclusion that God had done the greater thing for converts in their justification. Perhaps Paul's conclusion--if he really had a conclusion-- is the other way around: by their ultimate salvation God would do the greater thing for converts as members of his renewed covenant community. According to Paul, God did not cease to exist when Jesus came. God is always superior to Jesus for Paul and uppermost in his thinking. When Paul speaks about grace, it is almost always with reference to God, rarely to Christ. God acted in sending his Son, but God will also act in a final judgment still to come. Rom 2:6-11 makes that clear:

> For he [God] will repay to every person according to that person's works, to those who by patience in doing good seek glory and honor and immortality (there will be) eternal life, but for those who are ambitious and disobey the truth but obey unrighteousness (there will

be) wrath and fury. (There will be) affliction and anguish for every human being who does evil, the Jew first and also the Greek, but glory and honor and peace to every one who does good, the Jew first and also the Greek. For there is no partiality with God.

The wrath of God still has to be assuaged. Jews and Gentiles alike--God shows no partiality--still have to live the lives required of them by God, whether or not they are Christian converts, in order to escape God's wrath and attain ultimate salvation. Paul states this succinctly and to the point in 2 Cor 5:10: "For we all must appear before the tribunal (judgment seat) of Christ, in order that each person may receive either good or evil according to the things that person did in the body." The word translated as "receive" is komizo, which is really more forceful than the English word "receive." In the middle voice, as Paul uses it in 2 Cor 5:10, it means "get what has come to be one's own by earning." In other words, Paul says that there comes a time when each person will get what that person deserves because that person has earned it. He says the same thing in Rom 14:10-12 where, once again, the Jewish scriptures are the basis for his ideas: "For we shall all stand before the tribunal (judgment seat) of God, for it is written, 'As I live, says the Lord, every knee shall bow to me and every tongue shall confess to God.' So, then, all of us shall give account of ourselves to God" (see Isa 45:24; 49:18; Jer 22:24; Ezek 5:11).

Because some Judaizers, who insisted that Gentile converts had to be circumcised and obey Jewish law, caused a problem for Paul at Galatia, he wrote on the subjects of justification on the basis of the faithfulness of Christ, not works of the law, and on grace and salvation. In addition to Galatians he wrote Romans, which in itself contains inconsistencies and contradictions in thought. Paul can say, "So the law is holy and the commandment is holy and just and good" (Rom 7:12). God sent his Son "in order that the just requirement of the law might be fulfilled in us" (Rom 8:4). Yet Paul also says, "Christ is the end of the law for the purpose of righteousness to everyone who believes" in God (Rom 10:4). And Paul can deny categorically that faithfulness overthrows the law: "Do we, then, abolish the law by virtue of faithfulness? By no means! Rather, we establish the law" (Rom 3:31). These passages alone pose severe problems for the objective interpreter of Paul's thought.

The Ideas of Paul and Those of the Author of Hebrews

Perhaps the best evidence to support my interpretation of Paul's ideas on the subjects of faithfulness and works of the law and their relationship especially to justification and ultimate salvation is in several passages in the New Testament itself. In the letter to Hebrews, which was not written by Paul but by someone who may have been reflecting on Paul's message, the author says:

> For it is impossible to renew again to repentance those who have once been enlightened [that is, baptized] and have tasted the heavenly gift and have become partakers of the Holy Spirit and have tasted the goodness of the word of God and the powers of the coming age and fall back [into unbelieving and godless ways]. . . . For if we sin deliberately after receiving the knowledge of the truth, there no longer remains a sacrifice for sins, but a fearful expectation of judgment, and a fury of fire. . . . Someone who has broken the law of Moses dies without mercy at the testimony of two or three persons. How much worse punishment do you think will be deserved by the person who has treated the Son of God with disdain, and profaned the blood of the covenant by which that person was sacrificed, and outraged the Spirit of grace?" (Heb 6:4-6; 10:26-29).

The author of Hebrews continues by saying that vengeance belongs to God who will judge his people, as quoted from Deut 32:35 and Ps 134(135):14. Then the writer says: "It is a fearful thing to fall into the hands of the living God" (Heb 10:30-31). The author of Hebrews has a conception of the judgment that is more vivid than that of Paul's.

The writer of Hebrews is talking about persons who sin deliberately after baptism and about the consequences of such sin. But he seems confident that the readers of what he is writing are still on the right track because he assures them: "Although we speak thus, yet for you, beloved, we believe there are better things that belong to salvation. For God is not so unjust as to forget your work and the love that you showed for his name as you served the saints (holy ones) and are serving" (Heb 6:9-10; see also 12:17).

According to the author of Hebrews, sins of converts have been finally dealt with through the gracious sacrifice of Christ and the enlightenment that came with their baptism. Therefore, in the clearest statement in the New Testament of the second coming of Christ, the author writes: "Thus, also, Christ was offered once for all to bear the sins for the many; he will appear a second time, apart from (dealing with) sin, to those eagerly expecting him, for the purpose of salvation" (Heb 9:28). So, with the author of Hebrews, as with Paul in Phil 3:20, Christ's role as Savior will come at the end of the present age.

Thus, for the post-Pauline author of Hebrews, who says so much about faith, baptism and the reception of the Holy Spirit were not valid thenceforth apart from continuing in Christian faithfulness and works, which are required for ultimate salvation. So the writer feels it necessary to encourage his readers: "Let us hold fast the confession of our hope without yielding, for he who promised is faithful; and let us consider how to provoke one another for love and good works" (Heb 10:23-24). Only because his readers are continuing to work, love, and serve can the writer of Hebrews assure them of the "better things that belong to salvation" (Heb 6:9).

The author of Hebrews was only carrying Paul's argument in Romans to its logical conclusion. According to Paul, by virtue of baptism and justification converts were acquitted from sin and became new creations in Christ, but a continuation in their new existences free from sin was required for ultimate salvation. So, the conclusion about the ineffectiveness of repentance after baptism was the only one to which the author of Hebrews could logically come. He was simply completing the ideas of Paul where he left off.

What Paul Does Not Say

Repentance

Perhaps the best evidence that the writer of Hebrews has, indeed, interpreted Paul's thought correctly is the fact that Paul himself only rarely mentions anything about repentance. This is true in spite of the fact that genuine repentance was a main teaching in much of Judaism at the time of Paul. Paul mentions repentance only three times (2 Cor 7:8-10; 12:21; Rom 2:4). It is important to understand, above all else, that in the contexts of each of these passages Paul is addressing persons still in the process of becoming Christian converts. They had been converted from paganism to faithfulness toward God, but they were not yet fully established in the renewed covenant community of God (see comments on this subject below). This point is extremely important and cannot be emphasized too much.

Paul first brings up the subject of repentance with reference to his adversaries at Corinth. In 2 Cor 7:8-10 he speaks about making the Corinthian converts sorry because of the harsh letter he had written to them. Paul rejoices that the grief it caused them led to their repentance. And then he adds, "For grief of the kind God expects [literally, "according to God"--kata theon] effects repentance leading to salvation that is not to be repented of. But grief of a worldly kind produces death." The words "not to be repented of" translate a single word in Greek (ametameletos), and it is a kind of wordplay with the word "repentance" (metanoia). Metanoia really means "a change in the inner person." And ametameletos can also mean "about which no change of mind can take place." So, then, what Paul is actually saying in 2 Cor 7:8-10 is that he has become convinced to the point where he will not change his mind that the Corinthian converts are now on his side and no longer on the side of his adversaries. Titus has assured Paul of the obedience of all of them, so Paul is greatly encouraged by their changed behavior (2 Cor 7:13-16). This also means that, with respect to their religion, the converts are now on the right track, on the way toward ultimate salvation.

That the lack of morality on the part of some Corinthian converts was at least some of the problem for Paul in the controversy with his adversaries is clear from 2 Cor 12:21, a passage almost certainly written before the one in 2 Cor 7:8-10. Paul is afraid that when he visits the Corinthians again he may have to "mourn over many of those who sinned previously and have not repented of the uncleanness, sexual misconduct, and wantonness which they practiced."

As a result of their justification and the forgiveness of past sins converts became righteous and were expected to remain in that state before God. The substance of justification or forgiveness is the abandonment of evil deeds and even evil desires. As the prophet Isaiah says, "Let the ungodly forsake his ways, and the wicked man his designs; let him turn toward the Lord, and he shall be shown mercy, because he will abundantly forgive your sins" (Isa 55:7, LXX). After converts had turned to God from idols and subsequently been justified or forgiven of sins previously committed and become righteous-- symbolized in the rite of baptism--there should be no need for repentance and further forgiveness for members of the renewed covenant community of God. From his religious instruction as a Jew Paul knew that true repentance should effect a genuine change in the lives of converts. That is what Paul hoped for when he wrote 2 Cor 12:21 and which, apparently, he thought had been accomplished when he wrote 2 Cor 7:8-10. He hoped that the Corinthian converts would have become sincerely repentant for not siding with him instead of with his adversaries so that their inner beings would be changed and they would conduct their lives again by the Spirit. That would keep them on the way toward ultimate salvation, not on the way to death.

Once again, Paul shares the ideas of Judaism. God established repentance and forgiveness for sinners; but as a God of the righteous, he did not establish repentance for the righteous (Prayer of Manasseh 7-8). Sirach says: "Do not say, 'I sinned, yet what has happened to me?' for the Lord is slow to anger. Do not be so confident of forgiveness that you add sin to sin. Do not say, 'His mercy is great, he will forgive the multitude of my sins,' for both mercy and wrath are with him, and his anger will rest on sinners" (Sir 5:4-6; NRSV).

In Rom 2:4-5 Paul is also writing to converts who, although members of the church at Rome, have not yet entered the renewed covenant community of God. He asks them whether they do not know that the kindness of God is for the purpose of leading them to repentance. Then he adds: "But by your hard and impenitent heart you are storing up wrath for yourself on the day of wrath when the righteous judgment of God will be revealed" (Rom 2:5). This verse is the obverse of 2 Cor 7:10: "For grief according to God is repentance that works toward salvation that is not to be repented of." "True repentance according to God . . . leads the mind toward salvation" (Testament of Gad 5:7).

Forgiveness

In strong contrast to his Jewish predecessor Jesus, who often speaks about forgiveness, Paul rarely mentions it. He uses two verbs, aphiemi and charizomai, that may be translated with the English word "forgive." He uses the former in that way only in Rom 4:7 in the immediate context of Abraham's example of faithfulness. The larger context is that of God's forgiveness of the past sins of converts on the basis of faithfulness toward God, not works of the law (see Rom 3:21-4:12). Aphiemi in Rom 4:7 is used in a direct quotation from Ps 31(32):1: "Blessed are those whose iniquities are forgiven and whose sins are revealed; blessed is the person whose sins the Lord will not reckon." Paul prefaces the quotation by saying that David (who, according to Paul, wrote the Psalms) speaks a blessing upon the person to whom God reckons righteousness apart from works. Paul is speaking in the context of the justification of prospective converts, not persons already converted, as the words about believing on God "who justifies the impious" and about those against whom God will not reckon their sins clearly show.

The second word (charizomai) is the root from which charis ("grace") comes and means literally "graciously confer" and therefore "pardon" or "forgive." It is used with the first meaning in 1 Cor 2:12, where Paul speaks about understanding "the things graciously conferred upon us by God" through the Spirit which is from God. Charizomai is used the same way also in Gal 3:18; Rom 8:32; Phil 1:29; 2:9; and Phlm 22. Paul uses charizomai in the sense of forgive only in 2 Cor 2:7-10, in the context of members of the Corinthian community of converts forgiving fellow members of the community, and in 2 Cor 12:13 with reference to the converts' forgiveness of him.

The important thing is that Paul mentions forgiveness on the part of God only in one passage (Rom 4:7), and there, as with justification, it is used with reference to the past sins of potential converts. Elsewhere Paul speaks of forgiveness only on the part of converts toward fellow converts. Never--and this is most important!--does Paul speak of God's forgiveness with reference to the sins of converts committed after they were baptized and became members of the renewed covenant community of God (see comments on this subject below).

All of these things indicate that the author of Hebrews understood Paul's ideas of justification or forgiveness of the past, not future, sins of converts, along with the obligation to remain free from sin in order to obtain ultimate salvation. When the author of Hebrews wrote that there is no forgiveness after the enlightenment of baptism, he was simply carrying Paul's ideas to their logical conclusion. Paul himself must have come to the same conclusion in order to write as he does, but he did not get around to actually saying so, at least not in any letter known to us. At any rate, what Paul again does not say is as important for our understanding of his ideas of justification and salvation as what he actually does say.

The Ideas of Paul and Those of the Author of the Pastorals

Although the Pastoral Epistles purport to be written by Paul, they were not written by him but by someone who was familiar with his letters and wrote under his name. As with the writer of James, the writer of the Pastorals, in contrast to the real Paul, speaks of works in the sense of good deeds rather than works of the law. He mentions the word "law" (nomos) only once. This is probably true because by the time he wrote, Jewish law and its relationship to Christian faithfulness and life was not a major problem for the community or communities to which he was writing. He had to be more concerned with oppression from outside the church and with heresies within it than with Judaism. The author writes: "We know that the law is good, if any one uses it lawfully, understanding this, that the law is not laid down for the just, but for the lawless and unruly, the irreligious and sinners . . . immoral persons," and other wicked people (1 Tim 1:8-10). According to Gal 5:16-23 and Rom 7:12, 16, Paul would agree with the idea of the author of the passages from 1 Timothy.

In 2 Timothy there are echoes of Paul's views of justification and of being saved in the sense of becoming converts, except that the writer speaks of good works, not works of the law. The author writes that it was the power of God "who saved us and called us with a holy calling, not according to our works but according to his own purpose and the grace given us in Christ Jesus ages ago" (2 Tim 1:9). And from that point on in the letter, as with Paul, there is constant emphasis on moral and ethical behavior.

The addressee in 2 Timothy, whoever he was, in the midst of threatening false teachers, is exhorted to "offer" himself to God, "a workman who has no need to be ashamed" (2 Tim 2:15). The Greek verb translated as "offer" is <u>paristemi</u> and really means to offer oneself for service. The subsequent verses develop the idea of proper behavior in the service of the gospel in all its aspects of faithfulness and life. The addressee is to be "consecrated . . . prepared for any good work" (2 Tim 2:21). Practically speaking, the person addressed is to set himself apart from Hymenaeus, Philetus, and others who engage in "godless chatter" which leads people "into more and more ungodliness" and a departure from the truth (2 Tim 2:16-17; see also 3:17; 4:14, 18). This is reminiscent of Paul's advice to the converts at Corinth not to associate with immoral persons and to expel the wicked person from among them (1 Cor 5:1-2, 9-13; 2 Cor 6:14-7:1).

The same kind of language occurs also in three passages in the letter to Titus. Corrupt and unbelieving persons "profess to know God, but deny (him) by their works; they are detestable, disobedient, unfit for any good work" (Titus 1:15-16). Here the writer is speaking in the context of heretical threats to the Christian faith and life. For him heresy is as much a matter of improper conduct as of false or incorrect teaching. Consequently, the addressee is told: "Show yourself in all things a model of good works, and in your teaching (show) purity, seriousness, and sound speech that is beyond reproach, so that an opponent may be put to shame, not having anything evil to say about us" (Titus 2:7-8). Although Paul lived before the time the church was severely threatened by heretical teaching, he would have been glad to learn that what he had written had produced such fruit of the Spirit in a later follower of his.

Titus 2:11-14 reflects teaching of Paul:

> The grace of God has appeared for the salvation of all persons, educating us to abolish ungodliness and worldly desires, and to live sober, righteous, and godly lives in the present age, awaiting the blessed hope, and the appearing of the glory of the great God and of our Savior Jesus Christ, who gave himself on behalf of us, in order to ransom (redeem) us from all wickedness and to purify for himself a special people, zealous for good works.

As with Paul, so with the author of the letter to Titus, the very purpose of the redemptive work of God in Christ was to enhance the moral/ethical quality of life for those who became believers. Also, as with Paul, Christians are a community set apart for the service of God and Christ (see Gal 6:16; Phil 3:3), and the idea of such a community, as also with Paul, is derived from the Jewish scriptures (see, for example, Exod 19:5-6; Deut 7:6-11; 14:2; 26:16-19). And although salvation may be experienced to some degree "in the present age," ultimate salvation is still an eschatological hope and will be fully realized in the future when Christ will appear as Savior (see 1 Thess 1:9-10; 1 Cor 1:7; Rom 5:1-2; Phil 3:20-21). But the author of the Pastorals and Paul make it quite clear that there is no guarantee of such salvation apart from moral probity.

A parallel passage in Titus 3 confirms not only my interpretation of the above passages but my interpretation of Paul's central message as well. The writer speaks of former days: "We ourselves were once foolish, disobedient, deceived, slaves to various desires and pleasures, passing our time in depravity and envy, hated and hating one another." But such existence was changed:

> When the goodness and love for mankind of God our Savior appeared, he saved us, not because of works which we did in righteousness, but according to his own mercy, through the washing of regeneration and renewal of the Holy Spirit, which he poured out upon us richly through Jesus Christ our Savior, so that having been justified by his grace, we might become heirs according to the hope of eternal life (Titus 3:3-7).

This is the only place where the author of the Pastorals uses the verb dikaioo, and the passage reflects precisely Paul's views of justification and ultimate salvation. However, the author has changed Paul's idea of works of the law, which was no longer relevant for his situation, to good works, the message most apt for the community to which he was writing. The point is that the author of the Pastorals, as well as Paul, does not want the Christians in his communities to think that their salvation from or the forgiveness of their past sins was the result of any effort on their part, whether through works of the law, as with Paul, or by good works, as with the writer of the Pastorals.

According to Titus 3:3-7, as with Paul (for example, Gal 4:7; 6:7-10; Rom 2:7-11; 6:22-23; 8:15-17), Christian converts become heirs of eternal life through baptism and justification, but the actual inheritance of that life is dependent upon proper moral/ethical behavior in this life. For that reason the writer of the letter to Titus says immediately in what follows Titus 3:3-7: "I desire you to insist on these things, so that those who have believed in God may be intent on doing good works; these are excellent and profitable for humans. . . . As for a person who is factious . . . such a person is perverted and sins, being self-condemned" (Titus 3:8-11; see Rom 2:7-10; 16:17-20). The author is actually speaking in the context of Christian discussions and things that may disrupt the unity of the community addressed. Contentious persons are to be avoided, as are discussions that do not result in good deeds.

Finally, in 2 Tim 3:15 the author of the Pastorals speaks in a way quite unlike Paul. The writer reminds the addressee that he has known the sacred writings "that are able to make" him "wise for the purpose of (with a view to) salvation by virtue of faith, faith in [Greek, en] Christ Jesus" (see also 1 Tim 1:16). Paul never uses the expression "faith in Christ," here emphasized by the writer's Greek. Paul is primarily concerned about Christian converts' faithfulness toward God and only secondarily with their beliefs about Jesus.

<u>Observations and Summary</u>

According to the writer of the Pastorals, the Christian convert has experienced the forgiveness of a past life of sin and evil, knows the joy of a newly created life, and has the hope of salvation that is to be fully realized in the future when that life becomes eternal. But nowhere is eternal life guaranteed as a result of the forgiveness of the convert. Paul's views are precisely the same. Although the writer of the Pastorals puts much more emphasis on faith in the sense of assent as a part of the Christian life than does Paul, his writings lack none of Paul's emphasis on moral probity and ethical deeds arising from love. All of this means that the teaching of Paul was more effective and influential in subsequent decades of early Christianity than is frequently realized. The central message of his letters is not the so-called doctrine of justification by faith in Christ. Rather, Paul's emphasis is always on moral/ ethical life for converts who have faithfulness toward God and are preparing to enter the renewed covenant community of God.

Some Parting Thoughts on Paul's Silence

Paul's ideas of sinlessness and his silence on repentance and forgiveness may seem strange to Christians today who find it impossible to believe in the sinlessness of any human being and that there will not be a time for repentance after baptism. But there can be no doubt that Paul maintains precisely that for some converts. So, how can we reconcile Paul's views about sinlessness and his lack of teaching about repentance and forgiveness with his castigation of the holy ones (saints) for their many shortcomings, sometimes even their moral laxity? Perhaps the two simply cannot be reconciled, but I have some suggestions for a possible reconciliation of them.

It seems quite plausible that becoming members of the renewed covenant community of God did not just happen on a moment's impulse but involved a somewhat lengthy process, as it did to become full members in the community at Qumran. Indeed, Paul frequently exhorts converts, beginning with 1 Thessalonians, to continue in the moral/ethical instruction they received when they became converts to faithfulness toward God: "We beg and exhort you in the Lord Jesus that just as you received [instruction] from us how you ought to conduct your lives and to please God, just as you are conducting your lives, that you do so even more. For you know what rules [for living] we gave you through the Lord Jesus" (1 Thess 4:1; see also 1 Cor 14:6-12; Gal 6:6; Rom 6:17-18).

Presumably, according to Paul, there came a time when converts to faithfulness toward God were expected to become "mature" (1 Cor 2:6; Phil 3:15) members of the renewed covenant community of God and reach a point beyond which there was no return to the hope for ultimate salvation (see 1 Thess 4:13; 5:8; Rom 5:2). At the time of their baptism converts received the forgiveness of past sins, received the Holy Spirit, and were expected to remain sinless after that (Romans 6)-- which I have stressed, as Paul does. Although all this may seem strange to us, who study all of Paul's letters together, it probably did not seem so strange to converts in the individual churches, who, insofar as we know, received only the letter he wrote to them. We can, however, plausibly assume, it seems to me, that all converts received the same instruction in moral/ethical life. Nevertheless, this is one time when the silence of Paul does not provide us with as much learning as we might wish. Yet, if we reconsider some passages more carefully, perhaps we can learn more about the communities of converts to whom Paul writes.

Early Churches as Brotherhoods and as Renewed Covenant Communities of God

I have said that Paul mentions forgiveness on the part of God only in Rom 4:7. It is used with reference to past sins of prospective converts in general at the time they would be justified and baptized. We must remember that Paul does not speak of baptism with any substance before Romans 6, except in 1 Cor 12:13. There he had written: "For in one Spirit we were all baptized into one body--whether Jews or Greeks, whether slave or free--and all were made to drink of one Spirit." Thus, converts are brought into membership of a community of persons having received the Spirit at the dawn of the age of salvation. Paul identifies this community as the (spiritual) body of Christ (1 Cor 12:27), whose members individually and jointly function for the good of the whole, as with members of the physical body. This analogy gives concrete reality to the community and the responsibilities of its members to act toward one another in love: "Pursue love" (1 Cor 14:1; see also 1 Cor 13:1-13). It is God who sets all these things in operation (1 Cor 12:6; see also 12:18, 24, 28).

Presumably the teachings to which converts were subjected took place before their baptism with the forgiveness of past sins, reception of the Holy Spirit, and their entrance into the renewed covenant community of God. This would mean, then, that the first stage in conversion to Christianity, especially for Gentiles, but also for unbelieving Jews, was a profession of faithfulness toward God. All persons who professed such faithfulness would then be members of a church or community thought of as a brotherhood. They would not yet be members of the renewed covenant community of God, although they were regarded as set apart as holy ones, that is, persons whose purpose in life now was to become holy or righteous before God. Paul can, therefore, address all the members of his churches as holy ones. They would be subjected to a vigorous period of training in righteousness, or moral/ethical instruction, to which they had pledged themselves when they became converts to faithfulness toward God.

It was the moral aspect of the Thessalonian converts' faithfulness in time of suffering that needed to be established by Timothy (1 Thess 3:2) and that Paul hoped he and others would have the opportunity to supply (1 Thess 3:1-13). That this is the correct interpretation is clear from Paul's words in 1 Thess 3:11-13, continued in 1 Thess 4:1-12, part of which was quoted above. Paul hoped that he might get to Thessalonica and that the Lord (God) would "make you increase and abound in love toward one another and toward all persons, just as we do toward you."

There were no restrictions with respect to social status, race, or sex for entrance into the brotherhood or church. There was social diversity within the brotherhood at Corinth: circumcised and uncircumcised, slave and freed person (1 Cor 7:17-22). So, Paul says: "Fellow converts ("brothers"), in whatever (state) each was called, let each person remain in that (state) before God" (1 Cor 7:24).

Among some of the brothers at Corinth there was quarreling and dissension concerning baptism, so Paul appealed to them to break it up (1 Cor 1:10-17). What is significant about Paul's discussion concerning the dissension is that, in dealing with the differences among fellow converts, he does not reprimand them for any moral offense. He seems more embarrassed than anything else by their behavior and is thankful that he baptized only a few of those involved in the dissensions (1 Cor 1:13-17). Paul is defending himself against his missionary competitors, whom he does not accuse of deceitful or unethical motives as he sometimes does elsewhere. He accuses them indirectly only of speaking with more superior words of wisdom (1 Cor 2:1). Paul is addressing members of the community at Corinth who are "mature," to whom he can speak about the wisdom of God (1 Cor 2:6). There was a time when he could not speak to the brothers (fellow converts) as persons having the characteristics of the Spirit, but as persons having the characteristics of the flesh (1 Cor 3:1).

Instead of condemning those who were involved in the dissension, Paul says: "I do not write these things to shame you, but to admonish you as my beloved children." He continues by saying that he is their father in Christ Jesus by virtue of the gospel and urges them to be imitators of him. Paul concludes his discussion of the subject by saying: "For the kingdom of God is not in [characterized as] speech but in power" (1 Cor 4:14-20). Compare this with his references to the kingdom of God when later he asks if the converts do not know that unrighteous persons will not inherit the kingdom of God and warns that those who are immoral in various ways will not enter into it (1 Cor 6:9-10; see also 1 Thess 2:11-12; Gal 5:19-21; Rom 14:17).

Paul does go on to say, however, that the persons he addresses are still "fleshly" (sarkikos). "For wherever there is jealousy and strife among you, are you not fleshly and conducting your lives according to human standards?" (1 Cor 3:3). He does not condemn this kind of jealousy and strife (compare 2 Cor 12:20) as being among the works of the flesh as he does in Gal 5:20 (see also Rom 13:13-14). In fact, the group Paul is criticizing will, when the Lord comes, each receive praise from God (1 Cor 4:5). Because they had been baptized, they belonged to the renewed covenant community of God, those "on the inside," and they had not committed an offense great enough to warrant exclusion from that community (compare Gal 6:1-2). This is in sharp contrast to the immoral man Paul writes about, beginning in 1 Cor 5:1. It seems clear, then, that Paul is addressing persons of different ranks or stages in the brotherhood of believers in God. There were those involved in the dissensions over baptism, whose offenses were not serious, and those involved in immorality, whose offenses made them unworthy of membership in the renewed covenant community of God.

At Corinth also there were differences in preferences for worship style, even misconduct at the Lord's Supper (1 Cor 11:17-22; 14). Again, Paul doess not condemn the persons guilty of misbehavior. He simply says that he will not commend them in what they are doing (1 Cor 11:17, 22). Such persons do not judge themselves, but when they are judged by the Lord, they are chastised in order that they may not be condemned with the world (1 Cor 11:31-32). Their offense was not immoral behavior, but behavior unbecoming to Christian worshipers.

They could, therefore, remain within the renewed covenant community of God. Of course, I am sure they felt constrained to reform their behavior after Paul's rebuke.

The main concern for Paul from the beginning of his mission work was that all the brothers (fellow converts) be instructed in how they ought to live because they were called by God not for uncleanness but for holiness of life (1 Thess 4:1-8). They were called for the purpose of becoming holy ones (1 Cor 1:2; Rom 1:7). The passage from 1 Thess 4:1-8 provides insight into the crucial point with respect to the brotherhood. The basic distinction Paul made among members was the moral one. He wrote to some Corinthians not to associate intimately with anyone who has the name of brother if that person is guilty of immorality of various forms (1 Cor 5:11). Then he continues: "For what do I have to do with judging those on the outside? Is it not those on the inside whom you are to judge? God will judge those on the outside. Drive out the evil person from among yourselves" (1 Cor 5:12-13). Paul himself, although absent in person, had already made a judgment on the immoral man in the name of the Lord Jesus.

In Judaism the expression "those on the outside" sometimes meant those who belonged to another religious group. The last sentence in 1 Cor 5:13 is a direct quotation from the Septuagint of Deut 17:7 and was addressed to persons belonging to God's covenant people Israel. I suggest, therefore, that "those on the outside" are persons of the brotherhood at Corinth who do not yet belong to the renewed covenant community of God, that is, "those on the inside." The implication is that those belonging to the renewed covenant community of God who become immoral will not have the opportunity to repent and be forgiven. Members themselves are to drive out evil persons from among them. For those outside God is the judge.

In dealing with his adversaries at Corinth in 2 Corinthians 10-13 (recall comments on 2 Cor 7:8-10 above) Paul hopes that the faithfulness toward God of the Corinthian converts who are involved in the controversy with his adversaries will increase (2 Cor 10:15). He exhorts them to examine themselves to see whether they are still living in the faithfulness taught by him, not that taught by his adversaries (2 Cor 13:5). That their faithfulness was to include proper conduct as members of the brotherhood is clear from Paul's question: "Do you not perceive that Jesus Christ is in you?" (2 Cor 13:5). They will know that is true unless they are counterfeit (adokimos) Christians. The converts' changed way of life, doing what is morally/ethically right, not wrong, will be the best evidence of Paul's qualification as an apostle. His purpose was their edification, that is, to help them develop spiritual maturity. Paul prays for their proper condition (katartisin). And he finally exhorts the "brothers" to bring themselves into the proper condition, to encourage one another, to think about the same moral concerns, and to be at peace (2 Cor 13:11). The behavior of converts at Corinth who sided with Paul's adversaries was not yet what it ought to be for living as members of the brotherhood.

Paul uses the designation "brothers" both for members of a particular church or for the brotherhood in general. Gal 6:1 clearly suggests that in the churches of Galatia there were differences in status among the brotherhood: "Brothers, if a person (anthropos) is caught in any false step, you who have the characteristics of the Spirit bring that person into the proper condition in a spirit of gentleness, watching yourself, lest you also be tempted." Although here Paul uses anthropos ("person") instead of adelphos ("brother"), used in the passages from the Corinthian letters, he is surely referring to a member of the brotherhood, not to someone in paganism who lacks faithfulness toward God. Paul's words "lest you also be tempted" clearly imply that those who have the characteristics of the Spirit are sinless, or at least in a condition or rank above the person to be restored. Difference in rank is clearly implied also by the use of the verb katartizo, which I have porperly translated as "bring into the proper condition."

The persons having the characteristics of the Spirit should try to restore the person who makes the false step, at the same time trying not to commit the same offense themselves. If they live by the Spirit, they must "stay in line with the Spirit" (Gal 5:25). The verb I have translated as "stay in line with" is stoicheo and could also be translated as "stay in rank." In restoring the person who committed the false step (paraptoma), those who restore that person should not be "vainglorious, challenging one another, envying one another" (Gal 5:26). Those with the Spirit must be careful that they do not lose it in dealing with the offender and slip to a lower rank themselves.

In Gal 6:1 Paul's advice is obviously more gentle than his command to those in the higher rank in the Corinthian brotherhood to expel the evil person from among them. Apparently Paul did not consider the offense (paraptoma) of the person in Galatia so serious as that of the immoral man in Corinth. However, in Galatia, as in Corinth, there were ranks within the brotherhood. One of them was sinlessness, and Paul warns those within that rank also to watch their step when admonishing persons of a lower rank. This interpretation seems to be confirmed by Paul's conclusion to the passage in Phil 3:7-16, a passage discussed above (see also suggestions below).

Perhaps one would not expect to find the same kind of situation in Romans, written to a church Paul did not help to establish, at least directly. On the other hand, it is in that letter where Paul first actually argues for the sinlessness of converts after baptism. He wants converts there to be sure they understand the spiritual significance and the moral obligation of baptism into the renewed covenant community of God. Converts in the churches he directly helped to establish knew that.

There is one clear clue that there were also probably ranks within the brotherhood in the church at Rome. In Rom 16:17 Paul writes: "I exhort you, brothers, to watch out for those who cause dissensions and offenses in opposition to the teaching you have learned; keep away from them." Then Paul adds: "For such persons do not serve our Lord Christ but their own belly" (Rom 16:18). The words "but their own belly" (compare Phil 3:19) and others of the same kind that follow in Rom 16:19 indicate that the offenses referred to in this instance were immoral ones (compare also Rom 14:10-15:6) and that the teaching, therefore, was instruction in morality. Faithfulness toward God imposed the moral responsibility to the point of sinlessness as the basic requirement for persons striving to enter the renewed covenant community of God, the highest rank within Christian churches or brotherhoods, separately or collectively.

One of the moral ingredients lacking in some of the Roman converts' faithfulness was obedience, and Paul wanted to help bring it about (Rom 1:5). Moreover, obedience was "for the purpose of righteousness" (Rom 6:16). Some baptized converts, in contrast to others not yet baptized, "were once slaves of sin" but "have become obedient from the heart to the model of teaching" to which they were committed. And having been set free from sin, they became slaves of righteousness (Rom 6:17-18). These passages indicate that some converts at Rome were members of the renewed covenant community of God and had achieved the sinless status of righteousness. Others, although members of the brotherhood had not yet achieved that status.

As a final example of passages that indicate differences in status or rank within Christian brotherhoods I call attention again to Phil 3:7-16. This passage is a part of what probably was one of Paul's latest letters and gives us his autobiographical statements about his status as a Christian Jew, as compared with his former life as a Pharisaic Hebrew. These verses are a kind of public confession of his personal experience of a Christian Jew who has become a mature (Phil 3:15) member of the renewed covenant community of God.

For Paul nothing matters any more except "the surpassing worth of knowing Christ Jesus my Lord," that is, knowing him and the power of his resurrection (Phil 3:8, 10). All that is left for Paul in his spiritual development is "to attain the resurrection from the dead" (Phil 3:11), the ultimate status for members of the renewed covenant community of God who are completely good or mature (Greek, teleioi) in Christian character. But Paul still has to exhort those who share his status "to stay in line" (stoicheo) with what they have attained (Phil 3:16). Then he exhorts other "brethren" to join in imitating him and others who are models of moral life so that in their ultimate commonwealth in heaven the Lord Jesus Christ as Savior will change their lowly bodies to be like his glorious body. Those persons are placed in contrast to others whose "god is the belly" and whose "end is destruction" (Phil 3:17-21), persons not even members of the brotherhood and are pagans.

Summary

What I have been saying means, then, that there were sinful and sinless members in the churches or brotherhoods that Paul was instrumental in establishing. His exhortations to moral probity would be directed, on the one hand, to those sinners who were willing to turn to God from idolatry and who were, therefore, called to become holy ones, that is, set apart for the purpose of becoming holy persons and thereby potentially qualify for membership in the renewed covenant community of God and, therefore, for ultimate salvation. On the other hand, Paul also intended his moral exhortations for members who were already in the renewed covenant community of God in order to help them stay in line with their new moral existences as new creations having the characteristics of the Spirit.

The sinners were the evil persons like those listed in 1 Cor 6:9-10, for example. Paul reminds those on the inside, "Such were some of you" (1 Cor 6:11) and then adds: "But you were washed, you were sanctified, you were justified" (1 Cor 6:14). Those addressed there had been on the outside, but now they are on the inside. In contrast to the persons who are on the inside or in the renewed covenant community of God are the brothers Paul mentions in 1 Cor 6:1-8. They are still at the point where some have legal disputes with others and even go to trial before unrighteous judges in paganism who are among those who have not come to faithfulness toward God, that is, unbelievers. Such persons are to be ignored by other persons or holy ones belonging to the church or brotherhood for whom differences between brothers or members of the church should be settled among themselves. In contrast to the brothers among whom there were dissensions at Corinth and whom Paul does not write to shame (1 Cor 4:14), he does write for the shame of the brothers going to law outside the brotherhood (1 Cor 6:5). Paul accuses them of acting unjustly and repudiating each other and warns them that persons who behave in that way will not inherit the kingdom of God (1 Cor 6:2). They belong to the group not yet washed, sanctified, justified (1 Cor 6:11) and who are, therefore, not yet members of the renewed covenant community of God.

Presumably it took a long time for converts, especially Gentiles, to practice the stringent moral obligations to the degree required of them for entrance into the renewed covenant community of God. When they were able to meet those obligations, baptism marked the transition for them from one status to the other. After baptism and justification or the forgiveness of past sins and the reception of the Holy Spirit, converts were expected to remain sinless. For them there was no opportunity for repentance and forgiveness in the future. So Paul's exhortations are also directed toward them in an effort to help them remain in a state of sinlessness. All converts or members of the brotherhood, whether they are in the renewed covenant community of God or not, as well as persons not converted, will ultimately be judged by God on the basis of what they have done (2 Cor 5:10; Rom 2:6-11; 14:10-12).

Paul and the Community at Qumran

Again, Paul may well be influenced by a Jewish sect very much like that of Qumran, if not directly by that Sect. As we learn from the Manual of Discipline and other scrolls from Qumran, the ascetic sect there was an eschatological one, as were Paul and his converts. Members of the Qumran Sect believed they should prepare themselves for the final age when all evil would be abolished. They strove to transform their sinful human existences into some superior way of life by trying to eliminate all evil in their lives and by suppressing even evil desires that might cause sin.

Among designations by which the Sect of Qumran thought of itself was the Covenant, within which there were divisions and ranks and whose members were also referred to as holy ones. A judiciary Council was composed of laymen and priests who were to be perfect in everything revealed in the Torah, practice truth, righteousness, justice, loving kindness, and guard the faithfulness of the community with a steadfast purpose and a contrite spirit (1QS 8:1-3).

The Manual begins by stating the purpose and ideals of the Community. Every member is to obey the rules of the Community, to seek God and do what is good and right before him, to love everything that God has chosen and to hate everything that he has rejected, to keep from every form of evil, and to practice truth and righteousness and justice. Those wanting to enter the Community must pledge to obey God's commands and behave before him perfectly (1QS 1:1-8). There were severe punishments for various offenses to the rules, the worst of which was permanent exclusion from the community.

One of the basic principles of the Sect of Qumran was ritual purity, preserved through daily lustrations. But the Sect stressed emphatically that such lustrations alone did not purify. Rather, "By a spirit of uprightness and humility his sins shall be atoned" and by walking perfectly in all the ways of God (1QS 3:8-10).

If one listens to the silence in Paul's letters, one discerns ideas and practices of a renewed covenant community of God similar to those of the Qumran Sect. All this is to say nothing about the practice of a sacred communal meal and behavior at it (1QS 6:4-5; 1QSa 2:17-22; 1 Cor 11:17-34), the idea of converts as "chosen" or "elect" (1QS 8:6; 1QH 2:13; Gal 1:15; Rom 8:33), a new covenant (1QS 3:11; CD 8:21; 1 Cor 11:25; 2 Cor 3:6), and other similarities often recognized.

Paul thought of all persons in his churches or brotherhoods as converts to faithfulness toward God and refers to all of them as brothers. The designation "unbelievers" (apistoi) was used for persons who were not members of a church or brotherhood and who did not share converts' faithfulness toward God. The designation occurs only in the Corinthian correspondence (recall comments on the negative counterparts of words for believing in chapter 5 of this work). All members of a brotherhood were also thought of as hagioi, holy ones or saints, in the sense that they were set apart from others in the social world around them for the purpose of becoming a holy people of God. Obviously, not all remained on the course to moral holiness or sinlessness.

As with Jesus, Paul associated with evil persons, including those inside and outside his churches, in order to win at least some of them to his cause. The sole difference among ranks in the churches or brotherhoods was the practice of the stringent moral/ethical standards expected of those who joined the renewed covenant community of God. A member of the brotherhood who became immoral was not to be associated with by those inside the community of God. And one on the inside who became immoral was to be expelled from the community. As I said earlier, there is no evidence that anyone was ever expelled from a church or brotherhood because of differences of beliefs about Jesus or differences in practices at worship.

What I say, obviously, still leaves questions, proposed answers to which can come only from continued serious studies of the complex person of Paul and the many problems revealed through his letters. I hope I shall have inspired some readers to pursue plausible answers to problems that may have arisen in their own minds. There are times when I have felt inadequate for the task of trying to comprehend Paul's confused thought and many difficult texts. When interpreting any text or even when trying to determine Paul's thought in general, the interpreter can always expect the keen scholar and student of Paul to propose another view. As I said in the Preface, in this work I have tried to think otherwise. I shall be satisfied if a number of the suggestions I have made thus far will, at the least, seem plausible to many readers.

In the next and last chapters I have also thought otherwise by suggesting that there was law for Paul after all, law to be obeyed by all who became converts to faithfulness toward God and members of a church or brotherhood. The degree to which converts observed that law determined what rank or stage they held within the brotherhood. And all members of the brotherhood would ultimately be judged on the basis of their obedience to that law or their failure to obey it. Obedience was necessary to receive ultimate salvation.

Chapter 8

Law For Paul, After All

Paul, the Synagogue, and the Law

In the great Jewish institution known as the synagogue, law was central in all its functions for study, worship, and life. There is no evidence in any of Paul's letters or in the book of Acts to indicate that Paul ever was expelled from or disassociated himself from the synagogue. According to Acts, while on his missionary journeys, Paul regularly entered Jewish synagogues: in Salamis, on the island of Cyprus (Acts 13:5), Antioch of Pisidia (Acts 13:14), Iconium (Acts 14:1), Thessalonica (Acts 17:1-2), Athens (Acts 17:16-17), Corinth (Acts 18:1-4), and Ephesus (Acts 19:1-8). Also, according to Acts, Paul was sufficiently respected and persuasive to gain converts among both Jews and Gentiles who attended synagogue meetings (Acts 13:43; 14:1; 17:4, 11-12). If we had only the evidence from Acts--although rather convincing on this point, it seems to me--perhaps we could not be sure that Paul always remained associated with the synagogue and, therefore,

almost certainly also continued to have a positive interest in at least
some of the Jewish law.

It is true that Paul never writes anything about his own relationship
or the relationship of the recipients of his letters to the synagogue. This
is probably due to the fact that he was writing to a majority of persons
who were Gentiles and who had never become formally associated with
the synagogue. This is probably also the reason why Christian converts
met in the houses of members (see 1 Cor 16:19; Rom 16:5; Phlm 2).
There is, however, an important passage that confirms the fact that Paul
continued to be under the legal jurisdiction of the synagogue. That
passage is 2 Cor 11:24-25, where in narrating his sufferings as an
apostle he includes "forty lashes less one by the Jews" and being
stoned. Such lashings and stonings were standard punishments for
various offenses to the law (see, for example, Exod 21:20; Lev 24:15-
16; Deut 13:6-11; 17:2-7; 25:1-3). Paul would hardly have been the
victim of such beatings and stoning (for what offenses we do not know)
if he had not continued to be associated with the synagogue. If, indeed,
Paul never did disassociate himself from the Jewish synagogue, it
would be ridiculous to think that he disassociated himself from all
Jewish law. That law, or at least certain aspects of it, would be the one
means whereby he could best begin communicating with prospective
Jewish converts. There are, I believe, certain aspects of the law that
remained valid for Paul even after he became a Christian Jew. Those
laws, he believed, had lasting value not only for Jews but also for
Gentiles who became Christian converts.

In Romans, especially from chapter 7 on, Paul talks more about the
law and appears to be speaking more forcefully than anywhere else
against the law, even the law in general, not just circumcision and
dietary regulations. He does, indeed, seem to be saying that Christ has
delivered Christian converts from the law to give them freedom for life
by the Spirit or for life in Christ and that Christ, therefore, brought the
abolition of the law. A closer examination of his ideas, though, reveals
that there is law that should be fulfilled by those very Christian
converts themselves. This becomes clear from several terms Paul uses
almost exclusively in Romans. They add further evidence that the law
was no problem for Paul, even as a Christian Jew, until after the

conflict began with the Judaizers in the churches of Galatia. Dikaioma and Dikaiomata

Dikaioma (plural, dikaiomata) is a word derived from the same root as dikaioo, meaning "make or declare righteous," "acquit," "justify," and as dikaiosyne, meaning "righteousness" or "justification." Dikaioma is usually translated as "regulation," "requirement," or "commandment." Although, as with dikaioo, originally a legal term, dikaioma came to mean "a thing pronounced (by God) to be dikaios," that is, just or right. Dikaioma is used in the Septuagint in parallel with prostagma and entole, synonymous words meaning "injunction," "ordinance," or "commandment," and krima, "judgment" (for example, Gen 26:5; Num 36:13; Deut 4:40; 6:1; 7:11; Ps 17(18):23).

In addition to Romans, the word dikaioma occurs in the New Testament in Luke 1:6, where it is used as in the Septuagint. Zechariah and Elizabeth are characterized as "both righteous before God, walking in all the commandments [entolais] and ordinances [dikaiomasin] of the Lord blameless." The writer of Hebrews (9:1, 10) uses dikaiomata to refer to the ritualistic regulations or ordinances for worship under the first covenant. For the author of Hebrews the blood of Christ, as the mediator of a new covenant, made such regulations unnecessary because through his blood Christ brought the redemption which those regulations had sought to accomplish but failed to do so.

The meaning of the word dikaiomata in Rev 15:4 is uncertain. In a passage alluding to the Exodus and the song of Moses, it could mean "righteous deeds," "just decrees," or "sentences of condemnation." The Lamb is made to sing, with reference to God the Almighty: "All the nations shall come and bow down before you, for your dikaiomata were revealed." In Rev 19:8 the meaning seems to be "righteous deeds": "For the fine linen is the righteous deeds (dikaiomata) of the holy ones." In Rev 12:17 the synonymous word entolai has the same meaning: "Then the dragon . . . went off to make war on the rest of her [that is, the woman with a crown of twelve stars on her head] offspring, on those who keep the commandments [entolai] of God and bear testimony to Jesus" (see also Rev 14:12, quoted below).

Rom 1:28-32

With these passages as background, we turn now to the use of the noun dikaioma in Romans, the only letter in which it occurs. Speaking of Gentiles in Rom 1:28-32, Paul says: "Since they did not think it fitting to recognize God, God gave them over to a failing mind to do what is unfitting, filled with every kind of unrighteousness." After listing the many vices of the Gentiles, he continues: "Although they who know the commandment [dikaioma; NRSV, "decree"; REB and NAB, "just decree"] of God, that those who practice such things [all kinds of wickedness] are worthy of death, they not only do them, but also fully approve those who practice them" (Rom 1:32). Here Paul thinks of God as a lawgiver who decrees death for Gentiles who commit certain immoral/unethical acts not in accordance with the dikaiomata of God. Later, when speaking to such Gentiles, who by God's grace had become Christian converts, Paul asks: "What then? Are we to sin because we are not under law but under grace?" His answer, as we have seen, is an emphatic "By no means!" (Rom 6:15-19). And then in language so strong he felt some apology was necessary (Rom 6:19), Paul urges the obedience of the Roman converts, "who once were salves of sin" but "have become obedient from the heart to the model of teaching to which you were pledged" (Rom 6:17). It is clear that for Paul this model of teaching, which was not his teaching but early Christian teaching, was as binding upon the Christian converts at Rome as the law was for Jews. This Christian teaching for the purpose of moral/ethical life was a new revelation of God's will for those who are now members of the brotherhoods and trying to become worthy of entering the renewed covenant community of God.

Rom 2:25-29

Paul uses the word dikaioma again with reference to Gentiles in Rom 2:25-29: "If, then, the persons who do not practice circumcision keep the commandments [dikaiomata; NRSV, "requirements"; REB and NAB, "precepts"] of the law [nomos], will not their uncircumcision be reckoned for circumcision?" (Rom 2:26). Surely most Jews of Paul's day would have responded with a resounding "No!" But Paul is very liberal here. And he has in mind those Gentiles who, although "they do not have the law, do by nature the things of the law, those who do not have the law are a law to themselves. They show the work of the law written in their hearts" (Rom 2:14-15). The word Paul uses here for "law" is the one he most frequently uses--nomos. A little later he writes: "The person who is by nature uncircumcised who fulfills the law will judge you who through the letter and circumcision is a transgressor of the law. For the Jew is not one who appears as such, nor is circumcision that which appears in the flesh. But the Jew is one in inward nature [character], and circumcision is of the heart, in spirit not in letter" (Rom 2:27-29). As in the last passage quoted, the word for law is the usual one--nomos.

Here again, in the context of a discussion of law, Paul's thought reflects something of Hebrew law (Torah) itself. Consider, for example, Deut 10:16, "Circumcise therefore the foreskin of your heart," and Deut 30:6, "And the Lord your God will circumcise your heart and the heart of your offspring, so that you will love the Lord your God with all your heart and with all your soul, that you may live" (see also Jer 4:4).

The sense of the whole passage in Rom 2:25-29 is that what God requires (the dikaiomata) is not meant for people of a particular race and who have marks such as circumcision on their bodies. Rather, what God expects of all people is a distinctive kind of life, irrespective of whether they are Jews or not. In this respect Paul was different from other Jews of his time because he was neither "orthodox" Jew nor "orthodox" Christian, in the modern understanding of the terms. Paul was a Christian Jew whose views on the Jewish law were unique because he was a unique Christian Jewish person.

We are discussing Rom 2:25-29 because it contains the expression "the commandments of the law" (ta dikaiomata tou nomou). The passage clearly indicates that Paul does not negate all Jewish law. That he has in mind something which is in effect law, that is, "rules of conduct established and enforced by the authority," is made certain not only by the use of the term dikaiomata, but also by the addition of the words "the law" (tou nomou). Of course, for Paul God was the supreme authority. What Paul is really saying in Rom 2:25-29 is that there is a kind of righteousness which God expects and which, if practiced by Jew and non-Jew, is effective before God. Of the person who does practice such law Paul says: "That person's praise is not from humans but from God" (Rom 2:29).

Like Jesus, Paul stands in the unique moral/ethical tradition of the Hebrew prophets. For the prophets, for Jesus, and for Paul, religion is not a matter of outward signs or ceremonies, but of the heart and life (of many passages, see, for example, Deut 10:16; 30:6; Jer 4:1-4; Mic 6:8; Amos 5:10-15; Mark 7:20-23; Matthew 5-7; 12:33-37; 15:18-20; Luke 6:43-45).

Rom 5:16-18

The next time the word dikaioma appears is in the difficult passage on Adam and Christ in Rom 5:16-18:

> The free gift [of God] is not as if by virtue of the one [Adam] who sinned. For the verdict (resulting) from the one man was for condemnation, but the free gift (following) many transgressions was for an acquittal [dikaioma; NRSV, "justification"; REB and NAB, "acquittal"]. For if by the transgression of the one man [Adam], death ruled by virtue of the one, much more shall those who receive the abundance of [God's] grace and of the gift of righteousness rule in life by virtue of the one Jesus Christ. Therefore, as if by virtue of one transgression, the [outcome] was for condemnation for all persons, so also by virtue of one righteous act [dikaioma], the [outcome] was for the process of justification [dikaiosis] of life for all persons.

If the thought of Paul seems obscure, it is because his Greek abounds in obscurities. This is true in part also because these two verses contain many legal terms used in courts of law. Not only is the word dikaioma, by necessity translated two different ways--"acquittal" and "righteous act"--a legal term, but so are the words translated "verdict" (krima), "condemnation" (katakrima), and "process of justification" (dikaiosis). I have tried to bring out the sense--even though it may not make sense--of Paul's Greek as best I could with a rather literal translation that attempts to convey the meaning in harmony with his thought in general.

These verses are part of one of the most important and influential theological and Christological passages in the New Testament. On the basis of the legal terminology used, I believe the verses may be summarized thus: Paul places "condemnation" (katakrima) and "acquittal" (dikaioma)--however the two terms should be translated--in antithesis to each other. This indicates that he includes the two terms under the same category, namely, that of a court of justice in which God pronounces sentences on humankind. One sentence is that of condemnation as the result of Adam's sin, the other is a sentence of justification or acquittal by virtue of the action of God in Christ.

Paul has chosen the last legal term in the passage deliberately. It is dikaiosis. The suffix sis, added to the verbal root of the noun means that the action intended by the word is not completed but is still in the process of becoming complete. For Paul, the sinner's justification is not completed but is a process still in being and moving toward ultimate consummation. If we take "justification" in the sense of "acquittal," then acquittal means the acquittal or forgiveness only of converts' past sins. This point is confirmed not only by the use of the word dikaiosis, but also by the use of the preposition eis, which I have translated as "for a process of," before the word dikaiosis. It should be observed that even though Paul uses the same preposition (eis) before the word "condemnation," it does not have the same meaning. This is true because the word which follows it does not indicate something still in process. Paul seems also to have chosen the Greek word katakrima, rather than katakrisis, for "condemnation" deliberately. Those persons who do not become members of the renewed covenant community of God do not enter into the process which leads to eternal life. Their condemnation is final.

That the interpretation I have just given is the one intended by Paul is clear not only from Paul's use of the words dikaiosis and katakrima, but also from what follows in chapter 6 of Romans and in Rom 8:1-4, where the word dikaioma is used for the last time by Paul.

Rom 8:1-4

In the preceding passages Paul has used the term dikaioma with reference to Gentiles (Rom 1:32; 2:26) and to all persons who are to be the recipients of God's grace through their justification (Rom 5:16, 18). In Rom 8:1-4 Paul uses it in a discussion of law with reference to persons who are "in Christ," that is, are already Christians:

There is therefore now no condemnation [katakrima] for those who
are in Christ Jesus. For the law [nomos] of the Spirit of life in Christ
Jesus has set you free from the law [nomos] of sin and death. For
God, who sent his own Son in the likeness of sinful flesh and [to
atone] for sin, did what the law [nomos], because it was weakened on
account of the flesh, was unable to do, [God] condemned [katakrino]
sin in the flesh, in order that the just requirement [dikaioma] of the
law [nomos] might be fulfilled in us who conduct our lives not
according to the flesh but according to the Spirit.

This passage is comparable to the one in Rom 7:21-25 in that Paul
speaks about two aspects of law. There is no question that "the law of
sin and death" (Rom 8:2), as Paul refers to it-- presumably much of the
Jewish law as it was understood by persons not living in Christ or
experiencing life by the Spirit--was powerless in itself to effect
justification and ultimate salvation. But because of the efficacy of the
work of God through his Son, the condemnation, a life of sin and death
brought by the law, was transformed into a sentence with the
potentiality for restoring life anew as God himself requires. And the law
referred to as "the law of the Spirit of life in Christ Jesus," as the
antithesis of "the law of sin and death" (Rom 8:2), is a way of life in
which the mind is directed by the Spirit, the distinctive mark of the
Christian convert, not by the flesh. There is no better passage to prove
that the kind of law demanding moral probity we have been discussing
remained valid, according to Paul, than the following statement from
Rom 8:7: "Therefore, the mind that is on the flesh is hostile toward
God, for it does not submit to the law [nomos] of God, nor can it."

Entole and Entolai

As in the Septuagint and in Rev 12:17, Paul uses the word entole,
(plural, entolai) "command(ment)" or "ordinance," as synonymous with
dikaioma.

Rom 7:12; 13:8-10

Along with the law (nomos), the commandment (entole) "is holy
and just and good" (Rom 7:12). Entole is parallel to nomos in the
summary of Paul's love ethic: "Owe no one anything, except to love
one another; for the person who loves his neighbor has fulfilled the
law" (nomos). "'You shall not commit adultery, you shall not kill, you

shall not steal, you shall not covet,' and any other commandment [entole] is summed up in this sentence, 'You shall love your neighbor as yourself.' Love does not do wrong to a neighbor; therefore love is the fulfillment of the law" (nomos; Rom 13:8-10).

1 Cor 7:19; 14:37

To the Corinthian converts Paul writes: "Circumcision is nothing and uncircumcision is nothing, but keeping the commandments [entolas] of God" (1 Cor 7:19). Paul uses the same word (entole) in 1 Cor 14:37, where he is speaking about behavior during Christian worship. What Paul writes is "a command (entole] of the Lord" (Jesus), an allusion to instruction that had been transmitted under the name of Jesus and which Paul had learned when he became a Christian Jew. Paul refers to the same kind of instruction with the use of the word epitage ("command") in 1 Cor 7:6, 25, where he advises the Corinthian converts about marriage (see also 2 Cor 8:8).

Observations and Summary

Along with his profound faithfulness toward God and his beliefs about Jesus, Paul believes that there is a very real law for Christian converts. Not the ceremonial and ritualistic aspects of the Mosaic law, such as circumcision and dietary regulations, but moral/ethical probity is "the law of God" for the person, irrespective of race or status, who would live by the Spirit. The law represented by the words dikaioma and dikaiomata and entole and entolai is the only law, Mosaic or any other, for Christian converts. So the best understanding of what Paul means by those words is: "what is required for converts to enter the renewed covenant community of God and to keep persons already in the community righteous."

The explanation that I have been giving can now help us to understand such references in Romans to the law as the following. The law represented by Paul's four words is the law without which all who have sinned "will also perish without the law," and under which all who have sinned "will be judged by the law." It is the law by which all who do it will be justified and the law which those Gentiles who "do by nature" are "a law to themselves" (Rom 2:12-16). The law is the law that is not overthrown but rather upheld by faithfulness toward God (Rom 3:31). It is the law which, with the commandment, "is holy and just and good" (Rom 7:12). It is the law that is "spiritual" and "good" and which causes an inner struggle to do what is right in the person not living in Christ and by the Spirit (Rom 7:13-25). The law is that which is fulfilled by love of one's neighbor and that is the only debt of the Christian (Rom 13:8-10). It is the law that is fulfilled by love (Rom 13:10). The ultimate salvation of all Christian converts depends upon their fulfillment of that law.

Perhaps a passage in the book of Revelation reflects a tradition about the necessity for faithfulness and works in Christian life not unlike that which we have discerned in Paul's letters, especially in Romans. What Paul was saying in his usually complicated way in trying to characterize Christian faithfulness and life the writer of Revelation says clearly and succinctly: "Here is the patient endurance of the holy ones [ton hagion, that is, Christians], those who keep the commandments [entolas] of God and the faithfulness of Jesus" (Rev 14:12).

After all, the dikaioma tou theou, the "just requirement of God" (Rom 1:32); the dikaiomata tou nomou, the "just requirements of the law" (Rom 2:26), the dikaioma tou nomou, the "just requirement of the law" (Rom 8:4), and the entolai theou, the "commandments of God" (1 Cor 7:19), were still the law for Paul. After Paul developed beliefs about Jesus in addition to his profound faithfulness toward God, that law remained as much a requirement for him as a Christian Jew and for other Christians as well, he believed, as it had been for him as a pre-Christian Jew. As a Christian Jew Paul also included in that law certain commands of Jesus about which he learned when he became a Christian Jew. Paul himself actually says in 1 Cor 9:21 what we have been trying to say that he says: "To those without the law [of God] I became as one without the law--though not being without the law of God, but also obedient to the law of Christ."

Paul's Language

As with his discussion of the person not living in Christ and without the experience of life by the Spirit in Romans 7, so with his writing about the law for Christian converts, Paul speaks in a way that would be understood by many Gentiles, as well as Jews, in the church at Rome. Recall my remarks about "the law of God" in the discussion of Romans 7, and consider two passages from Epictetus quoted again here:

"Am I not wholly directed toward God and his commands [<u>tas entolas</u>] and ordinances [<u>prostagmata</u>]" (<u>Dis</u>. 3:24:114).

"These are the laws [<u>hoi nomoi</u>] sent to you from him [God], these are his ordinances [<u>diatagmata</u>]; you ought to become an interpreter of them, to these you ought to submit yourself, not to the laws of Masurius and Cassius" (<u>Dis</u>. 4:3:12).

The words in brackets are either identical to or synonymous with those Paul uses in the passages I have cited in the discussion of law for Paul. Again, the parallels in words and ideas are striking. They are also the words used in the passages quoted above from the Septuagint. Although Paul's language and thought are undoubtedly most influenced by the Jewish scriptures, his phraseology would certainly help him in trying to win Gentile as well as Jewish converts.

<u>Paul and the Jewish People</u>

As a person Paul was extremely complex. Who can claim to understand him completely? This difficulty is due in part to his background and training in Judaism which were also diverse and are not entirely comprehensible. Many factors from that background and training have influenced the language and thought that went into his writings. And his special religious experience of the spiritual Jesus to whose Spirit he was so devoted, but which is largely incomprehensible to his interpreters, was an important factor in his life.

In developing his ideas of the relationship of God to the people of the renewed covenant community of God or "the Israel of God," Paul as a Christian Jew was still primarily influenced by the scriptural ideas of God's relationship to his people Israel. Secondarily, Paul was influenced by the Judaism of his own time, especially aspects of it reflected in the community at Qumran. As with that community, so with Paul, to do what was good and right before God was an obligation of faithful Jews from the time of Moses (see 1QS 1:1-10). And as with the Sect of Qumran and the Jewish scriptures, so with Paul, the covenantal relationship with God involved the commitment to do the commandments of God (see 1QS 1:16-17; 1QpHab 8:1-3).

As a Christian Jew Paul came to believe that by virtue of the faithfulness of Christ, the unique element in his thought, God in his grace prepared the way that leads to ultimate salvation for all who were to come to faithfulness toward God and then also to certain beliefs about Jesus in the process of becoming Christian converts and entering into the renewed covenant community of God. As God had delivered his people Israel from bondage in Egypt and from Exile, so God in Christ was now reconciling to himself all sinners, both Jews and Gentiles, who had faithfulness toward God and held the prescribed beliefs about Jesus in the process of their entering the renewed covenant community of God.

Apparently Paul thought that Jews were restored to the covenant again when they became Christian converts, had their past sins forgiven, and were baptized into the renewed community of God. When Paul debates in his own being about the salvation of his people, the Jews, he quotes a combination of Jer 31:33-34, from Jeremiah's idea of the new covenant, and Isa 27:9: "And this is the covenant from me with them, when I take away their sins" (Rom 11:27). But, as with the ancient Israelites, once delivered from the bondage of sin and death (Gal 5:1; Rom 8:2, 21), members of the renewed covenant community of God had to serve God (1 Thess 1:9), Christ (Rom 14:18; 15:18) and one another (Gal 5:13). Christian converts living by the Spirit were to serve the Lord (Rom 12:11).

In his developing thought as a Christian Jew, when trying to present Christianity as a renewed covenant community of God, Paul uses a variety of terms and ideas. But let me stress here that no matter what terminology Paul uses, he has not the slightest notion that Christianity superseded or replaced Judaism (Rom 10:1-2; 11:1-12). Jews were not disinherited with the coming of Christ and Christianity. Rather, Christianity as a renewed covenant community of God was an institution that was not based on race, social status, or sex but was open to all who were willing to enter on the same terms. And, according to Paul, Jews were making a number of distinctive contributions to the renewed community that Paul and other Jews believed came from God (see especially Rom 9:4-5; 11:17-36).

Up to the time Paul wrote Romans he seemed to be mostly concerned with winning Gentiles to the Jesus movement. But the controversy in the churches of Galatia forced him to think about the justification of Gentiles and what the consequences of his newly developed views would be for his own people, the Jews. In spite of his concern for Gentiles, his heart was still with the Jews. Paul's ultimate objective was the eventual salvation of all Jews. His preaching to Gentiles, then, was to make the Jews jealous and thereby save some of them (Rom 11:11-27). Gentiles were just a wild olive branch grafted unto the real olive tree of Israel (Rom 11:17-24; see also Jer 11:16; Hos 14:6).

The wild olive was no good by itself and was usually unproductive. Grafting was a process normally used to give new life to the original tree itself. But Paul says that the branch grafted into the tree is to become "a joint partaker of the fatness of the root of the olive tree" (Rom 11:17). Gentiles who came to faithfulness toward God by necessity became part of the root of Judaism, but some Jewish branches were broken off because of disbelief (apistea) in God and were, therefore, temporarily cut off from the original tree, Israel. Apistea is always used by Paul for disbelief of Jews toward God and occurs only in Rom 3:3; 4:20; and 11:20, 23. Paul's main concern in Romans 11 is not to have the Jews left out in the cold with the coming of Jesus and his role in the justification and the eventual salvation of humankind.

That Paul did not think Christianity superseded or replaced Judaism becomes clearer if we look again at some statements in the gospel of John. The author of John, as with Paul, says that some Jews came to belief concerning Jesus, but the language and thought of John are quite different from those of Paul. "At the Passover Feast many [Jews] believed in his [Jesus'] name when they saw the sighs that he did; but Jesus did not trust himself to them" (John 2:23; see also 5:37-47). John writes that Jesus said the Jews would seek him but not find him and "where I am you cannot come" (John 7:34; see also 8:31-47; 11:45-53). Also, unlike Paul, the writer of John is not concerned with those who did not believe, including Jews. Those Jews who do not believe will die in their sins (John 8:24), and their guilt remains (John 9:41). The devil, not God, is the father of such Jews (John 8:44, 47).

For the writer of John, Christianity was something separate from Judaism, whereas for Paul Christianity was still authentic Judaism because of the faithfulness of Jesus the Messiah. Jesus' faithfulness toward God led God by his grace to forgive all persons who share that faithfulness of their past sins. According to Paul, both Jews and Gentiles lose their identity--"neither Jew nor Greek" (Gal 3:28)--when they become members of the brotherhood and prepare for entrance into the renewed covenant community of God, the roots of which are still in Judaism.

Moreover, as with Paul, the Johannine author thinks that some Jews rejected Jesus. "He came to the things that were his own, but his own people did not receive him, but as many as received him . . ." (John 1:11)--a frequently repeated theme in John. But in Paul's letters there is absolutely nothing to compare with the ideas of supersession or replacement of things Jewish, as in John. According to John, Jesus himself became the embodiment of the attributes of God in the covenant relationship with his special people Israel. God's loving kindness or graciousness (hesed) and truth (emeth) are inherent in Jesus himself, who was "full of grace and truth" (John 1:14; see also 1:17). The temple at Jerusalem no longer has validity because the body of Jesus is the true temple (John 2:19-21). These ideas of John show how different from them those of Paul really are.

Jews believed that the law was the gift of God, and Rabbis came to speak about "the gift of Torah." The idea of Torah as a gift is blended with the Hebrew idea of God's choice of Israel as his special people, beginning with the call of Abraham. Thus, Israel as the special people of God and the law were a blended union. The law had no significance apart from Israel, and Israel had no uniqueness without the law. In the same way, Christian converts, according to Paul, became God's special people living according to the moral instruction given them when they became converts. That instruction coupled with similar instruction from the Jewish law Paul thought of technically as the dikaioma tou theou, the "just requirement of God," the dikaioma tou nomou, the "just requirement of the law," the dikaiomata tou nomou, the "just requirements of the law," or the entolai theou, the "commandments of God." Apparently Paul thought of such laws as the law of Christ that he was under, though not being without law of God (1 Cor 9:21-22). Such laws are the law of Christ fulfilled by bearing one another's burdens (Gal 6:2). Such laws are the law written on the hearts of Gentiles who by nature do what the law requires (Rom 2:14-15). Especially for Paul himself, such laws are "the law of the Spirit of the life in Christ Jesus" that has set him "free from the law of sin and death" (Rom 8:2). And such laws (<u>dikaiomata</u> and <u>entolai</u>) are "the law of God" to which the persons whose mind is set on the flesh and, thus, hostile to God cannot submit (Rom 8:7). Thus, Christians, as members of the renewed covenant community of God, and their moral instruction were a blended entity. That instruction had no significance apart from the community of God, and without such instruction that community had no uniqueness in the social world in which it originated.

BIBLIOGRAPHY
BOOKS

Badenas, K. *Christ the End of the Law: Romans 10.4 in Pauline Perspective.* Sheffield: JSOT, 1985.

Bandstra, J. *The Law and the Elements of the World: An Exegetical Study in Aspects of Paul's Teaching.* Kampen: Kok, 1964.

Banks, R. *Paul's Idea of Community.* Grand Rapids: Eerdmans, 1980.

Barclay, J. M. G. *Obeying the Truth: Paul's Ethics in Galatians.* Minneapolis: Fortress, 1991.

Barnett, A. E. *Paul Becomes a Literary Influence.* Chicago: University of Chicago, 1941.

Barrett, C. K. *A Commentary on the Epistle to the Romans.* New York: Harper, 1957.

_____. *A Commentary on the First Epistle to the Corinthians.* New York: Harper & Row, 1968.

_____. *A Commentary on the Second Epistle to the Corinthians.* New York: Harper & Row, 1973.

_____. *Essays on Paul.* Philadelphia: Fortress, 1982.

_____. *Freedom and Obligation: A Study of the Epistle to the Galatians.* Philadelphia: Westminster, 1985.

_____. *Reading through Romans.* Philadelphia: Fortress, 1977.

Barth, M. *Ephesians.* 2 vols. Garden City: Doubleday, 1974.

_____. *Justification*. Trans. A. M. Woodruff III. Grand Rapids: Eerdmans, 1971.

_____. *The People of God*. Sheffield: JSOT, 1983.

Bassler, J. *Divine Impartiality: Paul and a Theological Axiom*. Chico: Scholars, 1982.

Beardslee, W. A. *Human Achievement and Divine Vocation in the Message of Paul*. London: SCM, 1961.

Beare, F. W. *A Commentary on the Epistle to the Philippians*. London: Black, 1973.

_____. *St. Paul and His Letters*. London: Black, 1962.

Beker, J. C. *Paul the Apostle*. Philadelphia: Fortress, 1980.

_____. *Paul's Apocalyptic Gospel*. Philadelphia: Fortress, 1982.

Best, E. *The First and Second Epistles to the Thessalonians*. New York: Harper & Row, 1972.

_____. *The Letter of Paul to the Romans*. Cambridge: University Press, 1967.

Betz, H. D. *Galatians*. Philadelphia: Fortress, 1979.

Bicknell, E. J. *The First and Second Epistles to the Thessalonians*. London: Methuen, 1932.

Black, M. *Romans*. Grand Rapids: Eerdmans, 1981.

Blank, J. *Paulus: Von Jesus zum Christentum: Aspekte der paulinischen Lehre und Praxis*. Munich: Kösel, 1982.

Bockmuehl, M. N. A. *Revelation and Mystery in Ancient Judaism and Pauline Christianity.* Tübingen: Mohr, 1990.

Borgen, P. *Paul Preaches Circumcision and Pleases Men.* Trondheim: Taper, 1983.

Bornkamm, G. *Early Christian Experience.* New York: Harper, 1969.

_____. *Paul.* Trans. D. M. G. Stalker. New York: Harper & Row, 1972.

Borse, U. *Der Brief an die Galater.* Regensburg: Pustet, 1984.

Bouttier, M. *Christianity according to Paul.* Trans. F. Clarke. London: SCM, 1966.

Breytenbach, C. *Versöhnung Eine zur paulinischen Soteriologie.* Neukirchen: Neukirchener, 1989.

Bring, R. *Christus und das Gesetz: Die Bedeutung des Gesetzes des Alten Testaments nach Paulus und sein Glauben an Christus.* Leiden: Brill, 1969.

Brinsmead, B. H. *Galatians--Dialogical Response to Opponents.* Chico: Scholars, 1982.

Brownlee, W. H. *The Dead Sea Manual of Discipline: Translation and Notes.* In *BASOR, Supplementary Studies 10-12* (1951).

Bruce, F. F. *The Epistle to the Galatians.* Grand Rapids: Eerdmans, 1982.

_____. *The Epistles to the Colossians, to Philemon, and to the Ephesians.* Grand Rapids: Eerdmans, 1984.

_____. *The Epistle of Paul to the Romans*. Grand Rapids: Eerdmans, 1982.

_____. *1 and 2 Corinthians*. Grand Rapids: Eerdmans, 1980.

_____. *1 and 2 Thessalonians*. Waco: Word, 1982.

_____. *Paul: Apostle of the Heart Set Free*. Grand Rapids: Eerdmans, 1977.

Buck, Charles, and G. Taylor. *Saint Paul: A Study of the Development of His Thought*. New York: Scribners, 1969.

Bultmann, R. *The Second Letter to the Corinthians*. Trans. R. A. Harrisville. Minneapolis: Augsburg, 1985.

_____. *Theology of the New Testament*. 2 vols. Trans. K. Grobel. New York: Scribners, 1951, 1955.

Burrows, M., J. C. Trever, and W. H. Brownlee, eds. *The Dead Sea Scrolls of St. Mark's Monastery; Vol. II, Fascicle 2: Plates and Transcription of the Manual of Discipline*. New Haven: American Schools of Oriental Research, 1951.

Burton, E. D. *The Epistle to the Galatians*. New York: Scribners, 1920.

Byrne, B. *Reckoning with Romans*. Wilmington: Glazier, 1986.

_____. "Sons of God"--"Seed of Abraham." Rome: Biblical Institute, 1979.

Caird, G. B. *Paul's Letters from Prison*. Oxford: University Press, 1976.

_____. *Principalities and Powers: A Study in Pauline Theology*. Oxford, Clarendon, 1956.

_____. *Principalities and Powers: A Study in Pauline Theology.* Oxford, Clarendon, 1956.

Campbell, D. A. *The Rhetoric of Righteousness in Romans 3:21-26.* Sheffield: Academic Press, 1992.

Carroll, J. T., et al. *Faith and History.* Part 2: "Studies in Paul." Atlanta: Scholars, 1990.

Cerfaux, L. *Christ in the Theology of Saint Paul.* New York: Herder & Herder, 1951.

_____. *The Christian in the Theology of St. Paul.* Trans. L. Soiron. New York: Herder and Herder, 1967.

_____. *The Spiritual Journey of Saint Paul.* Trans. J. C. Guinness. New York: Sheed and Ward, 1968.

Conzelmann, H. *1 Corinthians.* Trans. J. W. Leitch. Philadelphia: Fortress, 1975.

Collins, R. F. *Letters that Paul Did Not Write.* Wilmington: Glazier, 1988.

_____. *Studies on the First Letter to the Thessalonians.* Leuven: Peeters, 1984.

_____, ed. *The Thessalonian Correspondence.* Leuven: University Press, 1990.

Conzelmann, H. *An Outline of the Theology of the New Testament.* Trans. John Bowden. New York: Harper & Row, 1969.

Cosgrove, C. H. *The Cross and the Spirit: A Study in the Argument and Theology of Galatians.* Macon: Mercer, 1988.

Cousar, C. B. *Galatians*. Atlanta: John Knox, 1982.

Craddock, F. B. *Philippians*. Atlanta: John Knox, 1985.

Cranfield, C. E. B. *The Epistle to the Romans*. 2 vols. Edinburgh: T. & T. Clark, 1975, 1979.

Dahl, N. A. *The Crucified Messiah*. Minneapolis: Augsburg, 1974.

_____. *Studies in Paul*. Minneapolis: Augsburg, 1977.

Danker, F. W. *II Corinthians*. Minneapolis: Augsburg, 1989.

Daube, D. *The New Testament and Rabbinic Judaism*. London: Athlone, 1956.

Davies, G. N. *Faith and Obedience in Romans*. Sheffield: JSOT, 1990.

Davies, W. D. *Jewish and Pauline Studies*. Philadelphia: Fortress, 1984.

_____. *Paul and Rabbinic Judaism*. London: SPCK, 1955.

Davis, J. A. *Wisdom and Spirit: An Investigation of 1 Corinthians 1:18-3:20 against the Background of Jewish Sapiential Traditions in the Greco-Roman Period*. Lanham: University Press of America, 1984.

de Boer, M. C. *The Defeat of Death: Apocalyptic Eschatology in 1 Corinthians 15 and Romans 5*. Sheffield: JSOT, 1988.

Deidun, T. J. *New Covenant Morality in Paul*. Rome: Biblical Institute, 1981.

Deissmann, A. *Light from the Ancient East*. Trans. L. R. M. Strachan. New York: Doran, 1927.

_____. *Paul*. Trans. W. E. Wilson. New York: Harper, 1957.

_____. *The Religion of Jesus and the Faith of Paul*. Trans. W. E. Wilson. New York: Doran, 1926.

Derwachter, F. M. *Preparing the Way for Paul*. New York: Macmillan, 1930.

Dibelius, M., and W. G. Kümmel, ed. *Paul*. Trans. F. Clarke. Philadelphia; Westminster, 1953.

Dietzfelbinger, C. *Die Berufung des Paulus als Ursprung seiner Theologie*. Neukirchen-Vluyn: Neukirchener, 1985.

Dinkler, E. *"Prädestination bei Paulus," Signum Crucis*. Tübingen: Morh, 1967.

Dodd, C. H. *The Epistle of Paul to the Romans*. New York: Harper, n. d.

_____. *The Meaning of Paul for To-Day*. New York: Doran, n. d.

Donfried, K. P. *The Romans Debate*. Rev. and expanded ed. Peabody: Hendrickson, 1991.

Doohan, H. *Leadership in Paul*. Wilmington: Glazier, 1984.

_____. *Paul's Vision of Church*. Wilmington: Glazier, 1989.

Drane, J. W. *Paul, Libertine or Legalist?* London: SPCK, 1975.

Duncan, G. S. *The Epistle of Paul to the Galatians*. New York: Harper, n. d.

_____. *St. Paul's Ephesian Ministry*. New York: Scribner's, 1930.

Dunn, J. D. G. *Jesus, Paul, and the Law*. Louisville: Westminster/John Knox, 1990.

_____. *Romans*. 2 vols. Dallas: Word, 1988.

Dupont, D. J. *The Salvation of Gentiles*. Trans. J. Keating. New York: Paulist, 1979.

Dupont-Sommer, A. *The Essene Writings from Qumran*. Trans. G. Vermes. Cleveland: World, 1962.

Ebeling, E. *The Truth of the Gospel: An Exposition of Galatians*. Philadelphia: Fortress, 1985.

Edwards, J. R. *Romans*. Peabody: Hendrickson, 1992.

Edwards, T. C. *A Commentary on the First Epistle to the Corinthians*. London: Hamilton, 1985.

Ellis, E. E. *Paul's Use of the Old Testament*. Grand Rapids: Eerdmans, 1957.

Ellis, P. F. *Seven Pauline Letters*. Collegeville: Liturgical Press, 1982.

Enslin, M. S. *The Ethics of Paul*. New York: Harper, 1930.

_____. *Reapproaching Paul*. Philadelphia: Westminster, 1972.

Fallon, F. T. *2 Corinthians*. Wilmington: Glazier, 1980.

Fee, G. D. *The First Epistle to the Corinthians*. Grand Rapids: Eerdmans, 1988.

Feeley-Harnik, G. *The Lord's Table: Eucharist and Passover in Early Christianity*. Philadelphia: University of Pennsylvania, 1981.

Fitzmyer, J. A. "The Letter to the Galatians." Pp. 2:236-246 in *The Jerome Biblical Commentary (JBC)*. Ed. R. E. Brown, J. A. Fitzmyer, and R. E. Murphy. Englewood Cliffs: Prentice-Hall, 1968.

_____. "The Letter to the Philippians." Pp. 2:247-253 in *JBC*.

_____. "The Letter to the Romans." Pp. 2:291-331 in *JBC*.

_____. *Pauline Theology: A Brief Sketch*. Englewood Cliffs: Prentice-Hall, 1967.

Forestell, J. T. "The Letters to the Thessalonians." Pp. 2:227-235 in *JBC*.

Frame, J. E. *The Epistles of St. Paul to the Thessalonians*. New York: Scribners, 1912.

Freed, E. D. *The New Testament: A Critical Introduction*. Belmont: Wadsworth, 1991.

Fuller, D. P. *Gospel and Law: Contrast or Continuum?* Grand Rapids: Eerdmans, 1980.

Fung, R. Y. K. *The Epistle to the Galatians*. Grand Rapids: Eerdmans, 1989.

Funk, A. *Status und Rollen in den Paulusbriefen*. Innsbruck: Tyrolia, 1981.

Furnish, V. P. *The Moral Teaching of Paul*. Nashville: Abingdon, 1979.

_____. *Theology and Ethics in Paul*. Nashville: Abingdon, 1968.

_____. *II Corinthians*. Garden City: Doubleday, 1984.

Gager, J. G. *Kingdom and Community: The Social World of Early Christianity*. Englewood Cliffs: Prentice-Hall, 1975.

_____. *The Origins of Anti-Semitism*. Oxford: University Press, 1983.

Gale, H. M. *The Use of Analogy in the Letters of Paul*. Philadelphia: Westminster, 1964.

Gaston, L. *Paul and the Torah*. Vancouver: University of British Columbia, 1987.

Gaventa, B. R. *From Darkness to Light: Aspects of Conversion in the New Testament*. Philadelphia: Fortress, 1986.

Georgi, D. "Corinthians, First Letter to the." Pp. 180-183 in *The Interpreter's Dictionary of the Bible (IDB)*, supp. vol. New York: Abingdon, 1951-1957, 1976.

_____. "Corinthians, Second Letter to the." Pp. 183-186 in *IDB*, supp. vol.

_____. *The Opponents of Paul in Second Corinthians*. Philadelphia: Fortress, 1986.

Gerhardsson, B. *The Ethos of the Bible*. Trans. S. Westerholm. Philadelphia: Fortress, 1981.

Getty, M. A. *Philippians and Philemon*. Wilmington: Glazier, 1980.

Grant, M. *Saint Paul*. New York: Scribner's, 1976.

Grässer, E. *Der Alte Bund im Neuen*. Tübingen: Mohr, 1985.

Grassi, J. A. *A World to Win: The Missionary Methods of Paul the Apostle*. Maryknoll: Maryknoll Publications, 1965.

Grayston, K. *The Letters of Paul to the Philippians and to the Thessalonians*. Cambridge: University Press, 1967.

Grudem, W. *The Gift of Prophecy in 1 Corinthians*. Lanham: University Press of America, 1982.

Gundry, R. H. *Soma in Biblical Theology, with Emphasis on Pauline Anthropology*. Cambridge: University Press, 1976.

Gunther, J. J. *Paul: Messenger and Exile: A Study in the Chronology of His Life and Letters*. Valley Forge: Judson, 1972.

Guthrie, D. *Galatians*. Grand Rapids: Eerdmans, 1981.

Hagner, D. A., and M. J. Harns, eds. *Pauline Studies*. Grand Rapids: Eerdmans, 1980.

Hall, H. F. *According to Paul*. New York: Scribner's, 1945.

Hansen, G. W. *Abraham in Galatians*. Sheffield: JSOT, 1989.

Hanson, A. T. *The Paradox of the Cross in the Thought of St. Paul*. Sheffield: JSOT, 1987.

_____. *Studies in Paul's Technique and Theology*. Grand Rapids: Eerdmans, 1974.

Haufe, C. *Die sittliche Rechtfertigungslehre des Paulus*. Halle: Max Niemeyer, 1957.

Hays, R. B. *Echoes of Scripture in the Letters of Paul*. New Haven: Yale, 1989.

_____. *The Faith of Jesus Christ*. Chico: Scholars, 1983.

Heil, J. P. *Paul's Letter to the Romans*. Mahwah, NJ: Paulist, 1987.

Hering, J. *The First Epistle of Saint Paul to the Corinthians.* London: Epworth, 1962.

Hock, R. F. *The Social Context of Paul's Ministry.* Philadelphia: Fortress, 1980.

Hodge, C. *Commentary on the Epistle to the Romans.* Grand Rapids: Eerdmans, 1965.

Holladay, C. *The First Letter of Paul to the Corinthians.* Austin: Sweet, 1979.

Hooker, M. D. *A Preface to Paul.* New York: Oxford, 1980.

_____, and S. G. Wilson, eds. *Paul and Paulinism.* London: SPCK, 1982.

Houlden, J. L. *Paul's Letters from Prison.* Philadelphia: Westminster, 1977.

Howard, G. *Paul: Crisis in Galatia.* Cambridge: University Press, 1979.

Hübner, H. *Gottes Ich und Israel: Zum Schriftgebrauch des Paulus in Römer 9-11.* Göttingen: Vandenhoeck & Ruprecht, 1984.

_____. *Law in Paul's Thought.* Edinburgh: T. & T. Clark, 1984.

Hughes, P. E. *Paul's Second Epistle to the Corinthians.* Grand Rapids: Eerdmans, 1988.

Hultgren, A. J. *Paul's Gospel and Mission.* Philadelphia: Fortress, 1985.

Hurd, J. C. *The Origin of 1 Corinthians.* Macon: Mercer, 1983.

Jervell, J. *The Unknown Paul*. Minneapolis: Augsburg, 1984.

Jervis, L. A. *The Purpose of Romans*. Sheffield: Academic Press, 1991.

Jewett, R. *Christian Tolerance: Paul's Message to the Modern Church*. Philadelphia: Westminster, 1982.

_____. *A Chronology of Paul's Life*. Philadelphia: Fortress, 1979.

_____. *The Thessalonian Correspondence*. Philadelphia: Fortress, 1986.

Johnson, E. E. *The Function of Apocalyptic and Wisdom Traditions in Romans 9-11*. Atlanta: Scholars, 1989.

Käsemann, E. *Commentary on Romans*. Trans. and ed. G. W. Bromiley. Grand Rapids: Eerdmans, 1980.

_____. *Perspectives on Paul*. Trans. M. Kohl. Philadelphia: Fortress, 1969.

Kaye, B. N. *The Thought Structure of Romans with Special Reference to Chapter 6*. Austin: Schola, 1979.

Keck, L. E. *Paul and His Letters*. Philadelphia: Fortress, 1979.

_____, and V. P. Furnish. *The Pauline Letters*. Nashville: Abingdon, 1984.

Kepler, T. S., ed. *Contemporary Thinking about Paul*. New York: Abingdon-Cokesbury, 1950.

Kertelge, K. *The Epistle to the Romans*. New York: Herder & Herder, 1972.

_____. *"Rechtfertigung" bei Paulus*. Münster: Aschendorff, 1967.

Kim, S. *The Origin of Paul's Gospel*. Grand Rapids: Eerdmans, 1982.

Knox, J. *Chapters in a Life of Paul*. Nashville: Abingdon, 1950. Rev. ed. Ed. R. A. Hare. Macon: Mercer, 1987.

_____. *Philemon among the Letters of Paul*. London: Collins, 1960.

Knox, W. L. *St. Paul and the Church of the Gentiles*. Cambridge: University Press, 1939.

Kraeling, E. G. *I Have Kept the Faith: The Life of the Apostle Paul*. Chicago: Rand McNally, 1965.

Kreitzer, L. J. *Jesus and God in Paul's Eschatology*. Sheffield: JSOT, 9187.

Kuck, D. W. *Judgement and Community Conflict: Paul's Use of Apocalyptic Judgement Language in 1 Corinthians 3:5-4:5*. Leiden: Brill, 1992.

Kugelman, R. "The First Letter to the Corinthians." In *JBC* 2:254-275.

Lagrange, M.-J. *Saint Paul: Epitre aux Romains*. Paris: Gabalda, 1950.

Lake, K. *The Earlier Epistles of St. Paul*. London: Rivingtons, 1911.

Lapide, P., and P. Stuhlmacher. *Paul: Rabbi and Apostle*. Trans. L. W. Denef. Minneapolis: Augsburg, 1984.

Leenhardt, F. J. *The Epistle to the Romans*. London: Lutterworth, 1961.

Lightfoot, J. B. *The Epistle of St. Paul to the Galatians*. Grand Rapids: Zondervan, 1974.

Lincoln, A. T. *Paradise Now and Not Yet: Studies in the Role of the Heavenly Dimension in Paul's Thought with Special Reference to His Eschatology.* Cambridge: University Press, 1981.

Ljungman, K. *Pistis: A Study of Its Presuppositions and Its Meaning in Pauline Use.* Lund: Gleerup, 1964.

Lohse, E. *Colossians and Philemon.* Trans. W. R. Poehlmann and R. J. Karris. Philadelphia: Fortress, 1971.

Longenecker, R. N. *Galatians.* Dallas: Word, 1990.

_____. *Paul, Apostle of Liberty.* Grand Rapids: Eerdmans, 1964.

Luedemann, G. *Paul, Apostle to the Gentiles: Studies in Chronology.* Trans. F. S. Jones. Philadelphia: Fortress, 1984.

Lührmann, D. *Galatians.* Minneapolis: Fortress, 1992.

_____. *Glaube im frühen Christentum.* Göttingen: Gütersloh: Mohr, 1976.

_____. *Paulus und das Judentum.* München: Kaiser, 1983.

Lull, D. J. *The Spirit in Galatia.* Chico: Scholars, 1980.

Lyons, G. *Pauline Autobiography: Toward a New Understanding.* Atlanta: Scholars, 1985.

Maccoby, H. *The Mythmaker: Paul and the Invention of Christianity.* New York: Harper & Row, 1986.

_____. *Paul and Hellenism.* London: SCM, 1991.

MacDonald, D. R. *The Legend and the Apostle*. Philadelphia: Westminster, 1983.

MacDonald, M. Y. *The Pauline Churches*. New York: Cambridge: University Press, 1989.

Malherbe, A. *Moral Exhortation, A Greco-Roman Sourcebook*. Philadelphia: Westminster, 1986.

_____. *Paul and the Popular Philosophers*. Minneapolis: Fortress, 1989.

_____. *Paul and the Thessalonians*. Philadelphia: Fortress, 1987.

_____. *Social Aspects of Early Christianity*. Philadelphia: Fortress, 1983.

Maly, E. H. *Romans*. Wilmington: Glazier, 1983.

Marrow, S. B. *Paul: His Letters and His Theology*. New York: Paulist, 1986.

Marshall, I. H. *1 and 2 Thessalonians*. Grand Rapids: Eerdmans, 1983.

Martin, B. L. *Christ and the Law in Paul*. Leiden: Brill, 1989.

Martin, R. P. *Carmen Christi: Philippians ii.5-11 in Recent Interpretation and in the Setting of Early Christian Worship*. Grand Rapids: Eerdmans, 1983.

_____. *Colossians and Philemon*. Grand Rapids: Eerdmans, 1981.

_____. *Philippians*. Grand Rapids: Eerdmans, 1976.

_____. *Reconciliation: A Study of Paul's Theology*. Atlanta: John Knox, 1981.

_____. *2 Corinthians*. Waco: Word, 1986.

_____. *The Spirit and the Congregation*. Grand Rapids: Eerdmans, 1984.

Meeks, W. A., ed. *The Writings of St. Paul*. New York: Norton, 1972.

_____. *The First Urban Christians: The Social World of the Apostle Paul*. New Haven: Yale, 1983.

_____. *The Moral World of the First Christians*. Philadelphia: Westminster, 1986

_____, and Wilken, R. H. *Jews and Christians in Antioch in the First Four Centuries of the Common Era*. Missoula: Scholars, 1978.

Mell, U. *Neue Schöpfung*. Berlin: de Gruyter, 1989.

Michael, J. H. *The Epistle of Paul to the Philippians*. New York: Harper, n. d.

Michel, O. *Der Brief an die Römer*. Göttingen: Vandenhoeck & Ruprecht, 1963.

Minear, P. S. *The Obedience of Faith*. London: SCM, 1971.

Mitton, C. L. *Ephesians*. Grand Rapids: Eerdmans, 1981.

_____. *The Epistle to the Ephesians*. Oxford: Clarendon, 1951.

_____. *The Formation of the Pauline Corpus*. London: Epworth, 1955.

Moffatt, J. *The First Epistle of Paul to the Corinthians*. New York: Harper, n. d.

Moo, D. *Romans 1-8*. Chicago: Moody, 1991.

Mohrland, R. *Matthew and Paul: A Comparison of Ethical Perspectives*. Cambridge: University Press, 1984.

Morris, L. *The Epistles of Paul to the Thessalonians*. Grand Rapids: Eerdmans, 1983.

_____. *The Epistle to the Romans*. Grand Rapids: Eerdmans, 1988.

Morton, A. Q., and J. McLeman. *Paul: The Man and the Myth*. London: Hodder & Stoughton, 1966.

Moule, C. F. D. *The Epistle of Paul the Apostle to the Colossians and to Philemon*. Cambridge: University Press, 1958.

_____. *The Origin of Christology*. Cambridge: University Press, 1977.

Moxnes, H. *Theology in Conflict: Studies in Paul's Understanding of God in Romans*. Leiden: Brill, 1980.

Müller, C. *Gottes Gerechtigkeit und Gottes Volk*. Göttingen: Vandenhoeck & Ruprecht, 1964.

Munck, J. *Paul and the Salvation of Mankind*. Trans. F. Clarke. Richmond: John Knox, 1959.

Murphy-O'Connor, J. *1 Corinthians*. Wilmington: Glazier, 1982.

_____. *St. Paul's Corinth*. Wilmington: Glazier, 1983.

_____. *Becoming Human Together: The Pastoral Anthropology of St. Paul*. Wilmington: Glazier, 1982.

_____, ed. *Paul and Qumran: Studies in New Testament Exegesis.* London: Chapman, 1968.

Murray, J. *The Epistle to the Romans.* Grand Rapids: Eerdmans, 1987.

Mussner, F. *Der Galaterbrief.* Freiburg: Herder, 1974.

_____. *Die Kraft der Wurzel.* Freiburg: Herder, 1987.

Neil, W. *The Epistle of Paul to the Thessalonians.* London: Hodder & Stoughton, 1950.

_____. *The Letter of Paul to the Galatians.* Cambridge: University Press, 1967.

Newman, C. C. *Paul's Glory-Christology.* Leiden: Brill, 1992.

Neyrey, J. H. *Paul, in Other Words: A Critical Reading of His Letters.* Louisville: Westminster/John Knox, 1990.

Nickelsburg, G. W. E., and G. W. MacRae, eds. *Christians Among Jews and Gentiles.* Philadelphia: Fortress, 1986.

Nock, A. D. *Conversion.* Oxford: Clarendon, 1933.

_____. *St. Paul.* New York: Harper, 1938.

Ogg, G. *The Chronology of the Life of Paul.* London: Epworth, 1968.

O'Neill, J. C. *Paul's Letter to the Romans.* Baltimore: Penguin, 1975.

_____. *The Recovery of Paul's Letter to the Galatians.* London: SPCK, 1972.

Orr, W. F., and J. A. Walther. *1 Corinthians.* Garden City: Doubleday, 1976.

_____ and Walther, J. A. *I Corinthians*. Garden City: Doubleday, 1976.

O'Rourke, J. J. "The Second Letter to the Corinthians." Pp. 2:276-290 in *JBC*.

Osiek, C. *Galatians*. Wilmington: Glazier, 1980.

Pagels, E. H. *The Gnostic Paul: Gnostic Exegesis of the Pauline Letters*. Philadelphia: Fortress, 1975.

Patte, D. *Paul's Faith and the Power of the Gospel*. Philadelphia: Fortress, 1983.

Patzia, A. G. *Colossians, Philemon, Ephesians*. San Francisco: Harper & Row, 1984.

Pedersen, S. *Die paulinische Literatur und Theologie*. Göttingen: Vandenhoeck & Ruprecht, 1980.

Perkins, P. *Ministering in the Pauline Churches*. Ramsey: Paulist, 1982.

Petersen, N. R. *Rediscovering Paul*. Philadelphia: Fortress, 1985.

Piper, J. *The Justification of God: An Exegetical and Theological Study of Romans 9:1-23*. Grand Rapids: Eerdmans, 1983.

Plummer, A. *The First Epistle of St. Paul to the Corinthians*. New York: Scribners, 1911.

_____. *The Second Epistle of St. Paul to the Corinthians*. New York: Scribners, 1915.

Pobee, J. S. *Persecution and Martyrdom in the Theology of Paul*. Sheffield: JSOT, 1985.

Porter, F. C. *The Mind of Christ in Paul.* New York: Scribners, 1932.

Räisänen, H. *Paul and the Law.* Philadelphia: Fortress, 1986.

Reese, J. M. *1 and 2 Thessalonians.* Wilmington: Glazier, 1979.

Reinmuth, E. *Geist und Gesetz: Studien zu Voraussetzungen und Inhalt der paulinischen Parânese.* Berlin: Evangelische Verlag, 1985.

Reumann, J. *"Righteousness" in the New Testament.* Philadelphia: Fortress, 1982.

Rhyne, C. T. *Faith Establishes the Law.* Chico: Scholars, 1981.

Richardson, P. *Israel in the Apostolic Church.* Cambridge: University Press, 1969.

_____. *Paul's Ethic of Freedom.* Philadelphia: Westminster, 1979.

_____, P., and J. C. Hurd, eds. *From Jesus to Paul.* Waterloo: Wilfred Laurier University, 1984.

Ridderbos, H. *Paul: An Outline of His Theology.* Grand Rapids: Eerdmans, 1975.

Riddle, D. W. *Paul: Man of Conflict.* Nashville: Cokesbury, 1940.

Rigaux, B. *The Letters of St. Paul: Modern Studies.* Ed. and trans. S. Yonick. Chicago: Franciscan Herald Press, 1968.

Robinson, J. A. T. *The Body: A Study in Pauline Theolog* Philadelphia: Westminster, 1977.

_____. *Wrestling with Romans.* Philadelphia: Westminster, 1

Roetzel, C. J. *The Letters of Paul.* Louisville: Westminster/John Knox, 1991.

_____. *Judgment in the Community: A Study of the Relationship Between Eschatology and Ecclesiology in Paul.* Leiden: Brill, 1972.

Ruef, J. S. *Paul's First Letter to Corinth.* Baltimore: Penguin, 1971.

Rubenstein, R. L. *My Brother Paul.* New York: Harper & Row, 1972.

Sampley, J. P. *Pauline Partnership in Christ.* Philadelphia: Fortress, 1980.

Sanday, W., and Headlam, A. C. *The Epistle to the Romans.* New York: Scribners, 1895.

Sanders, E. P. *Paul, the Law, and the Jewish People.* Philadelphia: Fortress, 1983.

_____. *Paul and Palestinian Judaism.* Philadelphia: Fortress, 1977.

Sanders, J. T. *Ethics in the New Testament.* Philadelphia: Fortress, 1975.

Sandmel, S. *The Genius of Paul.* New York: Farrar, Straus & Cudahy, 1958.

Schelkle, K. H. *Paulus: Leben--Briefe--Theologie.* Darmstadt: Wissenschaftliche Buchgesellschaft, 1981.

Schlier, H. *Grundzüge einer paulinische Theologie.* Freiburg: Herder, 1978.

Schmidt, H. *Der Brief des Paulus an die Römer.* Berlin: Evangelische Verlaganstalt, 1972.

Schmithals, W. *Gnosticism in Corinth*. Trans. J. E. Steely. Nashville: Abingdon, 1971.

_____. *Paul and the Gnostics*. Trans. J. E. Steely. Nashville: Abingdon, 1972.

_____. *Paul and James*. London: SCM, 1965.

_____. *Paul and Jesus*. London: SCM, 1965.

_____. *Der Römerbrief*. Gütersloh: Gütersloher Verlagshaus, 1988.

Schmitt, R. *Gottesgerichtigkeit--Heilsgeschichte--Israel in der Theologie des Paulus*. Frankfurt am Main: Lang, 1984.

Schnelle, U. *Gerechtigkeit und Christusgegenwart: Vorpaulinische und paulinische Tauftheologie*. Göttingen: Vandenhoeck & Ruprecht, 1983.

_____. *Wandlungen in paulinischen Denken*. Stuttgart: 1989.

Schoeps, H. J. *Paul*. Trans. H. Knight. Philadelphia: Westminster, 1961.

Schrage, W. *The Ethics of the New Testament*. Trans. D. E. Green. Philadelphia: Fortress, 1988.

Schütz, J. H. *Paul and the Anatomy of Apostolic Authority*. Cambridge: University Press, 1975.

Schweitzer, A. *The Mysticism of Paul the Apostle*. Trans. W. Montgomery. New York: Holt, 1931.

_____. *Paul and His Interpreters*. Trans. W. Montgomery. New York: Schocken, 1964.

Schweizer, E. *The Holy Spirit*. Trans. R. H. Fuller and I. Fuller. Philadelphia: Fortress, 1980.

_____. *The Letter to the Colossians*. Trans. A. Chester. Minneapolis: Augsburg, 1982.

Scott, C. A. A. *Christianity according to St. Paul*. Cambridge: University Press, 1961.

Scroggs, R. *Paul for a New Day*. Philadelphia: Fortress, 1977.

Seeley, D. *The Noble Death: Graeco-Roman Martyrology and Paul's Conception of Salvation*. Sheffield: JSOT, 1990.

Segel, A. F. *Paul the Convert*. New Haven: Yale, 1990.

_____. *Rebecca's Children: Judaism and Christianity in the Roman World*. Cambridge, MA: Harvard, 1986.

Selby, D. J. *Toward the Understanding of St. Paul*. Englewood Cliffs; Prentice-Hall, 1962.

Shires, H. M. *The Eschatology of Paul in the Light of Modern Scholarship*. Philadelphia: Westminster, 1966.

Stambaugh, J. E., and Balch, D. L. *The New Testament in Its Social Environment*. Philadelphia: Westminster, 1986.

Stendahl, K. *Paul among Jews and Gentiles*. Philadelphia: Fortress, 1976.

Stowers, S. K. *The Diatribe and Paul's Letter to the Romans*. Chico: Scholars, 1981.

Strachan, R. H. *The Second Epistle of Paul to the Corinthians*. New York: Harper, n. d.

Stuhlmacher, P. *Der Brief an die Röer.* Göttingen: Vandenhoeck, 1989.

_____. *Gerechtigkeit Gottes bei Paulus.* Göttingen: Vandenhoeck & Ruprecht, 1966.

_____. *Das paulinische Evangelium.* Göttingen: Vandenhoeck & Ruprecht, 1968.

_____. *Reconciliation, Law, and Righteousness: Essays in Biblical Theology.* Philadelphia: Fortress, 1986.

_____. *Versöhnung, Gesetz, und Gerechtigkeit.* Göttingen: Vandenhoeck & Ruprecht, 1981.

Synge, F. C. *St. Paul's Epistle to the Ephesians.* London: Macmillan, 1959.

Talbert, C. H. *Reading Corinthians.* New York: Crossroad, 1987.

Tannehill, R. C. *Dying and Rising with Christ.* Berlin: Töpelmann, 1967.

Theissen, G. *Psychological Aspects of Pauline Theology.* Trans. G. P. Galvin. Philadelphia: Fortress, 1987.

_____. *The Social Setting of Pauline Christianity.* Ed. and trans. J. H. Schütz. Philadelphia: Fortress, 1982.

Thielman, F. *From Plight to Solution: A Jewish Framework for Understanding Paul's View of Law in Galatians and Romans.* Leiden: Brill, 1989.

Thompson, G. H. P. *The Letters of Paul to the Ephesians, to the Colossians, and to Philemon.* Cambridge: University Press, 1967.

Thompson, M. B. *Clothed with Christ: The Example and Teaching of Jesus in Romans 12.1-15.13.* Sheffield: Sheffield Academic Press, 1991.

Thrall, M. E. *The First and Second Letters of Paul to the Corinthians.* Cambridge: University Press, 1965.

Tobin, T. H. *The Spirituality of Paul.* Wilmington: Glazier, 1987.

Tomson, P. J. *Paul and the Jewish Law.* Minneapolis: Fortress, 1991.

Vanhoye, A., ed. *L'Apotre Paul.* Leuven: University Press, 1986.

van Dühnen, A. *Die Theologie des Gesetzes bei Paulus.* Stuttgart: Katholisches Bibelwerk, 1968.

van Unnik, W. C. *Tarsus or Jerusalem:The City of Paul's Youth.* Trans. G. Ogg. London: Epworth, 1962.

Volf, J. M. G. *Paul and Perseverance: Staying in and Falling Away.* Louisville: Westminster/John Knox, 1990.

Wanamaker, C. A. *The Epistles to the Thessalonians.* Grand Rapids: Eerdmans, 1990.

Watson, F. *Paul, Judaism and the Gentiles.* Cambridge: University Press, 1986.

Wedderburn, A. J. M. *Baptism and Resurrection: Studies in Pauline Theology against Its Graeco-Roman Background.* Tübingen: Mohr, 1987.

_____. *The Reasons for Romans.* Ed. J. Riches. Edinburgh: T. & T. Clark, 1988.

_____, ed. *Paul and Jesus: Collected Essays.* Sheffield: JSOT, 1989.

Westerholm, S. *Israel's Law and the Church's Faith: Paul and His Recent Interpreters*. Grand Rapids: Eerdmans, 1988.

Whiteley, D. H. E. *The Theology of St. Paul*. Philadelphia: Fortress, 1964.

Wikgren, A. *Early Christian Origins*. Chicago: Quadrangle Books, 1966.

Wilckens, U. *Der Brief an die Römer*. 3 vols. Cologne: Benziger, 1978, 1980, 1982.

Wiles, M. F. *The Divine Apostle*. Cambridge: University Press, 1967.

Williams, S. K. *Jesus' Death as Saving Event*. Missoula: Scholars, 1975.

Wire, A. C. *The Corinthian Women Prophets*. Minneapolis: Fortress, 1990.

Wise, A. C. *The Corinthian Women Prophets: A Reconstruction of Paul's Rhetoric*. Minneapolis: Fortress, 1990.

Wolter, M. *Rechtfertigung und zukünftiges Untersuchungen zu Röm 5, 1-11*. Berlin: de Gruyter, 1978.

Wright, N. T. *The Climax of the Covenant: Christ and the Law in Pauline Theology*. Edinburgh: T. & T. Clark, 1991.

Young, F., and D. F. Ford. *Meaning and Truth in 2 Corinthians*. Grand Rapids: Eerdmans, 1987.

Zeller, D. *Der Brief an die Römer*. Regensburg: Pustet, 1985.

_____. *Der Juden und Heiden in der Mission der Paulus: Studien zum Röerbrief*. Stuttgart: Katholisches Bibelwerk, 1972.

_____. *Charis bei Philon und Paulus*. Stuttgart: Katholisches Bibelwerk, 1990.

Ziesler, J. A. *The Meaning of Righteousness in Paul*. Cambridge: University Press, 1972.

_____, J. A. *Pauline Christianity*. Oxford: University Press, 1983.

_____. *Paul's Letter to the Romans*. London: SCM, 1989.

ARTICLES IN JOURNALS AND CHAPTERS IN BOOKS

Aageson, J. W. "Scripture and Structure in the Development of the Argument in Romans 9-11." *CBQ* 48 (1986): 265-289.

_____. "Typology, Correspondence, and the Application of Scripture in Romans 9-11." *JSNT* 31 (1987): 51-72.

Baird, W. "One Against the Other: Intra-Church Conflict in 1 Corinthians." In *The Conversation Continues*, 116-136, ed. R. T. Fortna and B. R. Gaventa. Nashville: Abingdon, 1990.

Barclay, J. M. G. "Thessalonica and Corinth: Social Contrasts in Pauline Christianity." *JSNT* 47 (1992): 49-74.

Barth, M. "The Faith of the Messiah." *HeyJ* 10 (1969): 363-370.

Baxter, A. G., and Ziesler, J. A. "Paul and Arboriculture: Romans 11.17-24." *JSNT* 24 (1985): 25-32.

Beale, G. K. "The Old Testament Background of Reconciliation in 2 Corinthians 5-7 and its Bearing on the Literary Problem of 2 Corinthians 6.14-7.1." *NTS* 35 (1989): 550-581.

Beker, J. C. "The Faithfulness of God and the Priority of Israel in Paul's Letter to the Romans." *HTR* 79 (1986): 10-16.

_____. "Paul's Theology: Consistent or Inconsistent?" *NTS* 34 (1988): 364-377.

Belleville, L. L. "'Under Law': Structural Analysis and the Pauline Concept of Law in Galatians 3.21--4.11." *JSNT* 26 (1986): 53-78.

Best, E. "Paul's Apostolic Authority." *JSNT* 27 (1986): 3-25.

Betz, H. D. "Geist, Freiheit und Gesetz." *ZTK* 71 (1974): 78-93.

_____. "The Literary Composition and Function of Paul's Letter to the Galatians." *NTS* 21 (1975): 353-379.

Boers, H. "Polarities at the Roots of New Testament Thought." In *Perspectives on the New Testament*, 55-75, ed. C. H. Talbert. Macon: Mercer, 1985.

_____. "We Who Are by Inheritance Jews; not from the Gentiles, Sinners." *JBL* 111 (1992): 273-281.

Boring, M. E. "The Language of Universal Salvation in Paul." *JBL* 105 (1986): 269-292.

Bowers, P. "Chruch and Mission in Paul." *JSNT* 44 (1991): 89-111.

_____. "'Fulfilling the Gospel: The Scope of the Pauline Mission." *JETS* 30 (1987): 185-198.

Brandenburger, E. "Paulinische Schriftauslegung in der Kontroverse um das Verheissungswort Gottes (Römer 9)." *ZThK* 82 (1985): 1-47.

Branick, V. P. "Apocalyptic Paul?" *CBQ* 47 (1985): 664-675.

_____. "The Sinful Flesh of the Son of God (Rom 8:3): A Key Image of Pauline Theology." *CBQ* 47 (1985): 246-262.

Brauch, M. T. "Perspectives on 'God's Righteousness' in recent German discussion." In E. P. Sanders, *Paul and Palestinian Judaism*, 523-542. Philadelphia: Fortress, 1977.

Breytenbach, C. "Versöhnung, Stellvertretung und Sühne." *NTS* 39(1993): 59-79.

Brooks, O. S. "A Contextual Interpretation of Galatians 3:27." In *Studia Biblica 1978*, III, 47-56, ed. E. A. Livingstone. Sheffield: JSOT, 1980.

Brown, R. E. "Not Jewish Christianity and Gentile Christianity but Types of Jewish/Gentile Christianity." *CBQ* 45 (1983): 74-79.

Bring, R. "Paul and the Old Testament: A Study of the Ideas of Election, Faith, and Law in Paul with Special Reference to Romans 9:30-10:13." *ST* 25 (1971): 25-28.

Bruce, F. F. "Paul and the Law of Moses." *BJRL* 57 (1974-75): 259-279.

_____. "The Romans Debate--Continued." *BJRL* 64 (1991-92): 334-359.

Burdon, C. J. "Paul and the Cricified Church." *ExpT* 95 (1984): 137-141.

Byrne, B. "Living out the Righteousness of God. The Contribution of Rom 6:1-8:13 to an Understanding of Paul's Ethical Presuppositions." *CBQ* 43 (1981): 557-581.

Cadbury, H. J. "Overconversion in Paul's Churches." In *The Joy of Study*, 43-50, ed. S. E. Johnson. New York: Macmillan, 1951.

Caird, G. B. "Predestination--Romans IX-XI." *ExpT* 68 (1957): 324-327.

Callan, T. "Pauline Midrash: The Exegetical Background of Gal 3:19b." *JBL* 99 (1980): 549-567.

Campbell, D. A. "The Meaning of *Pistis* and *Nomos* in Paul: A Linguistic and Structural Perspective." *JBL* 111 (1992): 91-103.

_____. D. H. "The Identity of *ego* in Romans 7:7-25." In *Studia Biblica 1978*, III, 57-64.

_____, W. S. "Christ and the End of the Law: Romans 10:4." In *Studia Biblica 1978*, III, 73-81.

_____. "The Freedom and Faithfulness of God in Relation to Israel." *JSNT* 13 (1981): 27-45.

_____. "The Romans Debate." *JSNT* 10 (1981): 19-28.

_____. "Salvation for Jews and Gentiles: Krister Stendahl and Paul's Letter to the Romans." In *Studia Biblica 1978*, III, 65-72.

Castelli, E. A. "Interpretations of Power in 1 Corinthians." *Semeia* 54 (1991): 197-22.

Clark, K. W. "Israel of God." In *Studies in the New Testament and Early Christian Literature*, 161-169, ed. D. E. Aune. Leiden: Brill, 1972.

Cohn-Sherbok, D. "Some Reflections on James Dunn's: 'The Incident at Antioch (Gal 2:11-18).'" *JSNT* (1983): 68-74.

Corsani, B. "*ek pisteos* in the Letters of Paul." In *The New Testament Age*, 87-105, ed. W. C. Weinrich. Macon: Mercer, 1984.

Cosgrove, C. H. "Justification in Paul: A Linguistic and Theological Reflection." *JBL* 106 (1987): 653-670.

Craig, W. L. "Paul's Dilemma in 2 Corinthians 5.1-10: A 'Catch-22'?" *NTS* 34 (1988): 145-147.

Cranfield, C. E. B. "Giving a Dog a Bad Name: A Note on H. Räisänen's *Paul and the Law*." *JSNT* 38 (1990): 77-85.

_____. "St. Paul and the Law." *SJT* 17 (1964): 43-68.

_____. "Some Notes on Romans 9.30-33." In *Jesus und Paulus*, 36-40, ed. E. E. Ellis and E. Grässer. Göttingen: Vandenhoeck & Ruprecht, 1975.

_____. "'The Works of the Law' in the Epistle to the Romans." *JSNT* 43 (1991): 89-101.

Crocket, W. V. "The Ultimate Restoration of All Mankind: 1 Corinthians 15:22." In *Studia Biblica 1978*, III, 83-87.

Crowther, C. "Works, Work and Good Works." *ExpT* 81 (1970): 166-171.

Dahl, N. A. "The Messiahship of Jesus in Paul." In *The Cricified Messiah and Other Essays*, 37-47. Minneapolis: Augsburg, 1974.

_____. "Paul and the Church at Corinth according to 1 Corinthians 1:10-4:21." In *Christian History and Interpretation*, 313-335, ed. W. R. Farmer, C. F. D. Moule, and R. R. Niebuhr. Cambridge: University Press, 1967.

Davies, W. D. "Paul and the People of Israel." *NTS* 24 (1977): 4-39.

Dawes, G. W. "'But if you can gain your freedom.'" *CBQ* 52 (1990): 681-697.

de Boer, M. C. "Paul and Jewish Apocalyptic Eschatology." In *Apocalyptic and the New Testament*, 169-190, ed. J. Marcus and M. L. Soards. Sheffield: JSOT, 1989.

Derrett, J. D. M. "Judgement and 1 Corinthians 6." *NTS* 37 (1991): 22-36.

Donaldson, T. L. "The 'Curse of the Law" and the Inclusion of the Gentiles: Galatians 3.13-14." *NTS* 32 (1986): 94-112.

_____. "'Riches for the Gentiles'" (Rom 11:12): Israel's Rejection and Paul's Gentile Mission." *JBL* 112 (1993): 81-98.

Donfried, K. P. "The Cults of Thessalonica and the Thessalonian Correspondence." *NTS* 31 (1985): 336-356.

_____. "Justification and Last Judgment in Paul." *ZNW* 67 (1976): 90-110.

_____. "Paul and Judaism: 1 Thessalonians 2:13-16 as a Test Case." *Int* 38 (1984): 242-253.

_____. "The Theology of 1 Thessalonians as a Reflection of Its Purpose." In *To Touch the Text*, 243-260, ed. M. P. Horgan and P. J. Kobelski. New York: Crossroad, 1989.

Dozeman, T. B. "*Sperma Abraam* in John 8 and Related Literature." *CBQ* 42 (1980): 342-358.

Dunn, J. D. G. "The Incident at Antioch (Gal. 2:11-18). *JSNT* 18 (1983): 3-57.

_____. "Jesus--Flesh and Spirit. An Exposition of Romans i.3-4." *JTS* 24 (1973): 40-53.

_____. "'A Light to the Gentiles': The Significance of the Damascus Road Christophany for Paul." In *The Glory of Christ in the New Testament*, 251-266, ed. L. D. Hurst and N. T. Wright. Oxford: University Press, 1987.

_____. "The New Perspective on Paul." *BJRL* 65 (1983): 95-122.

_____. "The Relationship between Paul and Jerusalem according to Galatians 1 and 2." *NTS* 28 (1982): 461-478.

_____. "Rom. 7.14-15 in the Theology of Paul." *TZ* 31 (1975): 258-273.

_____. "What was the Issue between Paul and 'Those of the Circumcision'?" In *Paulus und das antike Jundentum*, 295-317, ed. M. Hengel and U. Heckel. Tübingen: Mohr, 1991.

_____. "Works of the Law and the Curse of the Law (Galatians 3.10-14)." *NTS* 31 (1985): 523-542.

_____. "Yet Once More--'The Works of the Law': A Response." *JSNT* 46 (1992): 99-117.

Dupont, J. "The Conversion of Paul, and Its Influence on His Understanding of Salvation by Faith." In *Apostolic History and the Gospel*, 176-194, ed. W. W. Gasque and R. P. Martin. Grand Rapids: Eerdmans, 1970.

Ellison, H. L. "Paul and the Law--'All Things to All Men.'" In *Apostolic History and the Gospel*, 195-202, ed. W. W. Gasque and R. P. Martin. Grand Rapids: Eerdmans, 1970.

Engberg-Pedersen, T. "The Gospel and Social Practice according to 1 Corinthians." *NTS* 33 (1987): 557-584.

Epp, E. J. "Jewish-Gentile Continuity in Paul: Torah and/or Faith?" In *Christians among Jews and Gentiles*, 80-90, ed. G. W. E. Nickelsburg and G. W. MacRae. Philadelphia: Fortress, 1986.

Espy, J. M. "Paul's 'Robust Conscience' Re-Examined." *NTS* 31 (1985): 161-188.

Fee, G. D. "II Corinthians VI.14-VII.1 and Food Offered to Idols." *NTS* 23 (1977): 140-161.

Fiorenza, E. S. "Rhetorical Situation and Historical Reconstruction in 1 Corinthians." *NTS* 33 (1987): 386-403.

Fitzmyer, J. A. "Saint Paul and the Law." *The Jurist* xxvii no. 1 (Washington, D. C. January 1967).

Fortna, R. T. "Philippians: Paul's Most Egocentric Letter." In *The Conversation Continues*, 220-234.

Francis, J. "'As babes in Christ'--Some Proposals regarding 1 Corinthians 3.1-3." *JSNT* 7 (1980): 41-60.

Furnish, V. P. "Development in Paul's Thought." *JAAR* 38 (1970): 289-303.

_____. "Paul the Theologian." In *The Conversation Continues*, 19-34.

_____. "Pauline Studies." In *The New Testament and Its Modern Interpreters*, 321-350, ed. E. J. Epp and G. MacRae. Philadelphia: Fortress, 1989.

Gager, J. G. "Some Notes on Paul's Conversion." *NTS* 27 (1981): 697-704.

Gaston, L. "Abraham and the Righteousness of God." *HBT* 2 (1980): 39-68.

Gaus, E. "Christian Morality and the Pauline Revelation." *Semeia* 33 (1985): 97-108.

Gaventa, B. R. "Comparing Paul and Judaism: Rethinking our Methods." *BTB* 10 (1980): 37-44.

_____. "Galatians 1 and 2: Autobiography as Paradigm." *NovT* 28 (1986): 309-326.

Getty, M. A. "Paul and the Salvation of Israel: A Perspective on Romans 9-11." *CBQ* 50 (1988): 456-469.

Gillman, F. M. "Another Look at Romans 8:3: 'In the Likeness of Sinful Flesh.'" *CBQ* 49 (1987): 597-604.

Gordon, T. D. "A Note on *paidagogos* in Galatians 3.24-25." *NTS* 35 (1989): 150-154.

Goulder, M. D. "*Sophia* in Corinthians." *NTS* 37 (1991): 516-534.

Gundry, R. H. "Grace, Works, and Staying Saved in Paul." *Biblica* 66 (1985): 1-38.

Hahn, F. "Das Gesetzesverständnis im Römer-und Galaterbrief." *ZNW* 67 (1976): 29-63.

Hall, B. "All Things to All People: A Study in 1 Corinthians 9:19-23." In *The Conversation Continues*, 137-157.

_____. D. R. "Romans 3.1-8 Reconsidered." *NTS* 29 (1983); 183-197.

_____. R. G. "The Rhetorical Outline for Galatians: A Reconsideration." *JBL* 106 (1987): 277-287.

Hamerton-Kelly, R. G. "A Girardian Interpretation of Paul, Rivalry, Mimesis and Victimage in the Corinthian Correspondence." *Semeia* 33 (1985): 65-81.

_____. "Sacred Violence and Sinful Desire: Paul's Interpretation of Adam's Sin in the Letter to the Romans." In *The Conversation Continues*, 35-54.

_____. "Sacred Violence and 'Works of Law.' 'Is Christ Then an Agent of Sin?' (Galatians 2:17)." *CBQ* 52 (1990): 55-75.

Hanson, A. T. "The Origin of Paul's Use of PAIDAGOGOS for the Law." *JSNT* 34 (1988): 71-76.

Harris, G. "The Beginnings of Church Discipline: 1 Corinthians 5." *NTS* 37 (1991): 1-21.

Haufe, G. "Reich Gottes bei Paulus und in der Jesustradition." *NTS* 31 (1985): 467-472.

Hay, D. M. "*Pistis* as 'Ground for Faith' in Hellenized Judaism and Paul." *JBL* 106 (1989): 461-476.

Hays, R. B. "Christology and Ethics in Galatians: The Law of Christ." *CBQ* 47 (1987): 268-290.

_____. "'Have We Found Abraham to be our Forefather according to the Flesh?': A Reconsideration of Rom. 4:1." *NovT* 27 (1985): 76-98.

_____. "Psalm 143 and the Logic of Romans 3." JBL 99 (1980): 107-115.

_____. "'The Righteous One' as Eschatological Deliverer: A Case Study in Paul's Apocalyptic Hermeneutics." In *Apocalyptic and the New Testament*, 191-215.

Herbert, G. "'Faithfulness' and 'Faith.'" *Theology* 58 (1955): 373-379.

Hester, J. D. "The Use and Influence of Rhetoric in Galatians." *ThZ* 42 (1986): 386-408.

Hickling, C. J. A. "Centre and Periphery in the Thought of Paul." In *Studia Biblica 1978*, III, 199-214.

_____. "Paul's Reading of Isaiah." In *Studia Biblica 1978*, III, 215-223.

Hofius, O. "Das Gesetz des Mose und das Gesetz Christi." *ZThK* 80 (1983): 262-286.

Holladay, C. R. "1 Corinthians 13: Paul as Apostolic Paradigm." In *Greeks, Romans, and Christians*, ed. D. L. Balch, et al. Minneapolis: Fortress, 1990.

Hooker, M. D. "Interchange and Suffering." In *Suffering and Martyrdom in the New Testament*, 70-83, ed. W. Horbury and B. McNeil, Cambridge: University Press, 1981.

_____. "*Pistis Christou.*" *NTS* 35 (1989): 321-342.

Horsley, R. A. "Gnosis in Corinth: 1 Corinthians 8.1-6." *NTS* 27 (1980): 32-51.

Houlden, J. L. "A Response to James G. D. Dunn." *JSNT* 18 (1983): 58-67.

Howard, G. "The 'Faith of Christ.'" *Evt* 85 (1973-74): 212-215.

_____. "The Faith of Christ." *ExpT* 85 (1974): 212-215.

_____. "Notes and Observations on the 'Faith of Jesus Christ.'" *HTR* 60 (1967): 459-465.

_____. "Romans 3:21-31 and the Inclusion of the Gentiles." *HTR* 63 (1970): 223-233.

Hübner, H. "Rechtfertigung und Sühne bei Paulus." *NTS* 39 (1993): 80-93.

Hultgren, A. J. "The *Pistis Christou* Formulation in Paul." *NovT* 22 (1980): 248-263.

Hvalvik, R. "A 'Sonderweg' for Israel: A Critical Examination of a Current Interpretation of Romans 11.25-27." *JSNT* 38 (1990): 87-107.

Jewett, R. "The Law and Coexistence of Jews and Gentiles in Romans." *Int* 39 (1985): 341-356.

_____. "Romans as an Ambassadorial Letter." *Int* 36 (1982): 5-20.

Johanson, B. C. "Tongues, A Sign for Unbelievers?: A Structural and Exegetical Study of 1 Corinthians xiv.20-25." *NTS* 25 (1979): 180-203.

Johnson, D. G. "The Structure and Meaning of Romans 11." *CBQ* 46 (1984): 91-103.

Johnson, L. T. "Rom 3:21-26 and the Faith of Jesus." *CBQ* 44(1982): 77-90.

Karris, R. J. "Flesh, Spirit, and Body in Paul." *Bible Today* 70 (1974): 1451-1456.

Käsemann, E. "The 'Righteousness of God" in Paul." In E. Käsemann, *New Testament Questions of Today*. Trans. W. J. Montague. Philadelphia: Fortress, 1969), 168-182.

Keck, L. E. "The Function of Rom 3:10-18--Observations and Suggestions." In *God's Christ and His People*, 141-157, ed. J. Jervell and W. Meeks. Oslo: Universitetsforlaget, 1977.

_____. "'Jesus' in Romans." *JBL* 108 (1989): 443-460.

_____. "The Law and 'The Law of Sin and Death' (Rom 8:1-4): Reflections on the Spirit and Ethics in Paul." In *The Divine Helmsman*, 41-57, ed. J. Crenshaw and S. Sandmel. New York: Ktav, 1980.

Kertelege, K. "Gesetz und Freiheit im Galaterbrief." *NTS* 30 (1984): 382-394.

_____. "Zur Deutung des Rechtfertigungsbegriffs in Galaterbrief." *BZ* 12 (1968): 211-222.

Knox, J. "On the Meaning of Galatians 1:15." *JBL* 106 (1987): 301-304.

_____. "Romans." In *The Interpreter's Bible*, IX, 353-668, ed. G. A. Buttrick et al. New York: Abingdon, 1954.

Koenig, J. "The Knowing of Glory and Its Consequences (2 Corinthians 3-5)." In *The Conversation Continues*, 158-169.

Koptak, P. E. "Rhetorical Identification in Paul's Autobiographical Narrative." *JSNT* 40 (1990): 97-115.

Lambrecht, J. "The Line of Thought in Gal. 2.14b-21." *NTS* 24 (1978): 484-495.

Lampe, G. W. H. "Church Discipline and the Interpretation of the Epistles to the Corinthians." In *Christian History and Interpretaion*, 337-361, ed. W. R. Farmer, C. F. D. Moule, and R. R. Niebuhr. Cambridge: University Press, 1967.

Larsson, E. "Paul: Law And Salvation." *NTS* 31 (1985): 425-436.

Lategan, B. "Is Paul Defending His Apostleship in Galatians?" *NTS* 34 (1988): 411-430.

Lincoln, A. T. "Ephesians 2:8-10: A Summary of Paul's Gospel." *CBQ* 45 (1983): 617-630.

_____. "'Paul the Visionary': The Setting and Significance of the Rapture to Paradise in II Corinthians xii. 1-10." *NTS* 25 (1979): 204-220.

Little, J. A. "Paul's Use of Analogy: A Structural Analysis of Romans 7:1-6." *CBQ* 46 (1984): 82-90.

Longenecker, B. W. "Different Answers to Different Issues: Israel, the Gentiles and Salvation History in Romans 9-11." *JSNT* 36 (1989): 95-123.

_____. R. N. "The Nature of Paul's Early Eschatology." *NTS* 31 (1985): 85-95.

_____. "The Pedagogical Use of the Law in Galatians 3:19-4:7." *JETS* 25 (1982): 53-61.

Lührmann, D. "Paul and the Pharisaic Tradition." *JSNT* 36 (1989): 75-94.

Lull, D. J. "'The Law Was Our Pedagogue': A Study in Galatians 3:19-25." *JBL* 105 (1986): 481-498.

_____. "The Spirit and the Creative Transformation of Human Existence." *JAAR* 47 (1979): 39-55.

Luz, U. "Zum Aufbau von Röm. 1-8." *TZ* 25 (1969): 161-181.

MacArthur, S. D. "'Spirit' in Pauline Usage: 1 Corinthians 5.5." In *Studia Biblica 1978*, III, 249-256.

MacGorman, J. W. "The Law as Paidagogos: A Study in Pauline Analogy." In *New Testament Studies*, 103-111, ed. H. L. Drumwright and C. Vaughan. Waco: Baylor University, 1975.

Malherbe, A. J. "Exhortation in First Thessalonians." *NovT* 25 (1983): 246-249.

Marcus, J. "The Circumcision and the Uncircumcision in Rome." *NTS* 35 (1989): 67-81.

Martin, R. P. "Patterns of Worship in New Testament Churches." *JSNT* 37 (1989): 59-85.

Martyn, J. L. "A Law-Observant Mission to Gentiles: The Background of Galatians." *SJT* 38 (1985): 307-324.

_____. "Apocalyptic Antinomies in Paul's Letter to the Galatians." *NTS* 31 (1985): 410-424.

Matera, F. J. "The Culmination of Paul's Argument to the Galatians: Gal. 5.1-6.17." *JSNT* 32 (1988): 79-91.

McEleney, N. J. "Conversion, Circumcision and the Law." *NTS* 20 (1974): 319-341.

Meeks, W. A. "The Image of the Androgyne: Some Uses of a Symbol in Earliest Christianity." *HR* 13 (1973-74: 165-208.

_____. "On Trusting an Unpredictable God: A Hermeneutical Meditation on Romans 9-11." In *Faith and History*, 105-124, ed. J. T. Carroll, C. H. Cosgrove, and E. E. Johnson.: Scholars, 1990.

_____. "The Social Functions of Apocalyptic Language in Pauline Christianity." In *Apocalyticism in the Mediterranean World and the Near East*, 687-705, ed. D. Hellholm. Tüingen: Mohr, 1983.

Menoud, P. H. "Revelation and Tradition: The Influence of Paul's Conversion on his Theology." *Int* 7 (1953): 131-141.

Meyer, B. F. "The Pre-Pauline Formula in Rom. 3.25-26a." *NTS* 29 (1983); 198-208.

_____. P. W. "Romans 10:4 and the 'End' of the Law." In *The Divine Helmsman*, 59-78, ed. J. L. Crenshaw and S. Sandmel. New York: Ktav, 1980.

Mitton, C. L. "Romans vii Reconsidered." *ExpT* 65 (1953-1954): 78-81, 99-103, 132-135.

Moo, D. J. "Israel and Paul in Romans 7.7-12." *NTS* 32 (1986): 122-135.

_____. "'Law,' 'Works of the Law,' and Legalism in Paul." *WTJ* 45 (1983): 73-100.

_____. "Paul and the Law in the Last Ten Years." *SJT* 40 (1987): 287-307.

_____. "Romans 6:1-14." *TJ* 3 (1982): 215-220.

Moreton, M. J. "A Reconsideration of the Origins of a Christian Initiation Rite in the Age of the New Testament." In *Studia Biblica 1978*, III, 265-275.

Morris, L. "The Theme of Romans." In *Apostolic History and the Gospel*, 249-263, ed. W. W. Gasque and R. P. Martin. Grand Rapids: Eerdmans, 1970.

Moule, C. F. D. "Obligation in the Ethic of Paul." In *Christian History and Interpretation*, 389-406, ed. W. R. Farmer, C. F. D. Moule, and R. R. Niebuhr. Cambridge: University Press, 1967.

Moxnes, H. "Honour and Righteousness in Romans." *JSNT* 32 (1988): 61-77.

Murphy-O'Connor, J. "Relating 2 Corinthians 6.14-7.1 to its Context." *NTS* 33 (1987): 272-275.

Mussner, F. "Ganz Israel wird gerettet werden (Röm 11.26)." *Kairos* 18 (1976): 241-255.

Neugebauer, F. "Das paulinische 'In Christo.'" *NTS* 4 (1957-58): 124-138.

Neusner, J. "Comparing Religions." *HR* 18 (1978-79): 177-191.

Neyrey, J. H. "Bewitched in Galatia: Paul and Cultural Anthropology." *CBQ* 50 (1988): 72-100.

_____. "Body Language in 1 Corinthians: The Use of Anthropological Models for Understanding Paul and His Opponents." *Semeia* 35 (1986): 129-164.

Nolland, J. "Uncircumcised Proselytes." *JSJ* 12 (1981): 173-194.

Okeke, G. E. "I Thessalonians 2.13-16: The Fate of the Unbelieving Jews." *NTS* 27 (1981); 127-136.

Paige, T. "1 Corinthians 12.2: A Pagan *Pompe?*" *JSNT* 44 (1991): 47-65.

Perkins, P. "Pauline Anthropology in Light of Nag Hammadi." *CBQ* 48 (1986): 512-522.

Piper, J. "The Demonstration of the Righteousness of God in Romans 3:25, 26." *JSNT* 7 (1980): 2-32.

Plevnik, J. "The Center of Pauline Theology." *CBQ* 51 (1989): 461-478.

Popkes, W. "Zum Aufbau und Charakter von Römer 1.18-32." *NTS* 28 (1982); 490-501.

Räisänen, H. "Galatians 2.16 and Paul's Break with Judaism." *NTS* 31 (1985): 543-553.

_____. "Das 'Gesetz des Glaubens' (Röm. 3.27) und das 'Gesetz des Geistes' (Röm. 8.2)." *NTS* 26 (1979): 101-117.

_____. "Legalism and Salvation by the Law." In *Die paulinische Literatur und Theologie*, 63-84, ed. S. Pedersen. Aarhus: Aros, 1980.

_____. "Paul's Conversion and the Development of His View of the Law." *NTS* 33 (1987): 404-419.

_____. "Paul's Theological Difficulties with the Law." In *Studia Biblica 1978*, III, 301-320.

Reicke, B. "Paulus über das Gesetz." *TZ* 41 (1985): 237-257.

Reumann, J. "The Gospel of the Righteousness of God: Pauline Reinterpretation in Romans 3:21-31." *Int* 20 (1966): 432-452.

Rese, M. "Israel und Kirche in Römer 9." *NTS* 34 (1988): 208-217.

Rhyne, C. T. "*Nomos Dikaiosynes* and the Meaning of Romans 10:4." *CBQ* 47 (1985): 486-499.

Richardson, P. "Pauline Inconsistency: 1 Corinthians 9:19-23 and Galatians 2:11-14." *NTS* 26 (1980): 347-362.

Robertson, O. P. "Tongues: Sign of Covenantal Curse and Blessing." *WTJ* 38 (1975): 45-53.

Robinson, D. W. B. "'Faith of Jesus Christ'--A New Testament Debate." *RTR* 29 (1970): 71-81.

Rose, M. "Die Rettung der Juden nach Römer 11." In *L' Apotre Paul*, 422-430, ed. A. Vanhoye et al. Leuven: University Press, 1986.

Sampley, J. P. "Faith and Its Moral Life: Individuation in the Thought World of the Apostle Paul." In *Faith and History*, 223-238.

_____. "Romans and Galatians: Comparison and Contrast." In *Understanding the Word*, 315-339, ed. J. T. Butler, et al. Sheffield: JSOT, 1985.

Sanders, E. P. "Jewish Association with Gentiles and Galatians 2:11-14." In *The Conversation Continues*, 170-188.

_____. J. A. "Torah and Paul." In *God's Christ and His People*, 132-140, ed. J. Jervell and W. A. Meeks. Oslo: Universitetsforlaget, 1977.

Schenk, W. "Die Gerechtigkeit Gottes und der Glaube Christi." *TLZ* 97 (1972): 161-174.

Schnackenburg, R. "Römer 7 im Zusammenhang der Römerbriefes." In *Jesus und Paulus*, 283-300, ed. E. E. Ellis and E. Grässer. Göttingen: Vandenhoeck & Ruprecht, 1975.

Schreiner, T. R. "The Abolition and Fulfillment of the Law." *JSNT* 35 (1989): 47-74.

_____. "Paul and Perfect Obedience to the Law: An Evaluation of the View of E. P. Sanders." *WTJ* 47 (1985): 268-278.

_____. ""Works of the Law' in Paul." *NovT* 33 (1991): 217-244.

Schöllgen, G. "Was wissen wir über die Sozialstruktur der paulinischen Gemeinden?" *NTS* 34 (1988): 71-82.

Scroggs, R. "Paul as Rhetorician: Two Homilies in Romans 1-11." In *Jews, Greeks and Christians: Religious Cultures in Late Antiquity*, 271-298, ed. R. Hamerton-Kelly and R. Scroggs. Leiden: Brill, 1976.

Silberman, L. H. "Paul's Midrash: Reflections on Romans 4." In *Faith and History*, 99-104.

Sloyan, G. "Outreach to Gentiles and Jews: New Testament Reflections." *JES* 22 (1985): 764-769.

Smiga, G. "Romans 12:1-2 and 15:30-32 and the Occasion of the Letter to the Romans." *CBQ* 53 (1991): 257-273.

Snodgrass, K. R. "Justification by Grace--to the Doers: An Analysis of the Place of Romans 2 in the Theology of Paul." *NTS* 32 (1986): 72-93.

_____. "Spheres of Influence: A Possible Solution to the Problem of Paul and the Law." *JSNT* 39 (1988): 93-113.

Soards, M. L. "Käsemann's 'Righteousness' Reexamined." *CBQ* 49 (1987): 264-267.

Stanley, C. D. "'Under a Curse': A Fresh Reading of Galatians 3.10-14." *NTS* 36 (1990): 481-511.

Stegner, W. R. "Romans 9.6-29--A Midrash." *JSNT* 22 (1984): 37-52.

Stowers, S. K. "*Ek pisteos* and *dia tes pisteos* in Romans 3:30." *JBL* 108 (1989): 665-674.

_____. "Paul's Dialogue with a Fellow Jew in Romans 3:1-9." *CBQ* 46 (1984): 707-722.

Strelan, J. G. "Burden-Bearing and the Law of Christ: A Re-Examination of Galatians 6.2." *JBL* 94 (1975): 266-276.

Stuhlmacher, P. "Sühne oder Versöhnung." In *Die Mitte des Neuen Testaments*, 291-316, ed. U. Luz and H. Weder. Göttingen: Vandenhoeck & Ruprecht, 1983.

_____. "Zur Interpretation von Römer 11.25-32." In *Probleme biblischer Theologie*, 555-570, ed. H. W. Wolff. München: Kaiser, 1971.

Suggs, M. J. "'The Word is Near You': Romans 10:6-10 Within the Purpose of the Letter." In *Christian History and Interpretation*, 289-312, ed. W. R. Farmer, C. F. D. Moule, and R. R. Niebuhr. Cambridge: University Press, 1067.

Talbert, C. H. "Paul's Understanding of the Holy Spirit: The Evidence of 1 Corinthians 12-14." In *Perspectives on the New Testament*, 95-108.

Taylor, G. M. "The Function of PISTIS CHRISTOU in Galatians." *JBL* 85 (1966): 58-76.

Thielman, F. "The Coherence of Paul's View of the Law: The Evidence of First Corinthians." *NTS* 38 (1992): 235-253.

Thiselton, A. C. "Realized Eschatology at Corinth." *NTS* 24 (1978): 510-526.

Thrall, M. E. "The Origin of Pauline Christology." In *Apostolic History and the Gospel*, 304-316, ed. W. W. Gasgue and R. P. Martin. Grand Rapids: Eerdmans, 1970.

_____. "The Problem of II Cor. VI.14-VII.1 in Some Recent Discussion." *NTS* 24 (1977): 132-148.

Torrance, T. F. "One Aspect of the Biblical Conception of Faith." *ExpT* 68 (1957); 111-114.

Tyson, J. B. "'Works of Law' in Galatians." *JBL* 92 (1973): 423-431. Verseput, D. J. "Paul's Gentile Mission and the Jewish Christian Community." *NTS* 39 (1993): 36-58.

Walter, N. "Christusglaube und Heidnische Religiosität in Paulinischen Gemeinden." *NTS* 25 (1979); 422-442.

_____. "Zur Interpretation von Römer 9-11." *ZThK* 81 (1984):172-195.

Watson, N. M. "Justified by Faith; Judged by Works--An Antimony?" *NTS* 29 (1983): 209-221.

Wedderburn, A. J. M. "Hellenistic Christian Traditions in Romans 6." *NTS* 29 (1983): 337-355.

_____. "Some Observations on Paul's Use of the Phrases 'in Christ' and 'with Christ.'" *JSNT* 25 (1985): 83-97.

Weder, H. "Gesetz und Sünde Gedanken zu einem Qualitativen Sprung im Denken des Paulus." *NTS* 31 (1985): 357-376.

Welborn, L. L. "On the Discord in Corinth: 1 Corinthians 1-4 and Ancient Politics." *JBL* 106 (1987): 85-111.

Westerholm, S. "Letter and Spirit: The Foundation of Pauline *Ethics*." *NTS* 30 (1984): 229-248.

White, J. L. "Saint Paul and the Apostolic Letter Tradition." *CBQ* 45 (1983): 433-444.

Wilckens, U. "Zur Entwicklung des Paulinischen Gesetzesverständnisses." *NTS* 28 (1982): 154-190.

Williams, S. K. "The Hearing of Faith: *Akoe Pisteos* in Galatians 3." *NTS* 35 (1989): 82-93.

_____. "Justification and the Spirit in Galatians." *JSNT* 29 (1987): 91-100.

_____. "The 'Righteousness of God' in Romans." *JBL* 99 (1980): 241-290.

Willis, W. "An Apostolic Apologia? The Form and Function of 1 Corinthians 9." *JSNT* 24 (1985): 33-48.

Wilson, R. M. "How Gnostic were the Corinthians?" *NTS* 19 (1972-73): 65-74.

Witherington, B. "Rite and Rights for Women--Galatians 3.28." *NTS* 27 (1981): 593-604.

Wood, H. G. "The Conversion of St. Paul: Its Nature, Antecedents and Consequences." *NTS* 1 (1954-55): 276-282.

Yates, R. "Saint Paul and the Law in Galatians." *ITQ* 51 (1985): 105-124.

Young, N. H. "'Paidagogus': The Social Setting of a Pauline Metaphor." *NovT* 29 (1987): 150-176.

Zaas, P. S. "'As I Teach Everywhere in Every Church': A Study of the Communication of Morals in Paul." Dissertation, University of Chicago, 1982.

_____. "'Cast Out the Evil Man from Your Midst.'" *JBL* 103 (1984): 259-261.

Ziesler, J. A. "The Role of the Tenth Commandment in Romans 7." *JSNT* 33 (1988): 41-56.

INDEX